Social Media
in India

Social Media
in India

Regulatory Needs,
Issues and Challenges

Edited by
FRANCIS P. BARCLAY
BOOBALAKRISHNAN N.

Los Angeles | London | New Delhi
Singapore | Washington DC | Melbourne

First published in 2022 by

SAGE Publications India Pvt Ltd
B1/I-1 Mohan Cooperative Industrial Area
Mathura Road, New Delhi 110 044, India
www.sagepub.in

SAGE Publications Inc
2455 Teller Road
Thousand Oaks, California 91320, USA

SAGE Publications Ltd
1 Oliver's Yard, 55 City Road
London EC1Y 1SP, United Kingdom

SAGE Publications Asia-Pacific Pte Ltd
18 Cross Street #10-10/11/12
China Square Central
Singapore 048423

Published by Vivek Mehra for SAGE Publications India Pvt Ltd and typeset in 10.5/13 pt Bembo by AG Infographics, Delhi.

Library of Congress Cataloging-in-Publication Data Available

ISBN: 978-93-5479-075-1 (HB)

SAGE Team: Amrita Dutta and Vandana Gupta

*To our families and friends, for their encouragement
and support at difficult times.*

To the knowledge that kills ignorance.

To democracy.

Thank you for choosing a SAGE product!
If you have any comment, observation or feedback,
I would like to personally hear from you.

Please write to me at **contactceo@sagepub.in**

Vivek Mehra, Managing Director and CEO, SAGE India.

Bulk Sales

SAGE India offers special discounts
for purchase of books in bulk.
We also make available special imprints
and excerpts from our books on demand.

For orders and enquiries, write to us at

Marketing Department
SAGE Publications India Pvt Ltd
B1/I-1, Mohan Cooperative Industrial Area
Mathura Road, Post Bag 7
New Delhi 110044, India

E-mail us at **marketing@sagepub.in**

Subscribe to our mailing list
Write to **marketing@sagepub.in**

This book is also available as an e-book.

Contents

Part III: Balancing Autonomy and Regulation

List of Illustrations

FIGURES

TABLES

Foreword

THE BURDEN OF QUESTIONING SOCIAL MEDIA

Questions are meant to be questions, from the viewpoint of common sense. But, from a philosophical perspective, questions are meant to be doorways of epistemological and ontological universes and they are meant to keep the dialectical tensions between and among the plausible answers in motion forever. Deeply held philosophical questions seldom target easy pragmatic approaches to make sense of the questions. Pragmatism is borne of the need to address the questions and find their answers here and now, whereas philosophy seeks to address questions, both at their epistemological and ontological sites, and grapple with their complexities in an eternally relevant and meaningful manner.

Pragmatism is the defining characteristic of contemporary academic pursuits, particularly research. The governing principle here is to pose a question with an empirical or non-empirical posture to raise an issue, make scope for planes of encounters with the issues as problems and point to the way out of the problems. These exercises are meant to contribute to the advancement of knowledge concerning the area of research. One similarity that puts both philosophical questions and plain academic questions on the same mat is the challenge to carry the burden of connecting the existing with the non-existent planes of realities.

Both questions are the need of the hour in making sense of our social world and the implications of the presence or absence of 'policies' of the state apparatuses. The latter presents us with ideological frames of reference for the acts concerning the former. The latter also pushes us back to the times of the earliest usage of the term 'policy' alongside the term 'communication'. This was in the wake of the end of the Second World War, the period when communications studies became an intense preoccupation for sociologists, political scientists and social psychologists in the USA. The first two decades of the Cold War saw heightened activities in the power blocks of the then two superpowers, the USA and the Soviet Union, to forge policies linking communication media with their geopolitical agendas.

Policy studies that are organically fused with historical studies on the discipline of communication remain an under-explored area, even though the outcomes of the policies of the early Cold War period caused the birth of academic fields such as development communication and political communication. This is largely due to the uncritical manner in which the works of scholars who contributed to the making of these fields are dealt with even after several decades. Our urge to romanticize the origins of these fields and the contributions of scholars who helped in their formation blinds our view of the overt and subtle propaganda the communication policies spread across the world through the works of these scholars.

The urge to delink contemporary communication policy frameworks from the influences of such contexts is the need of the hour. Communication policy frameworks, if they exist, in many countries are the outcomes of the civil society and state interrelationships specific to the West European and North American milieu and the nature and characteristics of the sociality and the media that were born in such a milieu. When we speak of the need for a regulatory framework of media in India, we are parroting only the concerns that have been voiced in these regions for the past few hundred years with regard to the 'troubled' interface between the media and society there. This is not to say that we should deny the advantage of learning from their experiences, but the potential of a genuinely culture-specific communication policy framework becomes a casualty in such a case. The birth and circulation of media entities from outside the shores of any country or region, then and now, also entail the birth and circulation of ideas of policy and regulation from afar.

Moving from such a trajectory to the questions that are occupying the attention of the present work is revealing another problematic, the burden of questioning social media. The burden of the policy-related questions such as the one this book takes as its governing parameter (In the age of misuse and misinformation, what should India's social media policy be?) is the compulsion to connect the existing and non-existent planes of reality. Social media and their location in the 'age of misuse and misinformation' posits something that exists and the poser 'what should India's social media policy be?' is pointing to something that is a desired state of existence, one that is non-existent. This question can also be a bone of contention in other modes of scrutiny, for instance, (a) the exclusion of social media not as the cause of the 'age of misuse and misinformation' and (b) social media as sites of 'misuse and misinformation'. The other moot question is: Can social media policy, checkmate and contain misuse and misinformation in our age? Social media, after all, are embedded in the communication environments of the social worlds made possible by human beings, their non-living partners, particularly the media and their non-media counterparts, in their versions as objects, ideas and carriers of thoughts of life.

The primary burden of the question is not in the question's invoking of the missing relationship between the reality that exists and the reality that is desired, the desired being an imprint of the logic that regulations, policies that flow from the side of the state as well as the 'self-regulating' arms of the media themselves, are not only desirable but the need of the hour, in view of the problematic of social media and its growing complexities of existence in contemporary times. The problematic of social media is manifold. One important dimension of this relates to the predominant impression that media technologies constitute the media and the attendant interfaces with the members of the society. The problematic persists until the time when the media in question and the attendant relationships with the audience are normalized to the point where the problem imposed by the media technologies dissipate in thin air. This was argued by Hassan and Sutherland (2017, p. 2) as a case of sedimentation of media forms,

> The actual contrivance, be it the codex, the printing machine, the telegraph, the computer, soon becomes almost a part of nature. It becomes

sedimentary material and forms another layer of the fossil record of media, one that we may use still every day, but whose provenance and significance are obscure to all but the specialist. This process of sedimentation has been occurring since the very beginning of media forms....

Another dimension of the problematic relates to the key question that remains constant despite the rapid transformations of social media platforms and users who make them meaningful, as Miller et al. (2016) posed. From a common-sense perspective, this question is simplistically worded but raises important epistemological and ontological questions in turn. The question is 'What is Social Media?' Miller et al. answered the question in terms of how we make sense of sociality through social media in terms of what they termed as the 'scalable sociality'. They said:

> The core to the study of social science is the way in which people associate with each other to form social relations and societies. This is called sociality. The best way to define what is popularly called social media but also includes prior media is thus to describe the new situation as increasingly 'scalable sociality'. (2016, p. 3)

The secondary burdens of the question with which the present argument is constructed are in the radically different nature of the prefix, *social*, in social media, when compared with the prefixes previous generations of media had. The prefixes such as electronic (media), broadcast (media), print (media) had their locations in the technologies which spawned them. The prefix *social* is problematic as it lost its denotative meaning at the cost of the connotative meaning, which does not exist on a par with the social of the real social world but exists only as an allegory of the social all of us inhabit.

In this sense, the present work throws open myriad challenges in coming to terms with the realities of social media in India and the compulsions staring at us calling for policy interventions from the regulators, who are absent in India. The current regulator, TRAI, in my opinion, did not come into being to regulate the media sectors. It was established to regulate the telecom sector and along the way became an ad hoc regulator of the media sector. This anomalous condition is emblematic of the global flows of communication policies and regulatory frameworks gone astray. The rapid expansion of the telecom sector, particularly the advent of the mobile phone sector during the mid-1990s, across the world, also saw the expansion of the telecom sector and mobile phone sectors in India. This was part of the widening of the scope of the flow of technologies and the trades thereof made possible by the emergence of the new telecom technologies and their facilitation by the expansion of the sphere of influence of WTO. Telecom regulatory framework became anomalous as it missed its target constituency and became a site of fetish like a regulatory framework for non-telecom sectors such as media.

Another dimension of the problematic concerning social media relates to their geographical locations. Social media are not geographical entities and the national prism with which we seek to work with them has its own traps, particularly in defining a homogenous, geographically bounded category of users. We cannot speak of, as Morley (1980) did with his 'Nationwide Audience: Structure and Decoding' to engage with television in Britain, a national social media, even though we may speak of social media users within a national boundary.

Dr Francis P. Barclay and Dr Boobalakrishnan N. have marshalled a good thread of content to provoke our thoughts on the questions which motivated them to undertake this work.

The three-part book bristles with substantive content to hone our understanding of the social media contexts in India in terms of their 'users' and how they 'use' and 'misuse' social media. The second section, in particular, deserves attention and praise for deploying meaningful research studies to justify the question posed early on. The third section informs us about the road we should be taking in terms of the policy and regulatory initiatives.

The editors deserve appreciation for their unique contribution to the literature on social media in what is clearly one of the largest social media markets.

REFERENCES

Hassan, R. and Sutherland, T. (2017). *Philosophy of media: A short history of ideas and innovations from Socrates to social media.* Taylor and Francis.

Miller, D., Costa, E., & Haynes, N. (2016). *How the world changed social media.* UCL Press.

Morley, D. (1980). *Nationwide audience: Structure and decoding.* BFI.

G. Ravindran
Professor, Department of Media and Communication
Central University of Tamil Nadu
India

Acknowledgements

At times, the best of knowledge and insights come from unanticipated eye-opening sources. Such luck had us at our research expeditions to the far and wide corners and remote rural areas of Tamil Nadu, as part of a project sanctioned by the Indian Council of Social Science Research (ICSSR) under the Impactful Policy Research in Social Science (IMPRESS) scheme.

A plethora of curious and compelling discoveries thus made about social media usage and regulation inspired us to bring forth this book. We thank those organic, intelligible intellectuals and the politically aware and seasoned for their sincere and prodigious participation in our research and offering utile insights that have become incentives for this book—which beyond targeting the scholarly community and being an addendum to the scientific body of knowledge, advancing theory, is also aimed at the ordinary and everyday user of social media, for their knowledge, awareness and good use.

We record our faithful gratitude to ICSSR for funding our project titled 'Ethics, Autonomy, Privacy and Regulation: Balancing the Social Media Spheres of Political Influence' under the IMPRESS scheme. Four chapters of this book are born from the research we did for the project: Chapter 1 'Social Media Dependence and the Loss of Distinction and Detachment', Chapter 2 'Political Ideologies, Affiliation and Participation: Are These Related in Contemporary India?' Chapter 3 'Credibility of Social Media Messages and User Awareness' and Chapter 11 'Balancing Social Media Autonomy, Privacy and Regulation'. We thank the Central University of Tamil Nadu for providing the right ambience and motivation to conduct scholarly research and add to the academic contributions.

We thank our colleagues in the Department of Media and Communication at CUTN, Professor Ravindran G. (Head), Dr Manash Pratim Goswami, Dr B. Radha, Dr Nikhil Kumar Gouda, Dr Shamala R. and Mr Lakshminarayanan N. for their encouragement and support. Special thanks to Professor S. Ravi, Dean of the School of Communication, CUTN, for his help and support. We also thank our department scholars, especially Mr Naveen V., Mrs Malini S., Mrs Akhila S., Ms Malavika S., Mr Showkat Jan, Ms Amritha Balakrishnan and Mr Sathish Kumar V., for their enthusiasm and help. We record our appreciation and thanks to the scholars and seniors for their chapter contributions to this volume. We also appreciate the optimism and encouragements of the publishing team of SAGE.

We earnestly believe this book will be of use to all stakeholders of social media, including the users, intermediaries and the regulators, and help them make informed choices.

Introduction
Social Media Policy in the Age of Misuse and Misinformation

Francis P. Barclay

Thanks to immersive smartphone applications and the unregulated people's (social) media, we are suffering from new-found digital diseases and reeling under the side effects of information overdose. Medium is much more than the mere message; today, it has become a part of 'me'. For instance, for some of the digital natives, staying away from their smartphones for even a single day is unthinkable. It is hard to ignore those beeps (notifications) even when they are endless, day and night! Media may have become a highly personalized and immersive commodity, even while misinformation and disinformation are creating confusions about credibility and increasing cynicism.

What would the effect of such bombardment of media messages on human mentality, health, social understanding and well-being be? What will such overreliance and dependency amounting to addiction to media (old, new and the convergent) lead to? How are communications and relationships changing? How do social media messages reach millions in minutes? What triggers those shares? How are contemporary communication platforms perceived and used? To what extent and for what purposes? Does credibility matter? Is privacy intact? Is ethicality ignored? How is social media misused, intentionally and unintentionally? If these complicated communication networks are important for advancement, how are they regulated? To answer these pertinent and timely questions, this edited volume draws together a wide range of contributions that critically review contemporary social media uses and issues.

After the likes of Twitter, Facebook, WhatsApp and Instagram brought widespread popularity to the online social media platforms—aided by the availability of affordable smartphones—a dominant part of scholarly research in this area focused on the positive potentials of these platforms, viewing them as alternative media and decisive enablers booming the communicative capabilities of the humankind for their good. But now, online social media is evolving as a mainstream medium of mass communication, with advertorials and paid actions, and a view is emerging to subject them as well to the same regulations and ethical codes of conventional media organizations. Indian law regarding censorship in traditional media is fairly developed. With social media becoming an entwined part of our lives, thanks to its independent and undisciplined nature, it is prone to misuse and proving to be disturbing and deleterious at times, calling for regulation. This book binds chapters that critically review the usage and effects of online social media, building arguments for the regulation of these sprawling digital spaces. At this juncture, when social media adoption has surpassed media-information literacy, there is a clear lack of clarity and ordained documentation about where autonomy and privacy end and regulation should begin, adding to the mayhem.

This book reviews the values of freedom of expression, privacy and regulation and proposes strategies to balance the triad with the involvement of all stakeholders, aiding policy formation, at a time when the Indian government and significant social media intermediaries are in a stand-off over the Information Technology (Intermediary Guidelines and Digital Media Ethics Code) Rules of 2021. As a whole, this book examines the scope and nature of the issues and challenges related to social media regulation, argues why social media needs to have an updated regulatory framework, and thereby, aiding policymaking. Topical issues that are covered in this book include the opaque-invasive algorithms that induce social media addiction, data privacy, theft, misinformation and other kinds of misuse, user awareness, credibility, political usage, conflicts, legal frameworks, autonomy, privacy and regulation—contemporary and emerging issues related to social media that need to be examined for the overhaul of the IT Act (2000) or the introduction of secondary or subordinate legislation to the Act.

Though the legal framework comprises several provisions that can be used to censor online content and check misuse, timely remedies for the common users remain a far cry, when they are exploited or their privacy is invaded, and the social platforms are misused to harm them. This book brings to the limelight social and user-centric issues that threaten the sustainability of these online social network fabrics that can be checked with a balanced, pragmatic social media policy and robust regulatory framework, along with other means. It further argues why in this age of disinformation, conventional thoughts about social media and freedom need to be rethought to develop new social attitudes towards privacy and control the extent to which information is disseminated. It also discusses countermeasures to deal with these social media issues and concerns.

Some chapters of this book are part of the IMPRESS project (2019–2021) funded by the Indian Council of Social Science Research (ICSSR) and employ a mixed methods research (MMR) approach. It includes a survey of 2,500 respondents, focus group discussions (FGDs) and content analysis. Though a convergent parallel mixed method design—where the researchers concurrently conducted the quantitative and qualitative elements in the same phase of the research process, weighing in the methods equally, analysing the two components independently and interpreting the results together—was adopted in this study, at times, they used both exploratory and explanatory sequential approaches to design the instruments and interpret the results. For the survey part, the window of examination was January 2020–January 2021. A sample of 2,500 social media users were selected from across Tamil Nadu, using a multistage stratified sampling procedure. As many as 20 FGDs—with 10–12 participants in each—were also conducted during the same window of examination. Using the data and analysis, several categories and concepts were developed, related and mapped to build a unified theory to understand social media regulation. This study measures and discusses a range of variables and concepts such as political ideology, political affiliation, political participation, social network type, social media (SM) usage, SM motivations, SM dependency, exposure to political content, political information preferred, triggers for sharing political information, SM privacy, SM autonomy, SM credibility, SM awareness and SM regulation. The other studies included in this book use a plethora of research designs from quantitative survey and content analysis to qualitative analysis methods. A qualitative review is employed in the chapter which examines the legal frameworks of India related to online social media, which will help identify the popular concepts and knowledge gaps to further explore the issues.

A study of Twitter and political propaganda conducts an empirical investigation to examine the kinds of literary-rhetorical devices used in political tweets. Apart from the rhetorical test, the tweets are analysed for sentiment, form, topic, frames and responses and their relationships are tested. As many as 268 tweets were mined and manually content analysed. The most popular frames used in political tweets were morality and efficiency. Similarly, a study on memes and social media trolls and a study on Palk Bay conflict employ the manual content analysis technique. A study that tests the association between social media exposure and religious intolerance uses a survey of 215 millennials to measure their exposure to media along with their levels of religious intolerance, narcissism and pessimism. Based on self-reported data on the usages of diverse media—newspapers and magazines, radio, television, cinema, mobile phone, the Internet and online social media—three composite media usage patterns are identified employing factor analyses. A study on the role of social media in disaster management uses qualitative techniques to critically analyse the role of social media in rescue, relief and rehabilitation and also discusses the misuse of this new media platform by people with vested interests during natural disasters. Discourse analysis is adopted in a chapter to understand the medium and critically analyse civic participation. The 11 chapters of this book are organized under three main parts: Part I—Understanding Social Media Users; Part II—Use and Misuse of Social Media and Part III—Balancing Autonomy and Regulation.

PART I

UNDERSTANDING SOCIAL MEDIA USERS

Part I starts off with a chapter on social media addiction. Francis P. Barclay, Boobalakrishnan N. and Anushiya K. use an explanatory sequential MMR approach—first, critically and empirically examining the motivations to use the online social media platforms and the levels of clinical addiction of users and then employing a qualitative method to derive theoretical insights into the convoluted loss of distinction between the self and social media (or the actual and the virtual space) and the inability to detach from those applications—unravelling newer dimensions of social media addiction and asserting the new normal. These apart, the interaction of a moderator variable social network type with the motivations in their relationship with addiction is measured, alongside correlations between addiction and the triggers to share social media messages—with positive outcomes. Both the qualitative and quantitative analyses indicate alarming levels of social media use, with these applications and activities performed on them dominating their thinking and behaviours. Unlike other addictions such as that to drugs, these two new dimensions are especially specific to social media addiction, as they are easily accessible through handheld mobile devices that are perennially attached to users. The algorithms of these social media platforms are opaque and how these applications function is out of public knowledge. From privacy invasion and use of user data for commercial purposes to the employment of all means by these technologies to hook the users to their smartphones, several issues related to social media dependency have been raised of late and there is a need to make the tech firms more accountable.

In the next chapter the authors give insights to understand contemporary social media users and their online behaviours. The chapter examines the political ideologies, political affiliation and the levels of political participation of social media users both online and offline in the Indian context, apart from validating and standardizing instruments for these concepts. Political ideology, a convoluted system of beliefs that acts as a credo for political attitudes and behaviours, can be a challenging concept to understand and empirically measure—just as multifaceted political participation could be taking place in diverse media and platforms that are less coherent. As it is evident, individual voices communicated on the so-called people's media (social media), collectively, pave the way for democratic engagement and political deliberations. Consciously or not, it is here where intrinsic political ideologies—or the belief systems about politics and governance—influence such social media behaviour, which are exhibited in the form of agreements, arguments, or more often than not, trivial conversations. While political ideology has been an elusive concept not just within the realm of political science but in the whole of social sciences, a few recent studies have associated political participation with several factors. But in this chapter, the researchers venture to determine the relationship between political ideology and political participation (online and offline). Along with it, they also identify the relevance of political affiliation and check their web of relationships to test the theories that affiliation to a political party can leverage political participation and political ideology is synchronic with political participation and affiliation. For this, 2,500 social media users were surveyed across the Indian state of Tamil Nadu and the results helped identify four facets of political ideology: power structure, social freedom, economic freedom and social justice, with the latter being the most favoured of the four and economic freedom the least. Political participation online and offline was found to be abysmally low, while political participation is related to economic and social freedom.

The third and final chapter of Part I relates social media usage with levels of awareness and credibility, checking the relevance of cognitive dissonance.

Online social media applications have become widely prevalent in India—thanks to the so-called smartphone revolution offering affordable devices, spectrum surge offering high-speed internet and low-cost data plans that do not blow a hole in the pocket—refurbishing the communication system, but the low levels or the lack of media–information literacy and the inability to indifferently cognize and comprehend critical information that streams through these sophisticated social networks could mean more destruction than development. One of the major issues emerging in contemporary times seems to be the lack of mindful/fruitful use and etiquette on social media, courtesy the lack of opportunities to acquire awareness about ethical usage. Further, false or inaccurate information (misinformation and disinformation) finds this their primordial medium for circulation. In this chapter, levels of awareness of users about social media issues and their perceived credibility of social media messages are measured and related to demographic variables. Using a survey of 2,500 users, the study also examines how awareness and credibility relate to usage. Based on the study findings, the researchers propose strategies through more rigorous awareness and media-information literacy generation and regulation, aiding policy formation.

Though the study findings identify moderate-to-high levels of awareness about misinformation and disinformation on social media among a majority of the users, they tend to believe messages circulated on these unregulated networks to a large extent. They were also found to be highly active on social media, amounting to addiction. Awareness had a deterring effect on social media credibility. Highly active users, however, tend to attach high credibility to social media messages. There is still a need to raise awareness about the untrustworthiness of social media messages that are blindly circulated from sources that are hard to identify.

PART II

USE AND MISUSE OF SOCIAL MEDIA

Part II includes five chapters on the use and misuse of social media platforms. It begins with an empirical investigation into the kinds of literary-rhetorical devices used in political tweets. In the 2019 Lok Sabha elections, the popular microblogging website—Twitter—became one of the crucial tools for political propaganda, with political parties, news outlets and the electorate tweeting their stakes and stands. In Chapter 4, apart from the rhetorical test, Akhila S. and Francis P. Barclay analyse the tweets for sentiment, form, topic, frames and responses and their relationships are tested. While the window of the examination was October 2018, tweets were mined employing a systematic sampling procedure using the search terms: bjp and cong— with the Indian National Congress and Bharatiya Janata Party being the main contestants. As many as 268 tweets were mined and content analysed. The most popular frames used in political tweets are morality and efficiency. But the study findings suggest that it is the logic frame that draws the best of response: likes, comments and retweets. Sarcasm and hyperbole are the most popular devices used in the political tweets mined, and governance is the most popular topic discussed. While sarcasm is used to ridicule the corrupt, hyperboles are used to exaggerate poll issues. Twitter is also loaded with personal attacks. Study results are used to propose a communication model and theorize on the relationships among topics, frames and devices.

In the following chapter that attempts to map the millennial mind, Malini S. and Francis P. Barclay test the correlation between social media exposure and religious intolerance. Online social media surge could mean increased capabilities of information and opinion sharing. While, potentially, it could lead to an explosion of diverse—and an eruption of supposedly suppressed— viewpoints, popular beliefs could still sway social media conversations, deepening inherent discrimination and intolerance. To test this theory, a survey of 215 millennials is conducted and their exposure to the media is measured along with their levels of religious intolerance, narcissism and pessimism. Based on self-reported data on the usages of diverse media—newspapers and magazines, radio, television, cinema, mobile phone, the internet and online social media—three composite media usage patterns are identified employing factor analyses. Study results infer a correlation between online social media usage and religious intolerance. Further, newspapers and magazines are found to induce pessimism. With increased exposure to global media and diverse cultures—thanks to the pervasive smartphones—education and economic development, the millennials could embrace liberal, resilient and tolerant attitudes. But the study results show a positive association between the extent of social media usage and religious intolerance. Social media usage, however, has a negative association with narcissism and pessimism. These findings are used to theorize on media exposure and religious intolerance in the context of the Indian setting.

Chapter 6 analyses tweets employing the media framing idea to understand how a conflict is discussed online, apart from an editorial investigation. In this chapter, C. Pichandy, C. J. Ravikrishnan and Boobalakrishnan N. investigate the role of social media in carrying the messages about the conflict into mainland perception with or without the mainstream political overtones. It also attempts to answer the following questions based on the analysis: Are we justified in calling the print media depiction as the media frames and that of the social media as individual frames? How far are the media frames or individual frames dependent or independent and how do they interact? Which are the strong frames? When predefined frames are used in comparative analysis with deductive reasoning, which generic frames gain predominance? Their study results indicate that media coverage of the Palk Bay conflict has contributed to generate a regional and national level collective identity uniting the alienated intellectuals, urban middle-class and the fishermen. Repeated presentation of the plight of fishermen in the sea has generated a kind of emotional integration. Media coverages have to be perceived as strategic efforts to polarize individual actions into collective actions and the continuous framing of similar episodes develops a predictable pattern of reality and promotes organizational solidarity. The human rights violation frame has qualitative precedence over the other frames in the portrayal of the Palk Bay conflict in both print and social media.

Chapter 7 by C. Pichandy, S. Ramamurthy and V. Palaniappan elaborates on and reviews the world view of social movements and online social media. The efficacy of this digital media of both the online and offline protest mobilization is analysed using a discourse analysis citing important but critical contemporary mass movements, including the historical 'Jallikattu' movement in the Indian state of Tamil Nadu and the role played by social media.

The final chapter in this section by Binish Parveen and Nikhil Kumar Gouda examines the use and misuse of social media during disaster relief and rehabilitation. This chapter focuses on the role of social media in rescue, relief and rehabilitation work in the aftermath of the Kerala floods of 2018 and 2019. Unusual and unprecedented rainfall in the state of Kerala in 2018 had led to the worst flooding of the century. The disaster affected 5.4 million people, displaced 1.4 million and more than 400 lives were lost along with causing damage to infrastructure (UNDP, 2018). In 2019, the state experienced a flash flood that killed hundreds of people and brought down around 1,789 houses (Newsclick, 2019; PTI, 2019).

This chapter also discusses the misuse of this new media platform by people with vested interests during natural disasters.

PART III

BALANCING AUTONOMY AND REGULATION

This part of the book starts off with a chapter on understanding the fake news scenario and the challenges that it poses. Fake news is now a global phenomenon pervading through the internet of everything and its harmful repercussions are felt far and wide. Besides creating political and social issues, this problem is spread over domains such as healthcare where lack of verification and dissemination of unauthentic information can breed viral impacts on the lives and well-being of people. In India, fake news has threatened to weaken an already vulnerable thread of social fabric by spreading false information targeted at specific communities. This chapter by I. Arul Aram and Parama Gupta puts in perspective the issues surrounding fake news and its rampant proliferation in recent times using select cases of fake news and providing an overview of significant studies and initiatives that have been and continue to be undertaken by various stakeholders, including media and other organizations to fight the spread of the infodemic. They also report the findings from a survey and interviews that measure the level of awareness and perceptions of social media users with regard to fake news, which point towards awareness levels bordering on moderately high but still inadequate. Finally, the researchers outline the challenges in the battle against fake news.

Chapter 10 by Balashanmugam S. K. reviews Indian legal frameworks related to social media regulation to identify gaps and areas that need redaction. About 50 per cent of the world's population avail services of online social media. Despite its development, user privacy concerns have spiked in recent decades, leading to the deterioration of public trust, as control over their data has also been at stake. While this is the situation, there are no specific legislation to regulate the online social media platforms and the intermediaries across the globe. In addition to this, cybersecurity and data protection face a significant threat because of the absence of such an appropriate legislative and institutional framework. Therefore, the chapter attempts to evaluate the extent of development of the legislative and institutional frameworks concerning online social media, particularly data protection and data privacy among the domestic jurisdictions and especially in India.

The final chapter by Francis P. Barclay, Boobalakrishnan N. and Anushiya K. focuses on balancing social media autonomy, privacy and regulation. While online social media turns out to be an ideal tool for political deliberations and all other forms of communication, as a fallout, it has also raised several ethical issues, with fake messages used in unethical ways for propaganda and controversial regulatory measures drawing flak. Users—equipped and exhilarated with their new-found ability to broadcast and reach the masses in no time—knowingly or unknowingly, play a part in the spread of misinformation and disinformation. A lack of clarity and ordained documentation about where privacy and the freedom of expression end and regulation should begin adds to the mayhem. In this mixed methods research, a survey of 2,500 social media users is used to measure political ideology, the extent of usage of social media and online political participation and relate them with user perceptions about autonomy, privacy and regulation. Further, qualitative FGDs are conducted to propose strategies to balance these social media triad with the involvement of all stakeholders, aiding policy formation.

This book features a unique mix of contemporary sociopolitical issues related to social media in India and covers several aspects of social media, including information overdose, addiction, social media awareness, motivations, use and misuse, privacy, autonomy and regulation. We firmly believe that it will be useful to scholars of media, communication, psychology, political science and several other domains of social science. This book will also aid policy formation to regulate the mostly unregulated social media.

REFERENCES

Newsclick. (2019). Kerala Floods 2019: 121 dead, 1,789 houses collapsed. Retrieved May 10, 2021, from https://www.newsclick.in/kerala-floods-2019-121-dead-1789-houses-collapsed

PTI. (2019). Kerala flood water recedes, death toll rises to 104. Retrieved May 10, 2021, from https://www.indiatoday.in/india/story/kerala-flood-water-recedes-death-toll-rises-to-104-1581202-2019-08-15

UNDP. (2018). Post-Disaster Needs Assessment--Kerala. Retrieved May 10, 2021, from https://www.undp.org/publications/post-disaster-needs-assessment-kerala

PART I

Understanding Social Media Users

Chapter 1

Social Media Dependence and the Loss of Distinction and Detachment

Francis P. Barclay, Boobalakrishnan N. and Anushiya K.

INTRODUCTION

Online social media are conceivably distinct from the other communication technologies, as the lines that isolate the producers of content from their consumers are abbreviated. While there has long been a tendency to make everything possible technological and digital, shifting the most or best part of social networking, communication and relationships to the online space could have its own idiosyncratic fallout—being the logical detachment from actuality. To what extent the online avatars can compensate for their actual counterparts is a scholarly question to ponder over, given the hideous divergences and irrealizable snags that technology can cause.

Quite a few scholarly enquiries relating to social media addiction and allied issues have been made in the past decade (Alabi, 2013; Sharifah et al., 2011; Venkat, 2017).

Thanks to the new breed of low-cost smartphones and affordable internet, especially in the developing countries, users are suffering from new-found digital diseases and the side-effects of internet overdose. Emerging as a clear sign, for some of the digital natives, staying away from their smartphones for even a single day is unthinkable. It is hard to ignore those beeps [notifications] even when they are endless, day and night!

It is more relevant now than ever to delve deeper into these new-found digital diseases as social media adoption has been witnessing a steep rise in the past few years despite whistleblowing and warnings from several quarters. To provide a context, the number of internet users multiplied from 1.1 billion in 2005 to 2.035 billion in 2010 and to 4.66 billion in 2020 (Statista, 2021d; 2021e). Of that, about 4.14 billion are on social media.

In the Indian subcontinent, too, adoption and usage of social media have been witnessing a steep rise in the past few years—the internet user base of the country soared from 493.96 million in 2018 to 696.77 million in 2020 (Statista, 2021a), with social media users alone accounting for an estimated 376.1 million of them (Statista, 2021b), against an estimated Indian population of over 1.38 billion (United Nations, 2021). By the third quarter of 2019, the count of monthly active Facebook users was 2.45 billion, making it the most-used online social media platform in the world (Iqbal, 2020). At the start of 2020, in India, there were about 324 million Facebook users, accounting for about 23.2 per cent of the population and the majority being males—76 per cent—and aged 25–34 years—125 million (NapoleonCat, 2021). WhatsApp has over two billion monthly active users (MAUs) (Raj, 2020), sharing about 60 billion messages on an average day (FE Online, 2018). In India, WhatsApp is estimated to have over 281 million MAUs (Raj, 2020). In 2018, the microblogging website Twitter was projected to cross the 30-million mark, up from 11.5 million in 2013 (Statista, 2018).

India had surpassed the United States to become the country with the largest Facebook user base (Arora, 2017): Indian users were over 310 million, way ahead of the United States's 190 million (Statista, 2021c). About 90 per cent of Instagram users in India are below 30 years and the 18–24 age group is the most active (Quora, 2016). Between January 2017 and 2018, India posted a growth in social media users of 31 per cent (TNN, 2018). By 2018, YouTube had about 80 per cent of India's internet users using the video-sharing platform, with 225 million MAUs on mobile phones alone (Mitter, 2018). During the same time, LinkedIn, the networking site for professionals, had over 50 million users from India, its second-largest user base in the world, after the United States (Express Tech, 2018).

Indian internet user count crossed the 500-million mark in 2018, against the 481 million internet users as of December 2017. India's urban populace, which was estimated to be about 455 million, had 295 million of them browsing the web, while their rural counterparts (about 918 million as per the 2011 census) had 186 million active internet users (Agarwal, 2018).

If these numbers are any indication, then the online social networking applications such as Facebook, Twitter and WhatsApp are witnessing their soaring gains in India, with the numbers of takers increasing with each passing day.

After the arrivals of the popular social media platforms such as Facebook and Twitter, the bulk of the scholarly research before 2010 was on the positive potential of these online tools, ranging from fostering political participation and forecasting outbreaks of diseases to opinion mining and election prediction (Barclay et al., 2014, 2015, 2016, 2017; Nair & Barclay, 2017). After the turn of that decade, however, the focus shifted to the ill-effects of overdependence with studies on addiction and health issues.

Perhaps, overuse may be the earliest sign of addiction. As social media becomes increasingly prevalent in daily activities and dominates the thinking and behaviour, it is convincing to suspect that overuse may lead to the clinical state of addiction.

While several studies have suggested that use of over four hours a day may indicate addictive behaviour (Grindeland & Harrison, 2009; Sharifah et al., 2011), the use of social media may not always be continuous but rather intermittent or frequent.

Today, online social media platforms are wide and varied—some of them being partially closed social networks for virtual communities such as Facebook and a few others being open for online content-sharing such as YouTube. Applications such as LinkedIn offer an opportunity for building professional networks and sharing relevant data, while others such as WhatsApp allow easy group and one-to-one communication, adding the advantage of quick audio and video calls. While some of them allow creation of individual profiles to interact with real-life friends, a few others let them meet like-minded strangers to develop and maintain both online and offline relationships (Monacis et al., 2017).

RESEARCH PROBLEM

Signs of adverse effects of social media overuse and dependence have been well documented (Deragon, 2011; Leung & Lee, 2012). Examining the nature and effects of such overdependence on digital devices and their applications is the primary focus of this study.

To delve deeper into this research problem, the current study attempts to critically and empirically examine the motivations to use the online social media platforms and the levels of clinical addiction of users and thereby derive theoretical insights into the loss of distinction between the self and social media and the inability to detach from them, to check whether the latter can be seen as additional dimensions of social media overdependence or addiction. To bring in some clarity at this juncture, the following research questions are proposed:

RQ1. What are the motivations to use online social media applications?
RQ2. What are the levels of dependence or addiction?
RQ3. Are motivations and addiction related?
RQ4. Are demographic variables associated with motivations and addiction?
RQ5. Are users able to disengage from social media, when needed?
RQ6. Are users able to differentiate themselves and their real-world actions from their social media persona and behaviours online?

SOCIAL MEDIA ADDICTION: A REVIEW

While a handful of scholarly researchers (Byun et al., 2009; Khazaal et al., 2008; Lam et al., 2009; Ng & Wiemer-Hastings, 2005) had studied internet addiction prior to 2010, only a few had thought about social media addiction (Cabral, 2008). Several studies relating to internet and social media addictions have been made in the past decade, devising scales (Liu & Ma, 2018; Monacis et al., 2017; Nakaya, 2015; Tutgun-Ünal & Deniz, 2015) and associating them with several factors (Andreassen et al., 2017; Balakrishnan and Griffiths, 2017; Hou et al., 2019; Leong et al., 2019; Zivnuska et al., 2019), predominantly psychological (Hawi & Samaha, 2017; Turel & Bechara, 2018). Of the measurement scales devised, the Bergen Social Media Addiction Scale stands out, with several of its variants validated (Duradoni et al., 2020; Lin et al., 2017; Mahmood et al., 2020; Monacis et al., 2017) in several languages. From a biopsychological perspective, viewing behavioural addiction with the same lens of substance-related addiction, Griffiths (2005) proposed a model of addiction with six facets. Building upon this model, the Bergen Social Media Addiction Scale is developed with six dimensions: (a) salience (it becoming the most essential activity, dominating thinking (preoccupations and cognitive distortions); (b) feelings (cravings) and behaviour (deterioration of socialized behaviour); (c) tolerance (a condition where increasing amounts of the activity are required to achieve previous effects); (d) mood modification; (e) relapse (the tendency to revert to earlier patterns of the activity after abstinence or control) and withdrawal (eruption of obnoxious feelings when the activity is cut) and (f) conflict (interpersonal conflict between the addict and others or intrapsychic conflict within the individual addicts themselves). Several studies have identified similarities between social media (behavioural) and substance addictions (Echeburua & deCorral, 2010).

At the start of this decade, Karaiskos et al. (2010) conceptualized social media addiction as an internet spectrum addiction disorder. Several researchers have associated social media addiction with psychological traits and several other factors such as empathy (Dalvi-Esfahani et al., 2020), self-esteem and self-construal (Hawi & Samaha, 2019), neuroticism and extraversion (Marengo et al. 2020; Wilson et al., 2010), anxiety and insomnia (Younes et al., 2016) and self-identity and belongingness (Pelling & White, 2009), identifying some of them as indicators or predictors. Mostly, the scales used were the Bergen Social Media Addiction Scale or similar scales that measured problematic use or addictions to one of the social media applications. Such instruments have been criticized because they focus on an application rather than specific activities (Monacis et al., 2017) within those applications such as gaming, gambling, chatting, checking status updates and watching videos. To overcome this criticism, this chapter studies the varied motivations to use social media applications, along with social media dependence or addiction. Attempts have been made earlier, too, to relate motivations with addiction (Dhaha et al., 2014; Sharifah et al., 2011; Venkat, 2017).

THEORETICAL UNDERPINNINGS

Several studies (Bumgarner, 2007; Cheung et al., 2011; Dolan et al., 2016; Gan & Wang, 2015; Gruzd et al. 2018; Park et al., 2009; Quan-Haase & Young, 2010, Raaçke & Bonds-Raacke, 2008; Urista et al., 2009; Venkat, 2017; Whiting & Williams, 2013) have examined social media usage from the uses-and-gratifications perspective. The uses-and-gratifications hypothesis (Katz et al., 1974) posits that users are goal-directed in their use of media, well aware of their needs (Venkat, 2017) and use the media to fulfil those needs. As these become motivations to use social media applications, the handheld nature of the mobile device that provides access to the Internet and the applications and the plethora of uses that they offer enhances the chances of overuse.

Several motivations such as purposive value, self-discovery, entertainment value, social enhancement, maintaining interpersonal connectivity (Cheung & Lee, 2009); social, communication and companionship needs (Raacke & Bonds-Raacke, 2008); social-interaction, timepass, entertainment, companionship and communication (Sharifah et al., 2011); marketing (Choi et al., 2016) and engagement (Dolan et al., 2016); entertainment, socialization, information seeking and self-presentation (Hsu et al., 2015) have been studied. Hsu et al. (2015) integrated the perspectives of uses and gratifications and perceived interactivity to identify what leads to continuous use of social media applications. The researchers found associations between motivations and perceived interactivity (human–human interaction, human–message interaction and human–community interaction), which in turn determined satisfaction and continued use.

While one motivation could bring a user into social media applications (for instance, peer pressure), once there, they may go on to use it for several other purposes (Venkat, 2017) and eventually become dependent. The media dependency theory places media as influential, postulating that the greater the number of social functions a medium performs for the user, the greater the dependency will be on that medium (Ball-Rokeach & De Fleur, 1976).

Though anecdotal evidence had suggested that problematic use of social media is widespread, giving rise to behavioural and psychological problems, scholarly enquiries with theoretical underpinnings into those issues had still been considerably deficient (Wang et al., 2015). In this study, the 'theory of rational addiction' was used to investigate microblogging, assuming that media dependence develops from habit, initially, and then becomes problematic. Furthermore, this longitudinal study drew on the 'cognitive–affective–behavioural modelling paradigm' to hypothesize that 'maladaptive cognition and affect tend to distort habit into psychological dependence', leading to the clinical state of addiction.

SOCIAL NETWORKS AND TRIGGERS

Are the kinds of social networks that users build or are part of on social media applications relevant here? Do they moderate the relationship between the motivations to use social media and social media addiction? To answer these questions, the social network theory is consulted and the social networks that users have on social media applications are categorized as egocentric (networks with individuals as nodes connected to their close friends and relatives), sociocentric (where the users are part of closed educational or professional networks), open networks (where the boundaries are hard to identify) and mixed networks, where users are part of two or more of such networks. Also, the chapter intends to examine the relationship between social media addiction and the triggers to share social media messages, identified as informative, humour, shock or surprise, impact, human-interest and proximity. Accordingly, the following research questions are raised:

RQ7. Is Social Network Type associated with Social Media Addiction and does it interact with Motivations to use social media in their relationships with Social Media Addiction?
RQ8. Is Addiction associated with the Triggers to share social media messages?

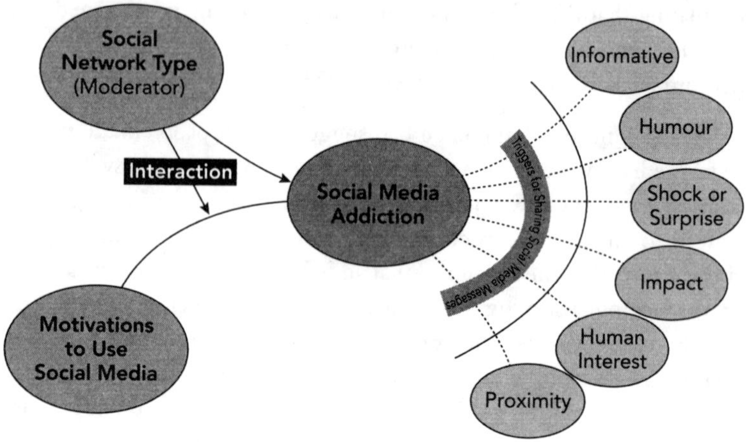

Figure 1.1 *Initial Model*

Based on the aforementioned research questions and assuming an association among these variables, a hypothetical model is presented in Figure 1.1.

RESEARCH METHOD

An explanatory sequential mixed methods research (MMR) approach is adopted for the study discussed in the chapter (refer to Figure 1.2 for the study design), with a quantitative survey followed by qualitative focus group discussions (FGDs) employing the grounded theory approach.

For the survey part, a sample of 2,500 social media users were selected from across the Indian state of Tamil Nadu, using a multistage-cluster sampling procedure during January 2020–January 2021. As many as 20 FGDs—with 10–12 participants in each of the discussions—were conducted during the period of study.

Survey Instrument

The survey questionnaire used to measure motivations and addiction was a part of a larger instrument that was created for a state-wide project funded by the Indian Council of Social Science Research (ICSSR) under

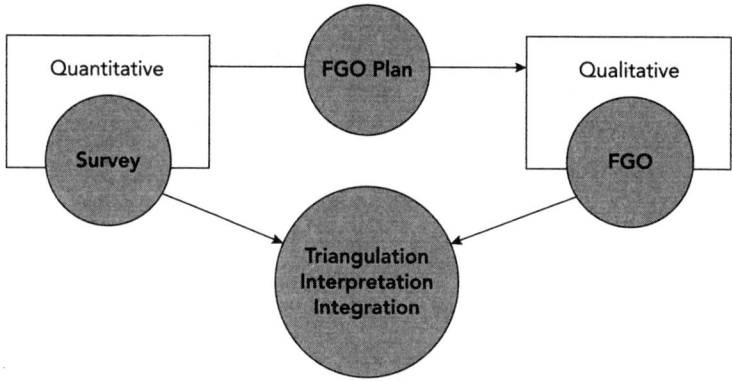

Figure 1.2 *Study Design*

the IMPRESS scheme. In this project, a range of variables are measured through a mixed methods research and the relationships that they share among them are examined to propose recommendations for the formation of policies to regulate the sprawling social media space. First, the state of Tamil Nadu was divided into five strata or zones: north, south, east, west and central. For each of these five zones, two or three districts were chosen as prime points for data collection, and respondents were chosen from each of these zones leading to a grand total of 2,500 respondents.

A pilot study was conducted using a survey questionnaire that had 135 items under 16 sections. Based on the feedback of the respondents, the questionnaire was revised to finally have 98 items under 16 sections. In the final questionnaire, there were 30 questions operationalizing the variables—motivations, addiction, social network type and triggers—apart from demographic variables—age, education, gender, occupation and family monthly income. Social interaction (with friends and relatives), timepass (to pass time when bored, for entertainment and check status updates), companionship (to communicate with partners and find long-lost friends or people with similar interests), information exchange (to view and share news, information and opinion and discuss issues) and education/profession (to build educational and professional groups, shares-related information and use the platforms for promotion) were the motivations analysed in the study, each with three items having three options (Yes, Maybe and No).

To measure social media addiction, we used an abbreviated version consisting of six items taken from the Bergen Facebook Addiction Scale which originally has 18 items (Andreassen et al., 2012), using six facets. These six items used a five-point Likert scale with the response format of strongly agree to strongly disagree.

FGD

For the qualitative analysis using FGD data, the grounded theory approach (Corbin and Strauss, 1990) was employed, where data were collected, coded and analysed simultaneously through constant comparison. Thus, data collection and analysis became an interrelated process in our study. At the start of the study, we made only tentative decisions about the initial collection of data instead of planning the entire procedure. Choices.regarding data collection were not entirely prearranged because the analysis was conducted simultaneously, and the analysis of data will reveal the need for more data. Theoretical sampling was performed until the point of saturation. Using the data and analysis, several categories and concepts were developed, related and mapped to build a unified theory.

Data Analysis

Quantitative Analysis

A quantitative survey was used to measure motivations and addiction—apart from demographic variables—age, education, gender, occupation and family monthly income. Their descriptive statistics are presented in Tables 1.1 and 1.2.

RQ1. What are the motivations to use online social media applications?
RQ2. What are the levels of dependence or addiction?

Of the 2,500 samples studied for the quantitative analysis, only a meagre 9.1 per cent (228) were unmotivated to use social media applications for social interaction. Similarly, 15.5 per cent (387) were not motivated to use those applications for timepass, 32.1 per cent (802) were unmotivated for companionship, 18.6 per cent (466) for

Table 1.1 *Descriptive Statistics: Demographics*

Frequencies					
Zone	Central	500	Gender	Male	1,320
	North	500		Female	1144
	South	500	Location	Rural	1,015
	East	500		Urban	1,485
	West	500	Occupation	Employed	810
Education	Plus two or below	587		Unemployed	308
	Undergraduate	1,233		Retired	148
	Postgraduate	680		Homemaker	266
Income	Less than ₹15,000	1,007		Student	968
	₹15,001 to ₹30,000	772	Age	Less than 23 years	1,184
	₹30,001 to ₹45,000	434		23–30 years	788
	Above ₹45,000	287		Above 30 years	528

Table 1.2 *Descriptive Statistics: Motivations and Addiction*

Frequencies					
Social Interaction	Unmotivated	228	Information Exchange	Unmotivated	466
	Likely to be motivated	1,045		Likely to be motivated	1,046
	Motivated	1,227	Location	Motivated	988
Timepass	Unmotivated	387	Education or Profession	Unmotivated	364
	Likely to be motivated	959		Likely to be motivated	1,008
	Motivated	1,154		Motivated	1,128
Companionship	Unmotivated	802	Addiction	Low	887
	Likely to be motivated	1,043		Moderate	1,429
	Motivated	655		High	184

information exchange and 14.6 per cent (364) for educational and professional reasons.

A majority of the respondents were either likely to be motivated or motivated to use social media applications for these purposes.

Similarly, 57.2 per cent (1,429) of the 2,500 respondents showed moderate symptoms of addiction and another 7.4 per cent (184) showed high levels.

RQ3. Are motivations and addiction related?

To check the associations among the motivational factors and the level of addiction, Pearson's product–moment correlation tests were performed, and the results are presented in Table 1.3.

Positive correlations were found among all the motivational factors and addiction. Only information exchange and addiction did not have a direct relationship and addiction and education or profession did not have direct relationship. Strong-to-moderate positive correlations were found between social interaction and timepass (0.404), social interaction and companionship (0.255), social interaction and information exchange (0.424), timepass and companionship (0.288), timepass and information exchange (0.358), companionship and information exchange (0.376), companionship and education or profession (0.373), and information exchange and education or profession (0.420).

Addiction has low but statistically significant levels of associations with the motivations to use social media applications, with the highest being with timepass (0.187).

RQ4. Are demographic variables associated with motivations and addiction?

To answer this research question, one-way ANOVA and t-test were conducted, and the results are presented in Table 1.4.

One-way ANOVA results indicated association between age and the motivational factors and addiction. While those belonging to the age group of 23 years and below were more inclined to use social media applications for social interaction, timepass, information

Table 1.3 Correlations: Motivations and Addiction

		Social Interaction	Timepass	Companionship	Information Exchange	Education or Profession
Addiction	Correlation	0.059**	0.187**	0.166**	0.037	0.047
	Sig.	0.003	0	0	0.067	0.019
Social interaction	Correlation		0.404**	0.255**	0.424**	0.219**
	Sig.		0	0	0	0
Timepass	Correlation			0.288**	0.358**	0.228**
	Sig.			0	0	0
Companionship	Correlation				0.376**	0.373**
	Sig.				0	0
Information exchange	Correlation					0.420**
	Sig.					0

** Correlation is significant at the 0.01 level (2-tailed); $N = 2,500$.

Table 1.4 *ANOVA and t-test Results: Demographic Variables vs Motivations and Addiction*

	Results	Social Interaction	Timepass	Comp	Information Exchange	Education or Profession	Addiction
Age	ANOVA (p)	0.024	0.000	0.015	0.005	0.000	0.000
	Highest	<23	<23	23–30	<23	<23	23–30
	Lowest	23–30	>30	>30	>30	>30	>30
Gender	t-test (p)	0.000	0.013	0.000	0.000	Not Sig.	0.015
	Highest	Female	Male	Male	Male	Male	Male
	Lowest	Male	Female	Female	Female	Female	Female
Education	ANOVA (p)	Not sig.	0.001	Not sig.	0.002	0.032	0.000
	Highest	+2	+2	PG	PG	PG	+2
	Lowest	PG	PG	UG	+2	+2	PG
Occupation	ANOVA (p)	0.000	0.000	0.000	0.000	0.000	0.000
	Highest	Student	Employed	Employed	Student	Student	Employed
	Lowest	Retired	Retired	Student	Homemaker	Homemaker	Homemaker
Income	ANOVA (p)	0.000	0.003	0.004	Not sig.	Not sig.	0.001
	Highest	15K–30K	>45K	15K–30K	15K–30K	30K–45K	<15K
	Lowest	30K–45K	30K–45K	>45K	<15K	>45K	>45K
Location	t-test	0.000	0.000	Not sig.	0.000	0.002	Not sig.
	Highest	Rural	Urban	Urban	Rural	Rural	Urban
	Lowest	Urban	Rural	Rural	Urban	Urban	Rural

exchange and educational and professional purposes, those belonging to the age group of 23–30 years were more motivated to use social media for companionship. The youngest group is also the one that showed the highest probability to get addicted to the online social media applications.

While male users were more interested in using social media for timepass, companionship and information exchange, their female counterparts were more motivated to use the applications for social interaction. Male groups were prone to addiction.

Similarly, those with low levels of education exhibited higher chances of getting addicted even though postgraduates had more motivations to get addicted. While students used social media platforms the most for social interaction, information exchange and educational and professional purposes, those employed used the applications for timepass and companionship and they were the ones who had the highest chances of getting addicted. The low-income groups were more inclined to use social media for companionship and get addicted. Both the rural and urban populace faced similar chances of getting addicted to social media.

RQ7. Is Social Network Type associated with Social Media Addiction and does it interact with Motivations to use social media in their relationships with Social media Addiction?

To answer this research question, one-way ANOVA and moderation analysis were conducted and the results are presented in Tables 1.5 and 1.6 and Figure 1.3.

Table 1.5 *One-way ANOVA: Social Network Type vs Social Media Addiction*

Dependent Variable	Mean Scores				Significance
	Egocentric	Sociocentric	Open	Mixed	
Social Media Addiction	15.8342	14.966	16.1159	16.2614	Significant at 0.05

Table 1.6 *Quadratic Regression: Motivations vs Addiction Moderated by Social Network Type*

Communication vs Dependency	Model Summary					Parameter Estimates		
Social Network Type	R Square	F	df1	df2	Sig.	Constant	b1	b2
Egocentric	0.016	11.311	2	1372	0.000	8.616	-0.157	0.006
Sociocentric	0.011	3.89	2	674	0.021	8.307	-0.176	0.006
Open	0.051	5.528	2	204	0.005	6.637	-0.055	0.004
Mixed	0.022	2.731	2	238	0.067	8.907	-0.26	0.008
Timepass vs Dependency	Model Summary					Parameter Estimates		
Egocentric	0.038	27.336	2	1372	0.000	6.531	0.033	0.001
Sociocentric	0.045	15.969	2	674	0.000	6.508	-0.006	0.002
Open	0.133	15.699	2	204	0.000	8.196	-0.308	0.012
Mixed	0.014	1.714	2	238	0.182	8.388	-0.23	0.007
Companionship vs Dependency	Model Summary					Parameter Estimates		
Egocentric	0.042	30.265	2	1372	0.000	4.209	0.18	-0.003
Sociocentric	0.006	2.031	2	674	0.132	5.291	0.106	-0.003
Open	0.081	8.99	2	204	0.000	5.427	0.021	0.002
Mixed	0.017	2.094	2	238	0.125	6.394	-0.057	0.003

Opinion-sharing vs Dependency	Model Summary					Parameter Estimates		
Egocentric	0.007	4.568	2	1372	0.011	5.786	0.15	−0.004
Sociocentric	0.01	3.298	2	674	0.038	6.74	−0.001	0.001
Open	0.007	0.721	2	204	0.488	7.368	−0.112	0.004
Mixed	0.018	2.133	2	238	0.121	9.052	−0.291	0.008

PE vs Dependency	Model Summary					Parameter Estimates		
Egocentric	0.008	5.714	2	1372	0.003	5.653	0.158	−0.004
Sociocentric	0.003	1.141	2	674	0.320	6.673	0.075	−0.002
Open	0.038	3.982	2	204	0.020	4.957	0.242	−0.006
Mixed	0.012	1.488	2	238	0.228	8.851	−0.172	0.005

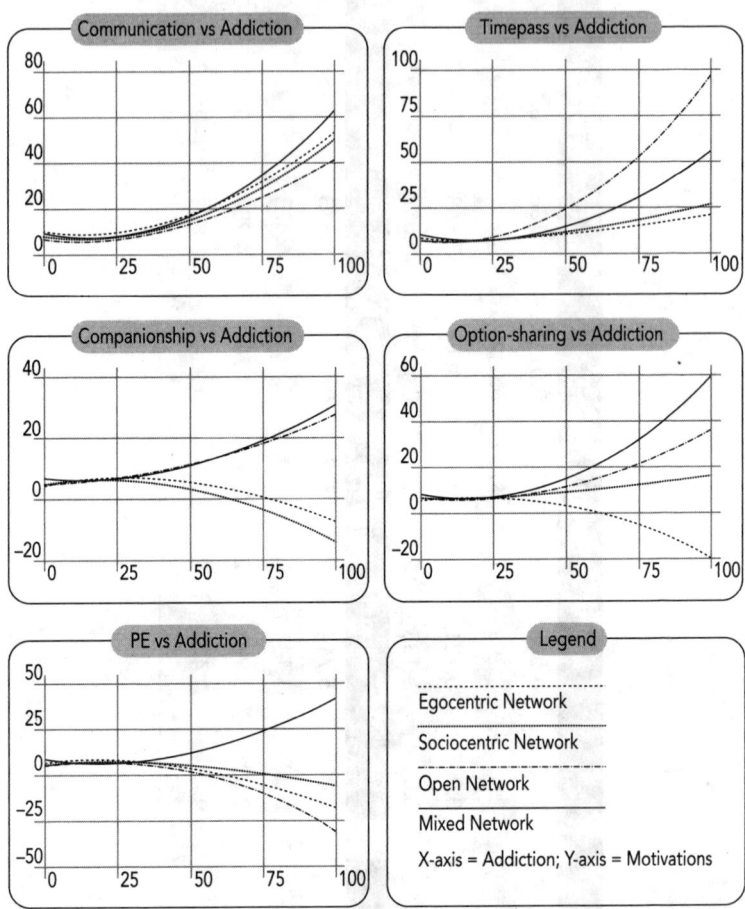

Figure 1.3 *Quadratic Regression Plots for Motivations vs Addiction, Moderated by Social Network Type*

Analysis results indicate that social network type is associated with the level of dependency or addiction, with those on the mixed networks showing high levels of addiction, followed by those on open social networks.

Study results indicate that social network type moderates the relationship between the motivations to use social media and social media dependency or addiction.

Those who are in mixed and egocentric networks have more chances of developing social media addiction when they use social media applications for communication.

Those who are in open and mixed networks have more chances of developing social media addiction when they use social media applications for communication. Similarly, those who are in mixed and open networks have more chances of developing social media addiction when they use social media applications for companionship. It could also be interpreted as those who use social media mainly for companionship purposes, that is, to develop and maintain relationships, tend to have open and mixed networks online.

Similarly, those who are in mixed and open networks have more chances of developing social media addiction when they use social media applications for opinion-sharing. Those who are in mixed and sociocentric networks have more chances of developing social media addiction when they use social media applications for professional and educational purposes.

RQ8. Is addiction associated with the triggers to share social media messages?

To test the relationship between social media dependency and triggers for sharing, t-tests were run, and the results are presented in Table 1.7.

All trigger variables barring shock, impact and human interest are associated with social media dependency. Those who tend to get

Table 1.7 *t-Test Results: Dependency vs Triggers*

Triggers	Mean Scores		Significance
	Not Triggered	Triggered	
Informative	15.2979	15.8608	Significant at 0.05
Humour	15.0467	16.2312	Significant at 0.05
Shock–surprise	15.7686	15.3926	Not significant
Impact	15.6879	15.5712	Not significant
Human interest	15.6202	15.7524	Not significant
Proximity	15.4655	16.456	Significant at 0.05

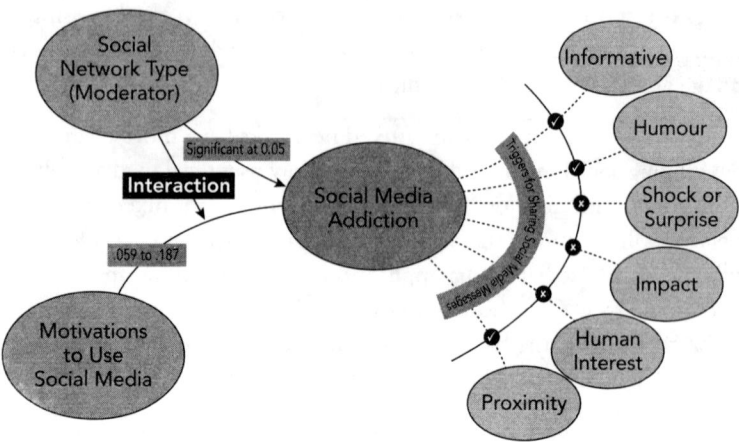

Figure 1.4 *Final Model*

addicted to social media platforms tend to share local, informative and humorous messages on social media.

Based on the study results, the final model is presented in Figure 1.4.

Qualitative Analysis

FGDs were conducted to answer the following research questions and the results are presented in Table 1.8 and Figure 1.5.

> RQ1. *What are the motivations to use online social media applications?*
> RQ2. *What are the levels of dependence or addiction?*
> RQ5. *Are users able to disengage from social media, when needed?*
> RQ6. *Are users able to differentiate themselves and their real-world actions from their social media persona and behaviours online?*

TRIANGULATION AND DISCUSSION

Though social interaction, timepass, information exchange, education and profession were the best motivators to use social media applications, it was companionship that drove users to addiction. A majority of the users showed moderate-to-high levels of addiction. The fact that about

Table 1.8 *FGD Results*

Categories	Themes	Overarching Concepts
Alternative media, citizen journalism	Activism	Motivations
Global reach, keyword search, timeliness, variety of options, verification	Capabilities	
Crisis communication, group communication, personal communication	Communication	
	Companionship	
Timepass	Entertainment	
Information exchange Information gain	Information	
	News	
Expression of feelings, expression of ideas, expression of thoughts, political discussion, public opinion	Opinion exchange	
	Peer pressure	
Education, file sharing, research, gaining fame, motivation, profession, business, marketing, advertising, professional skill development, showcasing talents, skill development	Personal development	
	Social learning	
Connecting with people, maintaining social relationship, socialization, socialization for introverts	Social networking	
	Conflict	Addiction
Avoiding loneliness	Mood modification	
Dominates behaviour, dominates thinking, health issues, information overdose, overdependence	Salience	

(Table 1.8 Continued)

(Table 1.8 Continued)

Categories	Themes	Overarching Concepts
	Withdrawal	
	Loss of detachment	
	Loss of distinction	

87 per cent of the users showed at least one symptom of addiction is an alarming finding. According to the study results, about 27 per cent of the users showed all signs of addiction.

Correlation test results also identified timepass and companionship as the motivators that best drive users to the pathological state of addiction. Positive intercorrelations were found among the motivational factors and addiction, indicating the soundness of the instrument and measurement. Further, linking companionship with addiction, it was those belonging to the age group of 23–30 years who used social media the most to find like-minded people online, develop relationships and communicate with their partners and also showed higher tendencies to develop social media addiction. Male, employed and economically weaker social media users were also more motivated to use applications for companionship purposes and more prone to addiction. It held good for both rural and urban social media users. Further, FGDs identified a range of factors that motivate people to use social media apps: activism, capabilities, communication, companionship, entertainment, information, news, opinion exchange, peer pressure, personal development, social learning and social networking.

Corroborating the findings of quantitative analysis and in line with the predilections, the qualitative analysis, too, indicated that social media applications had multiple uses and high levels of addiction. Further, the qualitative analysis also found support for the loss of distinction and detachment. Explaining this phenomenon, users reported to carry their digital devices wherever they go, even to their beds and

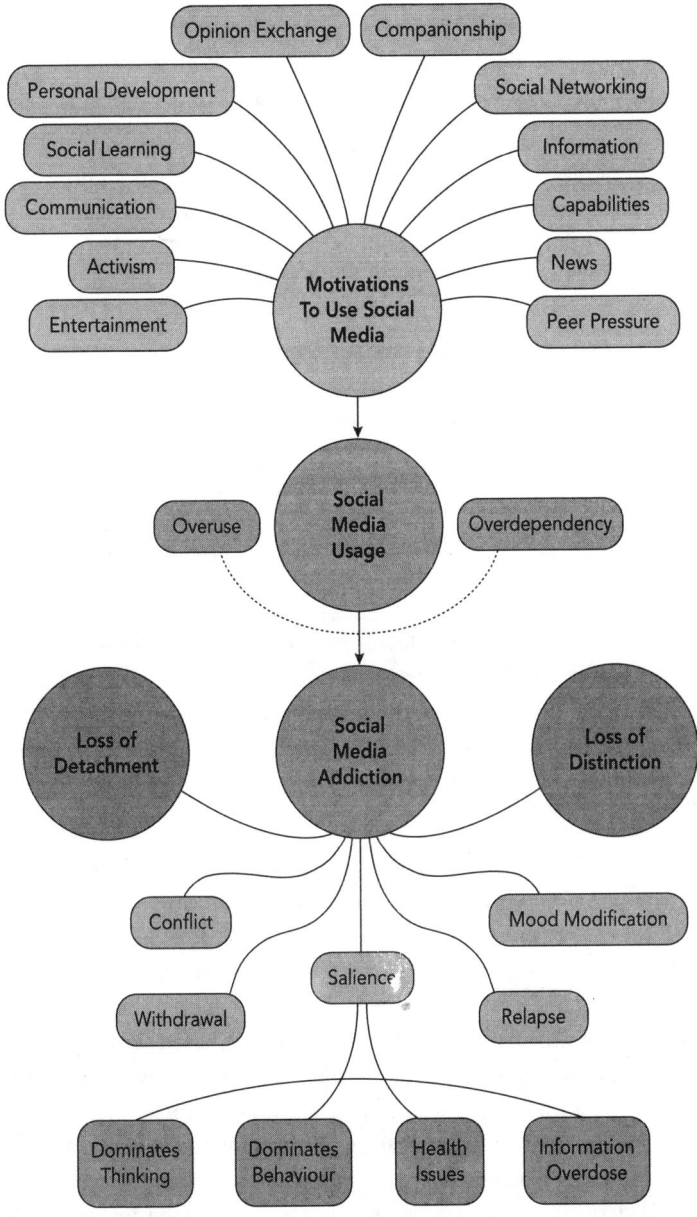

Figure 1.5 *FGD Results: Conceptual Model*

restrooms. They also reported withdrawal symptoms when they were not able to access the internet through their handheld devices.

Some of the users felt that there was no life without social media and even quoted communicating with their partners even when they were in the same place. Some of the partners were forced' to communicate via social media applications and maintain long-distance relationships, while a few others preferred online relationships to actual ones. It was also observed that users communicate so much through social media applications that they have lost the art of socializing with people in real life. Some of the users even felt that their devices and applications had become a part of them. While there was a clear lack of distinction between themselves and their real-world actions, from their social media persona and behaviours online in some cases, there were also cases which took their social media presence more seriously than their life or status offline. Users also reported to have experienced aggravating feelings when they faced threats online or when their expectations were not met on social media applications.

Most users accorded high levels of importance to their social media personage and spent considerable amounts of time and resources to maintain their social media exhibits. There were also instances of people forgetting their actual selves, during their indulgences online. Several such behaviours have also been studied (Bakhshi et al., 2015; Bell, 2019).

If people do not like their posts or status updates, or if their updates have not garnered enough views, users report getting upset. Wanting to record every (special or not) activity on social media applications and exhibit it to their social circles online for positive feedback has also had several detrimental effects, from not being able to indulge and enjoy the moment to being distressed when expected feedback is not received and developing personality disorders viewing the edited or unreal versions of people and their exhibits on social media. In the worst cases, users reported indications of detachment from actuality and to have developed psychological disorders such as anxiety, unreasonable fear and depression as a result of overuse, as reported in past studies (Venkat et al., 2014).

In line with the observations of several past studies (Deragon, 2011; Duradoni et al., 2020; Leung & Lee, 2012; Lin et al., 2017; Mahmood et al., 2020; Monacis et al., 2017), the current study also identified problematic social media use (overuse and addiction) from varied viewpoints, even though the users are more informed about these issues in the current times. The current study further validates the applicability of Bergen Social Media Addiction Scale and the model of addiction proposed by Griffiths (2005) with six facets in behavioural research.

While several studies (Cheung & Lee, 2009; Choi et al., 2016; Dolan et al, 2016; Hsu et al., 2015; Raacke & Bonds-Raacke, 2008; Sharifah et al., 2011) have identified a variety of motivations to use social media, qualitative analysis of the current study identified a few more.

To further corroborate the study findings that identify an addiction problem in India, a few of the local studies and their findings are consulted. Masthi et al. (2017), who investigated health issues related to social media usage and addiction in the Indian city of Bengaluru, and observed that such research on social media addiction were deficient in the Indian subcontinent where social media-related issues are burgeoning, found that about 20 per cent of the users suffered from the self-reported addiction syndromes, based on a survey. Further, addicted users were found to have a plethora of physical, psychological and behavioural issues, including sleep disturbances and neglected personal hygiene. Another similar survey conducted in South India also identified social media addiction among users and an association with loneliness (Shettar et al., 2017). Another Indian survey conducted among medical students in Delhi found an association between social media addiction and sleep deprivation (Basu et al., 2021).

CONCLUSION

Both the qualitative and quantitative analyses indicate alarming levels of social media use, with these applications and activities performed on them dominating their thinking and behaviours. The study also identified two new concepts, the lack of detachment from digital devices and loss of the ability of the users to differentiate themselves and their real-world actions from their social media persona and behaviours online, as newer dimensions to social media addiction, creating a new normal where smartphones are an undetachable part of human lives and such addictive behaviour is viewed as natural, normal and not a disorder.

Unlike other addictions such as that to drugs, these new dimensions are especially specific to social media addiction, as they are easily accessible through handheld mobile devices that are perennially attached to users, offer a plethora of uses and services, and most importantly, mediate social interaction and relationships.

Consulting the theoretical frameworks reviewed, from the uses and gratification and media dependency perspectives to the theory of rational addiction, the all-embracing premise that emerges is that users start social media use with rational intends, but maladaptive and detrimental usage reconstructs that habit into psychological dependence, leading to the clinical state of addiction. Understanding from the study findings, the archetype of a social media addict emerges to be male, employed but economically weaker or belonging to the age group of 23–30 years and motivated to use social media more for passing time and to build and maintain (more often than not, romantic) relationships online (companionship). A majority of the users showed moderate-to-high levels of addiction. That about 87 per cent of the users showed at least one symptom of addiction is an alarming finding. According to the study results, about 27 per cent of the users showed all signs of addiction.

REFERENCES

Agarwal, S. (2018, February 20). Internet users in India expected to reach 500 million by June: IAMAI. *The Economic Times*. Retrieved Jan 3, 2021, from https://economictimes.indiatimes.com/tech/internet/internet-users-in-india-expected-to-reach-500-million-by-june-iamai/articleshow/63000198.cms?utm_source=contentofinterest&utm_medium=text&utm_campaign=cppst

Alabi, O. F . (2013). A survey of Facebook addiction level among selected Nigerian university undergraduates. *New Media and Mass Communication*, 10, 70–80.

Andreassen, C. S., Torsheim, T., Brunborg, G. S., & Pallesen, S. (2012). Development of a Facebook addiction scale. *Psychological Reports*, *110*(2), 501–517.

Andreassen, C. S., Pallesen, S., & Griffiths, M. D. (2017). The relationship between addictive use of social media, narcissism, and self-esteem: Findings from a large national survey. *Addictive Behaviors, 64,* 287–293.

Arora, Kim. (2017, July 15). India has the most FB users: Report. Retrieved from https://timesofindia.indiatimes.com/india/india-has-the-most-fb-users-report/articleshow/59603509.cms

Bakhshi, S., Shamma, D., Kennedy, L., & Gilbert, E. (2015, April). Why we filter our photos and how it impacts engagement. In *Proceedings of the International AAAI Conference on Web and Social Media, 9*(1).

Balakrishnan, J., & Griffiths, M. D. (2017). Social media addiction: What is the role of content in YouTube? *Journal of Behavioral Addictions, 6*(3), 364–377.

Ball-Rokeach S. J., & DeFleur M. L. (1976). A dependency model of mass-media effects. *Communication Research, 3*(1), 3–21. doi:10.1177/009365027600300101

Barclay, F. P., Chinnasamy, P., & Pichandy, P. (2014). Political opinion expressed in social media and election outcomes—US presidential elections 2012. *GSTF International Journal on Media & Communications (JMC), 1*(2), 15–22.

Barclay, F. P., Pichandy, C., Venkat, A., & Sudhakaran, S. (2015). India 2014: Facebook 'like'as a predictor of election outcomes. *Asian Journal of Political Science, 23*(2), 134–160.

Barclay, F. P., Pichandy, C., Venkat, A., & Sudhakaran, S. (2016). Twitter sentiments: Pattern recognition and poll prediction. In Communication and Information Technologies Annual. Emerald Group Publishing Limited.

Barclay, F. P. (2017). Media effect on media: Progression of political news and tweets during India 2014. *Journal of Media and Communication, 1*(1), 1–28.

Basu, S., Sharma, R., Sharma, P., & Sharma, N. (2021). Addiction-like behavior associated with social media usage in undergraduate students of a government medical college in Delhi, India. *Indian Journal of Psychiatry, 63*(1), 35.

Bell, B. T. (2019). 'You take fifty photos, delete forty nine and use one': A qualitative study of adolescent image-sharing practices on social media. *International Journal of Child Computer Interaction, 20,* 64–71.

Bumgarner, Brett A. (2007). You have been poked: Exploring the uses and gratifications of Facebook among emerging adults. *First Monday, 12*(11). https://doi.org/10.5210/fm.v12i11.2026

Byun, S., Ruffini, C., Mills, J. E., Douglas, A. C., Niang, M., Stepchenkova, S., Lee, S. K., Loutfi, J., Lee, J. K., Atallah, M., & Blanton, M. (2009). Internet addiction: Metasynthesis of 1996–2006 quantitative research. *CyberPsychology & Behavior, 12*(2), 203–207.

Cabral, J. (2008). Is generation Y addicted to social media? *Future of Children, 2*(1), 5–14.

Cheung, C. M., & Lee, M. K. (2009). Understanding the sustainability of a virtual community: Model development and empirical test. *Journal of Information Science, 35*(3), 279–298.

Cheung, C. M. K., Chiu, P. Y. & Lee, M. K. (2011). Online social networks: Why do students use Facebook? *Computers in Human Behavior, 27*(4), 1337–1343.

Choi, E. K., Fowler, D., Goh, B., & Yuan, J. (2016). Social media marketing: Applying the uses and gratifications theory in the hotel industry. *Journal of Hospitality Marketing & Management, 25*(7), 771–796.

Corbin, J. M., & Strauss, A. (1990). Grounded theory research: Procedures, canons, and evaluative criteria. *Qualitative Sociology, 13*(1), 3–21.

Dalvi-Esfahani, M., Niknafs, A., Alaedini, Z., Ahmadabadi, H. B., Kuss, D. J., & Ramayah, T. (2020). Social media addiction and empathy: Moderating impact of personality traits among high school students. *Telematics and Informatics, 57*(6), 101516.

Deragon, J. (2011, January 11). What is your social media malady? NextGen Digital Strategis. Retrieved from http://www. Socialmediatoday.com/jderagon/260352/what-youy-social-media-malady

Dhaha, I. S. Y. A., & Igale, A. B. (2014). Motives as predictors of Facebook addiction: Empirical evidence from Somalia. *SEARCH: The Journal of the South East Asia Research Centre for Communication and Humanities, 2*(6), 1–22.

Dolan, R., Conduit, J., Fahy, J., & Goodman, S. (2016). Social media engagement behaviour: A uses and gratifications perspective. *Journal of Strategic Marketing, 24*(3–4), 261–277.

Duradoni, M., Innocenti, F., & Guazzini, A. (2020). Well-Being and social media: A systematic review of Bergen Addiction Scales. *Future Internet, 12*(2), 24.

Echeburua, E., & deCorral, P. (2010). Addiction to new technologies and to online social networking in young people: A new challenge. *Adicciones, 22*, 91–95.

Express Tech (2018, July 18). LinkedIn now has over 50 million users in India. Retrieved from https://indianexpress.com/article/technology/social/linkedin-now-has-over-50-million-users-in-india-5264336/

FE Online (2018, February 1). WhatsApp now has 1.5 billion monthly active users, 200 million users in India. Retrieved from https://www.financialexpress.com/industry/technology/whatsapp-now-has-1-5-billion-monthly-active-users-200-million-users-in-india/1044468/

Gan, C., & Wang, W. (2015). Uses and gratifications of social media: A comparison of microblog and WeChat. *Journal of Systems and Information Technology, 17*(4), 351–363. doi:10.1108/JSIT-06-2015-0052

Griffiths, M. D. (2005). A 'components' model of addiction within a biopsychosocial framework. *Journal of Substance Use, 10*, 191–197. doi:10.1080/14659890500114359

Grindeland, M., & Harrison, C. (2009). The power of social networking for women research study. Retrieved from www.shesconnectedmultimedia.com

Gruzd, A., Haythornthwaite, C., Paulin, D., Gilbert, S., & Del Valle, M. E. (2018). Uses and gratifications factors for social media use in teaching: Instructors' perspectives. *New Media & Society, 20*(2), 475–494.

Hawi, N. S., & Samaha, M. (2017). The relations among social media addiction, self-esteem, and life satisfaction in university students. *Social Science Computer Review, 35*(5), 576–586.

Hawi, N., & Samaha, M. (2019). Identifying commonalities and differences in personality characteristics of Internet and social media addiction profiles: Traits, self-esteem, and self-construal. *Behaviour & Information Technology*, *38*(2), 110–119.

Hou, Y., Xiong, D., Jiang, T., Song, L., & Wang, Q. (2019). Social media addiction: Its impact, mediation, and intervention. *Cyberpsychology: Journal of Psychosocial Research on Cyberspace*, *13*(1). doi:10.5817/CP2019-1-4

Hsu, M.-H., Chang, C.-M., Lin, H.-C., & Lin, Y.-W. (2015). Determinants of continued use of social media: The perspectives of uses and gratifications theory and perceived interactivity. *Information Research, 20*(2), paper 671. Retrieved from http://InformationR.net/ir/20-2/paper671.html (Archived by WebCite® at http://www.webcitation.org/6ZG2FYK7I).

Iqbal, Mansoor. (2020. October 30). Facebook revenue and usage statistics (2020). BusinessofApps. Retrieved from https://www.businessofapps.com/data/facebook-statistics/#:~:text=Alphabet%2C%20and%20Amazon-,Facebook%20User%20Statistics,world's%20largest%20social%20media%20platform

Karaiskos, D., Tzavellas, E., Balta, G., & Paparrigopoulos, T. (2010). Social network addiction: A new clinical disorder? *European Psychiatry*, *25*, 855. doi:10.1016/S0924-9338(10)70846-4

Karaiskos, Dimitris, Tzavellas, Elias, Balta, G., and Paparrigopoulos, Thomas. (2010). Social network addiction: A new clinical disorder? *European Psychiatry, 25*, 2–232.

Katz, E., Flumler, J. G., & Michael Gurevitch, M. (1974). *The uses and gratifications approach to mass communication.* SAGE Publications.

Khazaal, Y., Billieux, J., Thorens, G., Khan, R., Louati, Y., Scarlatti, E., & Zullino, D. (2008). French validation of the internet addiction test. *CyberPsychology & Behavior, 11*(6), 703–706.

Lam, L. T., Peng, Z. W., Mai, J. C., & Jing, J. (2009). Factors associated with Internet addiction among adolescents. *CyberPsychology & Behavior, 12*(5), 551–555.

Leong, L. Y., Hew, T. S., Ooi, K. B., Lee, V. H., & Hew, J. J. (2019). A hybrid SEM-neural network analysis of social media addiction. *Expert Systems with Applications, 133*, 296–316.

Leung, L., & Lee, P.S.N. (2012). The influences of information literacy, internet addiction and parenting styles on internet risks. *New Media & Society, 14*(1), 117–136.

Lin, C. Y., Broström, A., Nilsen, P., Griffiths, M. D., & Pakpour, A. H. (2017). Psychometric validation of the Persian Bergen Social Media Addiction Scale using Classic Test Theory and Rasch models. *Journal of Behavioral Addictions, 6*(4), 620–629.

Liu, C., & Ma, J. (2018). Development and validation of the Chinese social media addiction scale. *Personality and Individual Differences, 134*, 55–59.

Mahmood, Q. K., Jafree, S. R., & Sohail, M. M. (2020). Pakistani youth and social media addiction: The validation of Bergen Facebook Addiction Scale

(BFAS). *International Journal of Mental Health and Addiction*, 1–14. doi:10.1007/s11469-020-00391-0

Marengo, D., Poletti, I., & Settanni, M. (2020). The interplay between neuroticism, extraversion, and social media addiction in young adult Facebook users: Testing the mediating role of online activity using objective data. *Addictive Behaviors*, *102*, 106150.

Masthi, N. N. R., Pruthvi, S., & Mallekavu, P. (2017). A comparative study on social media addiction between public and private high school students of urban Bengaluru, India. *Journal of Psychiatry*, *18*(2), 206–215.

Mitter, Sohini. (2018, March 26). YouTube monthly user base touches 225 million in India, reaches 80 pc of internet population. Your Story. Retrieved from https://yourstory.com/2018/03/youtube-monthly-user-base-touches-225-million-india-reaches-80-pc-internet-population?utm_pageloadtype=scroll

Monacis, L., de Palo, Valeria., Griffiths, M. D., & Sinatra, M. (2017). Social networking addiction, attachment style, and validation of the Italian version of the Bergen Social Media Addiction Scale. *Journal of Behavioral Addictions*, *6*(2), 178–186.

Nair, Parvathy S., and Barclay, Francis P. (2017). Twitter usage patterns as a predictor of user gender. *Journal of Media and Communication*, *1*(2), 1–23.

Nakaya, A. C. (2015). Internet and social media addiction. *Webology*, *12*(2), 1–3.

NapoleonCat. (2021, January 6). Facebook users in India: January 2020. NapoleonCat.com, Retrieved from https://napoleoncat.com/stats/facebook-users-in-india/2020/01

Ng, B. D., & Wiemer-Hastings, P. (2005). Addiction to the internet and online gaming. *CyberPsychology & Behavior*, *8*(2), 110–113.

Park, N., Kee, K.F., & Valenzuela, S. (2009). Being immersed in social networking environment: Facebook groups, uses and gratifications, and social outcomes. *CyberPsychology & Behavior*, *12*(6), 729–733.

Pelling, E. L., & White, K. M. (2009). The theory of planned behaviour applied to young people's use of social networking sites. *CyberPsychology & Behavior*, *12*, 755–759.

Quan-Haase, A., & Young, A. L. (2010). Uses and gratifications of social media: A comparison of Facebook and instant messaging. *Bulletin of Science, Technology & Society*, *30*(5), 350–361.

Quora (2016, November 20). What's the user base of Instagram users in India currently? Any statistics available with a valid link to it? Retrieved from https://www.quora.com/Whats-the-user-base-of-Instagram-users-in-India-currently-Any-statistics-available-with-a-valid-link-to-it

Raacke, J., & Bonds-Raacke, J. (2008). MySpace and Facebook: Applying the uses and gratifications theory to exploring friend-networking sites. *CyberPsychology & Behavior*, *11*(2), 169–174.

Raj, Pritish. (2020, June 12). WhatsApp has most active users in India, followed by YouTube in May 2020. NextBigBrand. Retrieved from https://www.nextbigbrand.in/whatsapp-has-most-active-users-in-india-followed-by-youtube-in-may-2020/

Sharifah S. Z, Sofiah, Omar, S. Z. Bolong, J., & Osman, M. N. (2011). Facebook addiction among female university students. *Revista De Administratie Publica Si Politici Sociale*, 2(7): 95–109.

Shettar, M., Karkal, R., Kakunje, A., Mendonsa, R. D., & Chandran, V. M. (2017). Facebook addiction and loneliness in the post-graduate students of a university in southern India. *International Journal of Social Psychiatry*, 63(4), 325–329.

Statista. (2018, November 20). Digital population in India as of January 2018 (in millions), Retrieved from https://www.google.com/url?sa=t&rct=j&q=&es rc=s&source=web&cd=2&cad=rja&uact=8&ved=2ahUKEwiqsNLoreLeAh URfn0KHa89Dg4QFjABegQIBBAE&url=https%3A%2F%2Fwww.statista. com%2Fstatistics%2F309866%2Findia-digital-population%2F&usg=AOvVa w3otWa7eqmKRjKyAiGAlnVf

Statista. (2021a). Number of internet users in India from 2015 to 2020 with a forecast until 2025. Statista.com. Retrieved from https://www.statista.com/ statistics/255146/number-of-internet-users-in-india/

Statista. (2021b. Number of social network users in India from 2015 to 2018 with a forecast until 2023. Statista.com. Retrieved from https://www.statista.com/ statistics/278407/number-of-social-network-users-in-india/

Statista. (2021c). Leading countries based on Facebook audience size as of October 2020. Statista.com. Retrieved from https://www.statista.com/ statistics/268136/top-15-countries-based-on-number-of-facebook-users/

Statista. (2021d, January 27). Number of internet users worldwide from 2005 to 2019. Statista.com. Retrieved from https://www.statista.com/ statistics/273018/number-of-internet-users-worldwide/

Statista. (2021e). Global digital population as of October 2020. Statista.com, retrieved from https://www.statista.com/statistics/617136/digital-population-worldwide/

TNN (2018, June 27). After Saudis, most Indians got on social media last year. Retrieved from https://timesofindia.indiatimes.com/business/after-saudis-most-indians-got-on-social-media-last-year/articleshow/64707516.cms

Turel, O., Brevers, D., & Bechara, A. (2018). Time distortion when users at-risk for social media addiction engage in non-social media tasks. *Journal of Psychiatric Research*, 97, 84–88.

Tutgun-Ünal, A., & Deniz, L. (2015). Development of the social media addiction scale. *AJIT-e*, 6(21), 51.

United Nations. (2021). India: General Information. UNData App. Retrieved from http://data.un.org/en/iso/in.html

Urista, Mark A., Dong, Qingwen, and Day, Kenneth Day. (2009). Explaining why young adults use MySpace and Facebook through uses and gratifications theory. *Human Communication*, 12(2), 215–229.

Venkat, Anusha, Pichandy, C., Barclay, Francis P., and Jayaseelan, R. (2014). Facebook privacy management: An empirical study of awareness, perception and fears. *Global Media Journal-Indian Edition, 5*(1), 1–20.

Venkat, Anusha. 2017. A motivation-based perspective of Facebook addiction. *Journal of Media and Communication, 1*(1), 49–71.

Wang, C., Lee, M. K., & Hua, Z. (2015). A theory of social media dependence: Evidence from microblog users. *Decision Support Systems, 69*, 40–49.

Whiting, A., & Williams, D. (2013). Why people use social media: A uses and gratifications approach. *Qualitative Market Research: An International Journal, 16*(4). 1352–2752

Wilson K, Fornasier S., & White K. (2010). Psychological predictors of young adults' use of social net-working sites. *Cyberpsychology, Behavior and Social Networking, 13*(12), 173–177.

Younes, F., Halawi, G., Jabbour, H., El Osta, N., Karam, L., Hajj, A., & Rabbaa Khabbaz, L. (2016). Internet addiction and relationships with insomnia, anxiety, depression, stress and self-esteem in university students: A cross-sectional designed study. *PLOS One, 11*(9), e0161126.

Zivnuska, S., Carlson, J. R., Carlson, D. S., Harris, R. B., & Harris, K. J. (2019). Social media addiction and social media reactions: The implications for job performance. *The Journal of Social Psychology, 159*(6), 746–760.

Chapter 2

Political Ideologies, Affiliation and Participation
Are These Related in Contemporary India?

Boobalakrishnan N., Francis P. Barclay and Anushiya K.

INTRODUCTION

Associating an individual with single political ideology—given the complicated functions and nature of the ideological belief systems in varied sociopolitical contexts—may be impractical or an act of reductionism. Ideology could be a complicated concept (Szalay et al., 1972), with varying realities and expressions, and an umbrella term that could be determined with a combination of subsets or facets, which individuals use to take a stand on political institutions and governance. Conventional structure of an individual ideology is possessed by the environment and its prescription of how that should be structured, which also shares the mental models that a group of individuals carry (Denzau & North, 2000). From this point of view, people have to be well informed to adapt to a group of possibilities (various belief systems) which characterize the institution and the link between individual ideas and interests, which is said to be the 'selective process'. It would be interesting to address the belief system as an individual identity in India as a larger social process than as a selective process, for the reason that it has a governance structure and legacy with a track of centuries. Hence, political ideology and its affinity is continually in flux irrespective of the phenomena, emerging, adapted and transformed with influences from various parts of the world.

Ancient India had freedom of thought to some extent, which would mean it had democratic governance in the past and continued to persist which could be traced, providing evidence for democratic roots. The modern Indian political system may not be completely indigenous. India adopted the parliamentary democracy system only after the liberation from the British rule, which has protracted British influence in the Indian political system.

India, if you look at it as a sociopolitical system, is volatile, with alterations in ideas and interests of the political parties that vie for a chance to be in power. It is highly critical to conceive a political ideology and label it for a group of individuals, because of its presence in the factual track of events shaping them in unique ways. And, considering the regional reciprocation towards human values and attitudes in the milieu (Chakrabarty, 2008), it is obvious that nationalism and democratization were the two facets of identity that have crystallized during the pre- and post-Independence era.

Conceptualizing the political ideology of an individual as well as the parties and labelling it categorically is a challenging task, because the centrality of ideas of any political party is often far from comprehensible (Freeden, 2001). It should be studied in specific conditions and be tailored accordingly (Dommett, 2012). Various studies have attempted to put forward this variance and find out the degree to which the ideological inclination of one's belief in the political system and governance prevails (Delmonico, 2016; Lahoti et al., 2018; Northey et al., 2020; Nuechterlein, 1988; Ordabayeva & Fernandes, 2018; Rachlinski et al., 2017; Wänke, 2015).

Schematizing the notions of political ideology becomes an important examination in which individuals hold an opinion consciously or unconsciously called political ideology. Political perspectives need to be operationalized to identify the cluster and polarization (Bjornskov & Potrafke, 2012; Holbrook & Poe, 1987) of people's desire by exploring the political philosophies which are apparent and relevant to the contemporary sociopolitical system (Berry et al., 1998). In advancing the conceptual understanding, ingenious measures covering the holistic perspective of the political and governance system can be accommodated in the four dimensions (government, citizen, social, capital) which are also related (Ma, 2017) and relevant to any democratic government. Government functions as a system and it is evident to see the hierarchy among the members in the system, working under a set of roles and responsibilities between the authorities (policymakers), bureaucrats (executors) and citizens (consumers) in which they function. Policymakers mostly stand at a higher level in governance, and this is projected as hierarchy in the system and this operation is fluid, reciprocating and reinforcing among the citizens and the head of state in a democratic nation.

However, in such a system of governance, if the government becomes the sole authority in making decisions, suppressing the opposition and demanding the citizens to accept, it may face consequences. Conversely, the hierarchical mode of governance can help in executing the programmes and making decisions at multiple levels by granting autonomy (Cai, 2008). As these claims reflect the two-dimensional facet of governance, as authoritarian and autonomous, which is imbibed by the power structure among the stakeholders in the state.

It is something of which the system is in control, and in particular, it is essential in a democracy that the citizens participate in governance or else they would be forced to fight for freedom. Hence, it is necessary to identify the freedom of choices (Pettit, 2014), socially and politically justified as individuals' belief in a state like India. 'Social freedom' is defined as 'to enable individuals and groups with divergent political and moral views to agree on what it is they disagree about on the normative level' (Oppenheim, 2004). Without considering economics, studying and measuring the political ideology becomes void, and as aforementioned, to bring up the freedom of choice with respect to economy is about an individual's control over their wages and assets, which as a result supports an environment for the citizens to work, produce and do businesses freely. After schematizing control and freedom (social and economical) as political ideological stands, it leads to look into how far these are apparent in society. Within this context, this chapter has taken political ideology by conglomerating the ideological beliefs articulated by political philosophies across the world and development of the state to pre- and post-Independence, which are pertinent in grasping contemporary Indian politics. Remarkably, ideology has come up as a decisive attitude and insists on the need for enquiry among the individuals and groups in this contemporary scenario. It produces a specific model that may be applicable to the Indian socio-economic and cultural circumstances, which is perhaps the most populous democracy in the world.

In this line, identifying one's own ideological preferences towards politics and governance becomes convoluted, and hence, participation becomes a serious concern that needs to be addressed. The earliest political participation studies concentrated on willingness to vote and mostly examined the voting behaviour of citizens (Milbrath, 1981). Later, researchers started enquiring into other activities allied with political participation such as attending party meetings, increasing memberships, financial donations and so on.

Sparing time, spending money and civic skills like voting are termed to be the individual's resources to participate in political activities, which are mostly acquired during early life, that too in the non-political institutions (Brady et al., 1995). Apart from casting votes, political participation, in these times, is not limited to conventional acts such as taking part in party meetings and rallies, or it may even be argued that such traditional modes of political participation are limited and bygone. A political vacuum thus created is being compensated by the digital space where individuals choose political information that they prefer to consume or of their interest, and they express their insights with embedded ideologies, either consciously or unconsciously, devising the mise en scene of the political drama played out on a plethora of digital platforms. Political participation in non-political institutions in the modern times is inevitable and at the same time, the techno-friendly features of the new medium is well built to voice one's opinions and its rapid growth is undeniable.

Political participation online, attributing the aforementioned acts, varies distinctively or desegregates based on the social media type they use and that may be fostered by this online medium (Gibson & Cantijoch, 2013). Other forms of participation using digital technologies, which covers opinion development towards governance and commenting on the policy decisions taken affect civic life and nations' welfare.

Social media plays a vital role in people's choice of media, where it unites them coherently, and a majority of research focuses on examining the effects of such engagement with the democratic process. This may in turn establish the connection between social media usage and political expression and participation. It has been shown that social media has an apparent stand in demonstrating the democratic process (Boulianne, 2019; Gil de Zuniga et al., 2014). There are two contradictory perspectives about the internet when it comes to political participation. One, the Internet provides citizens with the feeling that they can leverage the government and the government will pay heed to their concerns, which will motivate them to involve more actively and mobilize people.

Two, there is not much evidence that the Internet plays a major role in the democratic process, which requires further research (Di Gennaro & Dutton, 2006). It is more relevant to examine the effects and relationships of demographic variables (gender, age, education etc.,) and their association (Boulianne, 2019; Brady et al., 1995; Hirzalla et al., 2011; Kim, 2019) with political interests and expressing them online and offline, though inconsistent (Kim et al., 2017). When it comes to interest among various age groups, it is observed that often the driving factors, 'friendship driven' and 'interest driven', influence the political engagement among weak ties more than among strong ties (Kahne & Bowyer, 2018).

Office-bearers of political parties play a major role in mobilizing and disseminating information among the party and non-party members through conventional acts. Political parties mostly rely (Fisher et al., 2014) on party members that they would accomplish the tasks assigned to them. If this alone determines the success of political and election campaigns, then why do some parties with large memberships not come out with effective and successful campaigns (Boulianne, 2015; Fisher et al., 2014; Whiteley & Seyd, 2003)?

Though political parties encourage their partisans to propagate (Lilleker, 2013) their messages for maximum reach, committed party members may be limited, and hence, mediated actions may be necessary for a wider coverage, to enable non-partisan participation online, create a massive followership and result in less divisive campaigns (Asencio & Sun, 2015; Lilleker & Koc-Michalska, 2017).

Social media usage and its effect on political participation of citizens has become the focal point of many researchers because of the Arab spring (2010 to 2012) and Obama's campaign (2008 and 2012). Also, some studies have shown a positive relationship between social media usage and political participation (Boulianne, 2015; Kim, 2019) because of the technological revolution across the globe which has increased the use of social networking sites and its tools utmost for political activities (Boulianne, 2020).

Social media can be helpful for ordinary citizens to express their views openly about the functioning, shortcomings and opinions of the state machinery. It is evident that it works diligently to convey one's views on political issues and politicians, especially during elections. Social networking sites have become an important component in the political sphere and an inevitable platform for politicians in the contemporary scenario. Social media platforms offer opportunities to engage young audiences (Howard, 2019) and enable politicians to build their populist relationship with and articulate their ideologies among the masses without gatekeeping, which mainstream media has to comply with (Bartlett, 2014; Engesser et al., 2017).

Politicians become brands during the election campaigns just as traditional marketing campaigns. Social media usage during campaigns depends on the issue they address and acts as a marketing stratagem in the election campaign arena. Because of the features such sites have, they get direct, cost-effective contact with voters with instant feedback (Magic Mile Media, 2019). In addition, the efforts that candidates build to brand themselves on social media can lead to increasing the attention of the traditional mainstream media and sometimes turning into headlines. According to Trilling (1972), credibility and honesty are the two facets which describe a person's trueness to inner-self and to others respectively. Politicians are considered to be most honest on social media (Enli & Rosenberg, 2018).

On the other hand, when left uncontrolled, it would be a challenge for politicians and the political contents posted online becomes questionable in terms of trustworthiness. Fake messages have become one of the major issues on social media. One of the biggest challenges politicians face in using social media is their lack of knowledge about the structure of social networking sites and the lack of technical skills required to use it (Howard et al., 2016). Many politicians and parties hire professionals, proxying them for their political activities. This raises the question of direct linkage between politicians and voters, and in many cases this leads to issues and politicians losing their credibility with their followers and public.

Social media has become one of the major platforms for political participation to share political information and engage themselves in many political activities (Ahmad et al. 2019). As yet, research on social media usage and political participation is expediting and producing diverse results. On the one side, the kind of social media use determines the relationship between its usage and political participation (Gil de Zúñiga et al., 2012; Vitak et al., 2011).

Further, an obvious prediction like positive relationship between social media use and various factors of political involvement (Bode, 2012; Valenzuela et al., 2009; Zhang et al., 2013) is also suggested by various studies. Diverse and sometimes contradictory claims have been made by researchers who have studied the relationship between political activities, online and offline (Kim et al., 2017), such as online and offline political participation are independent of each other (Emmer et al., 2012); they are highly associated with each other (Bode et al., 2014; Gil de Zúñiga et al., 2014); and participation online and offline could be mutually encouraging (Harlow & Harp, 2012; Vissers & Stolle, 2014).

Social media and its features including expressing their views through various forms provide more opportunities for political parties and politicians to mobilize and engage social media users in political activities (Metkar & Aade, 2020). Social networking sites such as Facebook, Twitter facilitate politicians to have instant and direct messaging and contact with their followers and public. Policymakers and many governments have accepted that mobilizing people on social media to protest and raise questions leads to promotion of good governance in the country (Dwivedi, 2011). Social media has become an integral part of youth and in near future it will be used to engage youngsters in political activities, and during election times social media plays a major role in promoting the images and political messages among people (Adhana & Saxena, 2018; Meti et al., 2015; Parida & Das, 2014).

Our research explores the political ideology of an individual in this contemporary scenario and aims to study the relationship between political ideology and online and offline political participation. It also attempts to examine the connection between political party affiliation and participation and political ideology. To address these, the following research questions have been raised.

RQ1: *What political ideology exists among the civic?*
RQ2: *What are the online and offline political participations engaged in?*
RQ3: *Are political ideology and political participation (online and offline) related?*
RQ4: *Does party affiliation have any effect on the political participation (online and offline) of individuals?*

METHODOLOGY

In this quantitative survey, a multistage cluster sampling procedure was employed to sample 2,500 social media users across the Indian state of Tamil Nadu. Political ideology, affiliation and political participation are the major variables measured. The survey questionnaire used to measure political ideology is developed with the following four factors: power structure, social freedom, economic freedom and social justice using a five-point Likert scale. These variables are predetermined with theoretical and literature support. Political affiliation is measured with the following three categories: no party affiliation, just affiliated to a party and office-bearer of a party. Political participation (online and offline) variable is measured using six items in a five-point Likert scale.

ANALYSIS AND RESULTS

Exploratory factor analysis was performed among the political ideology items to identify the strongest items underpinned under this construct, and then the instrument was developed, and validation was performed. Kaiser–Meyer–Olkin value of 0.826 suggested sampling adequacy and Bartlett's test of sphericity is significant and provided evidence to reject the null hypothesis that the correlation matrix is not identical. After these test values were obtained, the principal component method was adopted for the factorial analysis (see Table 2.1 and Figure 2.1).

Table 2.1 *Factor Loadings*

Political Ideology Items	PS	SJ	EF	SF
Government decisions should always be accepted.	0.705			
Court decisions are final.	0.668			
Government should be the sole decision-making authority.	0.743			
The best way to ensure peace is through military strength.	0.711			
One should always support his/ her country, whether it was right or wrong.	0.611			
Same-sex marriage should be legalized.				0.803
Smoking is a personal choice, and the government should ignore.				0.585
Homosexuality should be accepted by society.				0.795
Minimum-wage laws are important.			0.693	
Business corporations make too much profit.			0.668	
The economic system in this country unfairly favours powerful interests.			0.673	

(Table 2.1 Continued)

(Table 2.1 Continued)

Political Ideology Items	PS	SJ	EF	SF
Income redistribution is more important than economic growth.			0.561	
Reservations are important for the upliftment of the downtrodden.		0.529		
Populist schemes for the down-trodden should be encouraged.		0.625		
Alleviation of poverty should be the first priority.		0.742		
Establishments should prioritize the welfare of the workers.		0.752		
Gap between rich and poor should be reduced.		0.614		

PS: Power Structure; SF: Social Freedom; EF: Economic Freedom; SJ: Social Justice

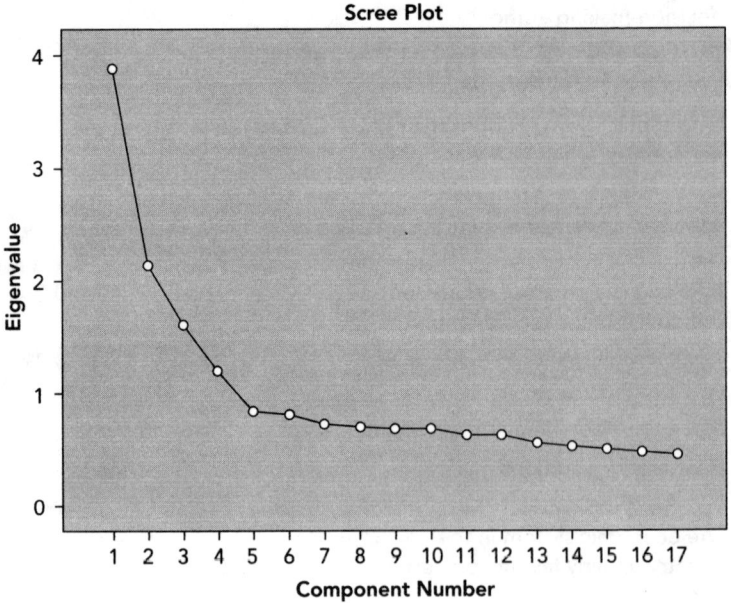

Figure 2.1 *Scree Plot*

Factorability of the 17 political ideology items was explored. It was observed that the 17 items are correlated with at least 0.3 with at least one other item, suggesting logical factorability (correlation matrix). Further, the Kaiser–Meyer–Olkin measure of sampling adequacy was 0.82, which was above the suggested value of 0.6, and Bartlett's test of sphericity was significant (χ^2 (136) = 8677.05, $p < 0.05$). The communalities of the proposed items were all above 0.3 (see Table 2.1). Given these indications, factor analysis was suitable with all the 17 items. The four-factor solution explained 52 per cent of the variance and it supports the theoretical background, with the scree plot 'levelling off' of eigenvalues shown after four factors. Cronbach's alpha was used to examine the reliability for each of the constructs.

The alpha values were highly moderate 0.75 for power structure (5 items), 0.60 for social freedom (3 items), 0.64 for economic freedom (4 items), 0.74 for social justice (5 items). No considerable increase of alpha value was achieved by removing any of the items.

Descriptive statistics for the four political ideology factors are presented in Table 2.2. Composite scores were computed for the four factors, higher the scores indicated more inclination towards that particular ideology. Social justice was the ideology that respondents reported having the most, with a negatively skewed distribution, followed by power structure. Social freedom and economic freedom were noticeably less

Table 2.2 *Descriptive Statistics: Political Ideology Factors*

	No. of Items	Mean ± SD	Skewness	Kurtosis	Cronbach's Alpha
Power Structure	5	2.29 ± 0.57	–0.469	–0.702	0.75
Social Freedom	3	1.76 ± 0.61	0.397	–0.818	0.60
Economic Freedom	4	1.47 ± 0.49	0.901	0.099	0.64
Social Justice	5	2.60 ± 0.45	–0.273	1.279	0.74

Table 2.3 *Descriptive Statistics for Political Participation (Online and Offline)*

Political Participation	Mean ± SD
Voting in elections	3.85 ±1.08
Tracking political news	3.57 ±.99
Discussing political issues	3.38 ±1.05
Participating in protests	2.86 ±1.24
Posting online	3.06 ±1.26
Sharing online	3.08 ±1.27

among respondents with positively skewed distributions. On the whole, this analysis determined that four factors were rooted in the political ideology responses and that these factors were internally consistent.

Table 2.3 presents the descriptive statistics for political participation which consists of six items (voting in elections, tracking political news, discussing political issues, participating in political protests, posting contents online, sharing contents online), which showed highly moderate internal consistency of 0.70 Cronbach's alpha. Mean scores show that people voting during elections is the priority of the respondents followed by tracking of political news and discussing political issues. Participating in protests is considerably less among the respondents when it comes to offline participation.

When it comes to online political participation, people weigh equally on posting and sharing online contents after giving top priority to tracking political news.

Correlation test was performed to identify the relationship between political ideologies (power structure, social freedom, economic freedom, social justice) and political participation. Table 2.4 shows the Pearson correlation coefficients and it revealed that there is a significant relationship between social freedom, economic freedom and political participation at 0.01 level of significance. It was also observed in the table that the relationship among the political ideologies, where power structure had a significant positive relationship with social justice and

Table 2.4 *Correlation between Political Ideologies and Political Participation*

	Power Structure	Social Freedom	Economic Freedom	Social Justice
Social Freedom	–0.160**			
Economic Freedom	–0.281**	0.064**		
Social Justice	0.234**	–0.123**	–0.457**	
Participation	0.018	0.130**	–0.141**	0.013

** Correlation is significant at the 0.01 level (2-tailed).

negative relationship with social freedom and economic freedom at the 0.01 level of significance.

To test the association between party affiliation and political participation (online and offline) and political ideology, one-way ANOVA was conducted, and the results are presented in Table 2.5. The ANOVA test result indicated that the mean scores of political affiliation group had statistically significant differences with regard to the four facets of political ideology (power structure, social freedom, economic freedom, social justice) and political participation.

Table 2.5 *ANOVA Test Results for Party Affiliation*

DV	Highest Mean Score	Lowest Mean Score	Significance
Political participation	Just affiliated to a party	No party affiliation	<0.0005
Power structure	Just affiliated to a party	Office bearer of a party	<0.0005
Social freedom	Office bearer of a party	Just affiliated to a party	<0.0005
Economic freedom	Office bearer of a party	Just affiliated to a party	<0.0005
Social justice	No party affiliation	Just affiliated to a party	<0.0005

ANOVA test results have come up with several interesting findings. Those with just an affiliation to a party tended to participate in politics-related activities, online and offline, actively. Those without a party affiliation were the ones with the least involvement in political affairs. When it comes to opinion about the power distance, those affiliated to a party seemed to favour hierarchy the most, while, interestingly, it was the party office-bearers who had equality as their ideology. Those who are office-bearers of a party favour social freedom and economic freedom the most, and the group just affiliated to a party supported these concepts the least. Social justice was favoured most by the group which did not have any party affiliation, and the group just affiliated to a party were the least inclined towards social justice.

The study findings are presented as a conceptual model in Figure 2.2.

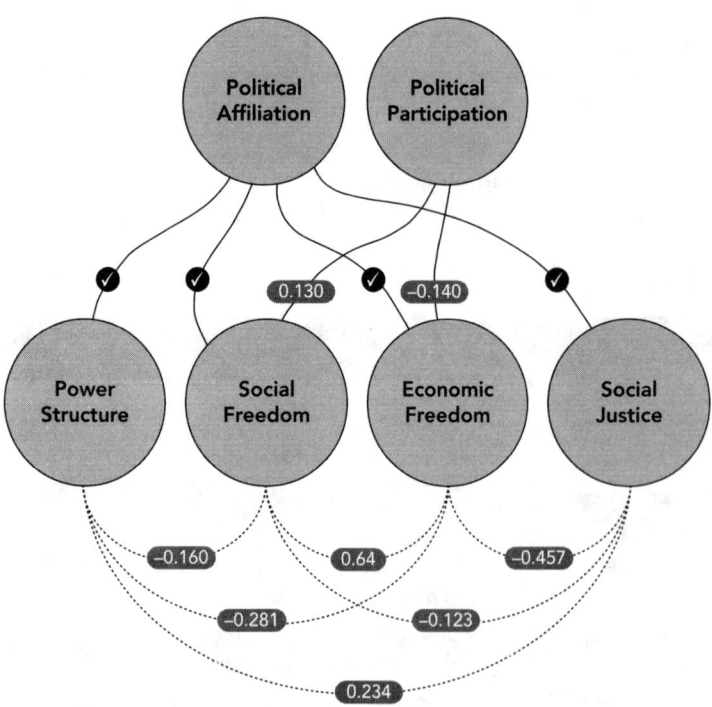

Figure 2.2 *Conceptual Model*

DISCUSSION

In this study, 20 items were used to determine the four facets of political ideology. Exploratory factor analysis settled for 17 items validating the four facets of political ideology (Ma, 2017), namely power structure (measured using five items), social freedom (measured using three items), economic freedom (measured using four items), social justice (measured using five items), with acceptable levels of reliability and validity. This test also provided a standardized and validated instrument to measure political ideology in the Indian context. Several of the existing political ideology measurement tools (Ahn et al. 2014; Bjornskov & Potrafke 2012; Carmines & D'Amico 2015; Gerring, 1997; Giannone 2010; Holbrook & Poe 1987; Jordan & Ferguson 2016; Jungkunz, 2019; Knight 1985; Laméris, Jong-A-Pin & Garretsen 2018; Marcus, Tabb & Sullivan, 1974; Smith et al., 2011) were not designed to suit the pluralistic nature of Indian political ideology and belief system (Dommett, 2012). Among the four facets of political ideology validated in the Indian context, the highest priority was attached to social justice, followed by political hierarchy and social freedom. Economic freedom was the least of their concern. Of the 2,500 respondents studied, over 50 per cent (1,284) favoured political hierarchy, while only a meagre 15 per cent (379) stood for equality. It is interesting to note that while the pep talk is all about equality in this largest democracy, a major section of the population still favours a certain level of hierarchy to maintain the status quo. This is also in opposition to the Marxist ideology that sees hierarchy as the bane of the established systems. Is it the failure of communism and fascist fears that favour hierarchy? Or is it the simple inclination to not disturb the existing social and political understructures?

Only 12 per cent (318) of the respondents favour social freedom and are open to individual choices. Even though India stands in a global arena on par with developed nations, consuming Western fashion and outlooks, deep down under it is still largely conservative sticking to tradition. Such conservative beliefs make India stand out even today in the contemporary world giving it a distinctive colour. In the same line, economic freedom is also disfavoured widely (66%, 1,662 respondents). The possible reasons could be the general disdain for the super-rich and their corporate conglomerates with a deluge of instances of lobbying, violations, economic offences and disregard to agricultural, environmental and societal considerations. That is also why, as the data suggests, the popular opinion is for stricter laws rather than economic freedom for development.

Social justice stands out as the primordial ideology among the four facets, with over three quarter of the respondents (1,913) favouring the welfare of the poor, schemes benefitting the underprivileged and rights of the needy. Such a stronger preference for the upliftment of the downtrodden compared to economic progress of the elitist accounts for the state's strong lineage to the liberal federation movement of South India for more than a century since its inception in 1916, a stronghold that continues even till this day. Social justice has been the fundamental tenet of this social movement, which propagated the ideals of social, rational and radical activism with a possible populist stance and metamorphosed into a political ideology termed Dravidianism. Instrument items for social justice reflect the ideological concepts of equality, upliftment of the downtrodden and marginalized and reduction of divides, the primary principle of the Dravidian ideology that fought against oppression in a caste-ridden society. It is strongly believed by the people that an egalitarian outlook could be a way to cater to the rights of the needy, as propagated by the Dravidianism movement engendered by Erode Venkatapathy Ramasamy Naicker, popularly called Periyar. It is evident in the findings, and no wonder social justice turns out to be a predominant ideology.

It is noted that the power structure precursored with social justice also reflects the Dravidian ideology during its growth. Recognizing the limitations of a social movement and that societal transformation could be easier with power and political base, the Dravidian social movement led to a successful political outfit. Study findings also show that the masses are for social justice and a strong political leadership. In this political milieu and the consecutive rule of Dravidian parties for more than half a century, the populist needs remain predominant. While economic freedom could be favourable to spur growth, it is least favoured in the state compared to the rest of the ideologies. This shows their concern for the upliftment of the marginalized and reduction of widespread social and economic inequalities. Overviewing these results, what emerges as an overarching ideology is that the popular Indian is an anti-capitalist strongly favouring social justice, but he still believes in a leader to uphold this ideal.

Numbers don't lie! A majority of the Indian population is moderate in political participation (64%, 1,601). Of the 2,500 respondents, about 71 per cent (1,772) reported participating in the primary duty of a citizen, not missing voting during general elections. As many as 1,469 (58.8%) reported to track political developments using the news outlets, while only 1,202 (48%) engage in discussing political issues offline. When it comes to participation in conventional political acts such as protests and demonstrations, the numbers further went down to 792 (32%) (Kahne and Bowyer, 2018). Even while the online social media is hugely popular in the Indian subcontinent, only about 41 per cent posted political and social messages online (1,032) and responded to such online postings (1,005) (Ahmad et al., 2019; Gibson & Cantijoch, 2013; Kim et al., 2017).

A majority of the Indian electorate did not have a party affiliation (65%, 1,628 respondents). Party office-bearers were an elite group accounting for 5 per cent (127), even though 35 per cent (872) reported having a party affiliation.

Among the facets of political ideology, social justice was positively correlated with power structure and economic freedom was positively correlated with social freedom. In other words, people wanted political leaders to redeem the downtrodden, while those who favoured social freedom with forward thinking also supported economic freedom for quick development.

Interestingly, those who favoured social freedom were against hierarchy and social justice. Those who favoured economic freedom also had a disdain for the hierarchical political system, mainly because it is the legal framework and governing institutions that are against social and economic freedom. Naturally, those who favour economic freedom that supports the interests of the capitalist and upper classes were not for social justice that works for reduction of inequality and support those at the bottom of hierarchy.

While those who favoured social freedom showed active levels of political participation offline and online, those who favoured economic freedom disengaged from political participation as it was politics and governance that they wanted to break free from.

CONCLUSION

The study discussed in this chapter developed and validated an instrument to measure the political ideology in the Indian setting with four facets—power structure, social freedom, economic freedom, social justice. A contradiction was observed in the Indian mindset to favour social justice even while maintaining political hierarchy. Social justice, however, prevails as the predominant want. Economic freedom stands to be the least favoured. A majority of the electorate stay away from formal political partisanship, even while their involvement in tracking and discussing political affairs is at a high. On the online space, however, politics is yet to catch up, with only about 40 per cent of the electorate posting and sharing social and political issues. As the correlation results reveal, thoughts of social and economic freedom were against political hierarchy and social justice. When it comes to political participation, those favouring social freedom showed much interest while those favouring economic freedom were the ones who try to abstain from.

REFERENCES

Adhana, D. K., & Saxena, M. (2018). Role of social media in the changing face of Indian politics: A study with special reference to Facebook. *International Journal of Research and Analytical Reviews (IJRAR)*, 6(1): 935–951. eISSN 2348–1269.

Ahmad, T., Alvi, A., & Ittefaq, M. (2019). The use of social media on political participation among university students: An analysis of survey results from rural Pakistan. *SAGE Open*, 9(3), 2158244019864484.

Ahn, W. Y., Kishida, K. T., Gu, X., Lohrenz, T., Harvey, A., Alford, J. R., Smith, K.B., Yaffe, G., Hibbing, J.R., Dayan, P., & Montague, P. R. (2014). Nonpolitical images evoke neural predictors of political ideology. *Current Biology*, 24(22), 2693–2699.

Asencio, H. and Sun, R. (Eds.). (2015). *Cases on strategic social media utilization in the nonprofit sector*. IGI Global.

Bartlett, J. (2014). Populism, social media and democratic strain. In Sandelind, C. (Ed.), *European populism and winning the immigration debate* (pp. 99–116). Fores.

Berry, W. D., Ringquist, E. J., Fording, R. C., & Hanson, R. L. (1998). Measuring citizen and government ideology in the American states, 1960–93. *American Journal of Political Science, 42*(1), 327–348.

Bjornskov, C., & Potrafke, N. (2012). Political ideology and economic freedom across Canadian provinces. *Eastern Economic Journal, 38*(2), 143–166.

Bode, L. (2012). Facebooking it to the polls: A study in online social networking and political behavior. *Journal of Information Technology & Politics, 9*, 352–369. doi:10.1080/19331681.2012.709045

Bode, L., Vraga, E. K., Borah, P., & Shah, D. V. (2014). A new space for political behavior: Political social networking and its democratic consequences. *Journal of Computer-Mediated Communication, 19*(3), 414–429.

Boulianne, S. (2015). Social media use and participation: A meta-analysis of current research. *Information, Communication & Society, 18*(5), 524–538.

Boulianne, S. (2019). Revolution in the making? Social media effects across the globe. *Information, Communication & Society, 22*(1), 39–54.

Boulianne, S. (2020). Twenty years of digital media effects on civic and political participation. *Communication Research, 47*(7), 947–966.

Brady, H. E., Verba, S., & Schlozman, K. L. (1995). Beyond SES: A resource model of political participation. *American Political Science Review, 89*(2): 271–294.

Cai, Y. (2008). Power structure and regime resilience: Contentious politics in China. *British Journal of Political Science, 38*(3), 411–432.

Carmines, E. G., & D'Amico, N. J. (2015). The new look in political ideology research. *Annual Review of Political Science, 18*, 205–216.

Chakrabarty, B. (2008). *Indian politics and society since independence: Events, processes and ideology.* Routledge.

Delmonico, J. R. (2016). Personality factors, ideology, and sensitivity to change. MSU Graduate Thesis. 2959. Retrieved from https://bearworks.missouristate.edu/theses/2959

Denzau, A. T., & North, D. C. (2000). Shared mental models: ideologies and institutions. In A. Lupia, M.C. McCubbins & S.L. Popkin (Eds.), *Elements of reason: Cognition, choice, and the bounds of rationality* (pp. 23–46). Cambridge University Press.

Di Gennaro, C., & Dutton, W. (2006). The Internet and the public: Online and offline political participation in the United Kingdom. *Parliamentary Affairs, 59*(2), 299–313.

Dommett, K. (2012). *Conceptualising party political ideology: An exploration of party modernisation in Britain* [Doctoral Dissertation] University of Sheffield.

Dwivedi, M. R. (2011). The penetration of social media in governance, political reforms and building public perception. *International Journal of Mass Communication, 6*(2011), 163–167.

Emmer, M., Wolling, J., & Vowe, G. (2012). Changing political communication in Germany: Findings from a longitudinal study on the influence of the internet on political information, discussion and the participation of citizens. *Communications, 37*(3), 233–252.

Engesser, S., Ernst, N., Esser, F., & Büchel, F. (2017). Populism and social media: How politicians spread a fragmented ideology. *Information, Communication & Society, 20*(8), 1109–1126.

Enli, G., & Rosenberg, L. T. (2018). Trust in the age of social media: Populist politicians seem more authentic. *Social Media+ Society, 4*(1), 2056305118764430.

Fisher, J., Denver, D., & Hands, G. (2006). The relative electoral impact of central party co-ordination and size of party membership at constituency level. *Electoral Studies, 25*(4), 664–676.

Fisher, J., Fieldhouse, E., & Cutts, D. (2014). Members are not the only fruit: Volunteer activity in British political parties at the 2010 general election. *The British Journal of Politics and International Relations, 16*(1), 75–95.

Freeden, M. (2001). Ideology. Political Aspects. In N. J. Smelser, & B. Baltes (Eds.), *International Encyclopedia of the Social and Behavioral Sciences* (pp. 11–7174). Elsevier.

Gerring, J. (1997). Ideology: A definitional analysis. *Political Research Quarterly, 50*(4), 957–994.

Giannone, D. (2010). Political and ideological aspects in the measurement of democracy: The Freedom House case. *Democratization, 17*(1), 68–97.

Gibson, R., & Cantijoch, M. (2013). Conceptualizing and measuring participation in the age of the internet: Is online political engagement really different to offline? *The Journal of Politics, 75*(3), 701–716.

Gil de Zúñiga, H., Jung, N., & Valenzuela, S. (2012). Social media use for news and individuals' social capital, civic engagement and political participation. *Journal of Computer-Mediated Communication, 17*(3), 319–336.

Gil de Zúñiga, H., Molyneux, L., & Zheng, P. (2014). Social media, political expression, and political participation: Panel analysis of lagged and concurrent relationships. *Journal of Communication, 64*(4), 612–634.

Harlow, S., & Harp, D. (2012). Collective action on the Web: A cross-cultural study of social networking sites and online and offline activism in the United States and Latin America. *Information, Communication & Society, 15*(2), 196–216.

Hirzalla, F., Van Zoonen, L., & de Ridder, J. (2011). Internet use and political participation: Reflections on the mobilization/normalization controversy. *The Information Society, 27*(1), 1–15.

Holbrook-Provow, T. M., & Poe, S. C. (1987). Measuring state political ideology. *American Politics Quarterly, 15*(3), 399–416.

Howard, M. (2019, January 11). 'Don't Be Awkward' and other advice for politicians on Instagram. Retrieved Oct 10, 2021, from https://www. wbur.org/cognoscenti/2019/01/11/elizabeth-warren-alexandria-ocasio-cortez-social-media-miles-howard

Howard, P. N., Savage, S., Saviaga, C. F., Toxtli, C., & Monroy-Hernández, A. (2016). Social media, civic engagement, and the slacktivism hypothesis: Lessons from Mexico's 'El Bronco'. *Journal of International Affairs, 70*(1), 55–73.

Jordan, S., & Ferguson, G. (2016). Extremism in survey measures of ideology. *Research & Politics, 3*(3), 2053168016669743.

Jungkunz, S. (2019). Towards a measurement of extreme left-wing attitudes. *German Politics, 28*(1), 101–122.

Kahne, J., & Bowyer, B. (2018). The political significance of social media activity and social networks. *Political Communication, 35*(3), 470–493.

Kim, S. B. (2019). Political engagement of social media users in Korea. *Korea Observer, 50*(4), 587–618.

Kim, Y., Russo, S., & Amnå, E. (2017). The longitudinal relation between online and offline political participation among youth at two different developmental stages. *New Media & Society, 19*(6), 899–917.

Knight, K. (1985). Ideology in the 1980 election: Ideological sophistication does matter. *The Journal of Politics, 47*(3), 828–853.

Lahoti, P., Garimella, K., & Gionis, A. (2018, February). Joint non-negative matrix factorization for learning ideological leaning on Twitter. In *WSDM '18: Proceedings of the Eleventh ACM International Conference on Web Search and Data Mining* (pp. 351–359). Association for Computing Machinery, New York.

Laméris, M. D., Jong-A-Pin, R., & Garretsen, H. (2018). On the measurement of voter ideology. *European Journal of Political Economy, 55*, 417–432.

Lilleker, D. G., & Koc-Michalska, K. (2017). What drives political participation? Motivations and mobilization in a digital age. *Political Communication, 34*(1), 21–43.

Lilleker, D. G. (2013). Empowering the citizens? Political communication, coproduction and the harnessed crowd. In R. Scullion, R. Gerodimos, D. Jackson, & D. Lilliker (Eds.), *The media, political participation and empowerment* (pp. 24–38). Routledge.

Ma, L. (2017). Political ideology, social capital, and government innovativeness: Evidence from the US states. *Public Management Review, 19*(2), 114–133.

Magic Mile Media. (2019, April 15). How social media is changing the way politicians communicate. https://www.magicmilemedia.com/blog/2019/4/15/how-social-media-is-changing-the-way-politicians-communicate

Marcus, G. E., Tabb, D., & Sullivan, J. L. (1974). The application of individual differences scaling to the measurement of political ideologies. *American Journal of Political Science, 18*, 405–420.

Meti, V., Khandoba, P. K., & Guru, M. C. (2015). Social media for political mobilization in India: A study. *Journal of Mass Communication & Journalism, 5*(9), 1–4.

Metkar, A. B. and Aade, A., Role of social media in political management in India (June 29, 2020). Available at SSRN: https://ssrn.com/abstract=3637843 or http://dx.doi.org/10.2139/ssrn.3637843

Milbrath, L. W. (1981). Political participation. In Samuel Long (Ed.), *The handbook of political behavior* (pp. 197–240). Springer.

Northey, G., Dolan, R., Etheridge, J., Septianto, F., & Van Esch, P. (2020). LGBTQ imagery in advertising: How viewers' political ideology shapes their emotional response to gender and sexuality in advertisements. *Journal of Advertising Research*, *60*(2), 222–236.

Nuechterlein, J. (1988). Athens and Jerusalem in Indiana. *The American Scholar*, *57*(3) 353–368.

Oppenheim, F. E. (2004). Social freedom: Definition, measurability, valuation. *Social Choice and Welfare*, *22*(1), 175–185.

Ordabayeva, N., & Fernandes, D. (2018). Better or different? How political ideology shapes preferences for differentiation in the social hierarchy. *Journal of Consumer Research*, *45*(2), 227–250.

Parida, S. K., & Das, A. (2014). Social media in relation to politics in Odisha, India: An Overview. *International Journal of Interdisciplinary and Multidisciplinary Studies*, *1*(2), 45–47.

Pettit, P. (2014). Three kinds of freedom. *Journal of Zhejiang University*, (0) 1–5.

Rachlinski, J. J., Wistrich, A. J., & Guthrie, C. (2017). Judicial politics and decisionmaking: A new approach. *Vanderbilt Law Review*, *70*(6), 2051.

Smith, K. B., Oxley, D. R., Hibbing, M. V., Alford, J. R., & Hibbing, J. R. (2011). Linking genetics and political attitudes: Reconceptualizing political ideology. *Political Psychology*, *32*(3), 369–397.

Szalay, L. B., Kelly, R. M., & Moon, W. T. (1972). Ideology: Its meaning and measurement. *Comparative Political Studies*, *5*(2), 151–173.

Trilling, L. (1972). *Sincerity and authenticity*. Harvard University Press.

Valenzuela, S., Park, N., & Kee, K. F. (2009). Is there social capital in a social network site?: Facebook use and college students' life satisfaction, trust, and participation. *Journal of Computer-Mediated Communication*, *14*, 875–901.

Vissers, S., & Stolle, D. (2014). The Internet and new modes of political participation: Online versus offline participation. *Information, Communication & Society*, *17*(8), 937–955.

Vitak, J., Zube, P., Smock, A., Carr, C. T., Ellison, N., & Lampe, C. (2011). It's complicated: Facebook users' political participation in the 2008 election. *Cyberpsychology, Behavior, and Social Networking*, *14*(3), 107–114.

Wänke, M. (2015). Its All in the Face: Facial Appearance, Political Ideology and Voters Perceptions. In J. P. Forgas, K. Fiedler, & W. D. Crano (Eds.), *Social Psychology and Politics* (pp. 143–160). Psychology Press, Taylor & Francis, New York.

Whiteley, P., & Seyd, P. (2003). How to win a landslide by really trying: the effects of local campaigning on voting in the 1997 British general election. *Electoral Studies*, *22*(2), 301–324.

Zhang, W., Seltzer, T., & Bichard, S. L. (2013). Two sides of the coin: Assessing the influence of social network site use during the 2012 U.S. presidential campaign. *Social Science Computer Review*, *31*(5), 542–551.

Chapter 3

Credibility of Social Media Messages and User Awareness

Francis P. Barclay, Boobalakrishnan N. and Anushiya K.

INTRODUCTION

Even after the onslaught against fake messages on online social networks from several quarters, such applications are still rife with recent instances in India, fuelling mob lynching (Krishnan, 2018), leading to protests and riots (Sharon, 2018), causing political deceptions of disparate proportions during the 2019 Lok Sabha elections (Fact Check Bureau, 2019), complicating the combat against COVID-19 with a range of rumours, fake messages and conspiracy theories about its origin and cure (Sahoo, 2020), and even about one of the most popular social media applications WhatsApp that informed its users of a revision in its privacy policy, terms and conditions (Dasgupta, 2021). In the spread of each of these false or inaccurate messages, the naive and uninformed users had a role to play. Misinformation—false or inaccurate information—isn't a new concept or problem (Fox, 1983; Godfrey-Smith, 1989; Kuklinski et al., 2000), but the emergence of online social media has elaborated concerns to alarming levels, shifting the focus of recent scholarly research to the digital space (Allcott et al., 2019; Bode & Vraga, 2018; Bursztyn et al., 2020; Chou et al., 2018;

Del Vicario et al., 2016; Valenzuela et al., 2019; Wang et al., 2019; Wu et al., 2019).

A kind of misinformation with deceptive intention, disinformation is also being studied on online social media networks in the contemporary times (Bradshaw & Howard, 2018; Chadwick & Vaccari, 2019; Colliander, 2019; Gottlieb & Dyer, 2020; Tandoc Jr et al., 2020; Tucker et al., 2018;), with several of the studies focusing on how to combat this rising issue (Napoli, 2019; Saurwein & Spencer-Smith, 2020; Shu et al., 2020). In India, social media usage has been witnessing a steep rise in the past few years—the internet user base of the country soared from 493.96 million in 2018 to 696.77 million in 2020 (Statista, 2021a), with social media users alone accounting for an estimated 376.1 million of them (Statista, 2021b), against an estimated Indian population of over 1.38 billion (United Nations, 2021). Social media has diverse uses for research as well, ranging from fostering political population and forecasting outbreaks of diseases to opinion mining and election prediction (Barclay et al., 2014, 2015, 2016; Nair & Barclay, 2017).

Furthermore, most people are confined to the safety of their homes, courtesy the COVID-19 pandemic and resultant lockdowns that have opened only a palm-size digital window to the world outside and the developments around them. It becomes, hence, crucial to study the levels of awareness of Indian social media users about fake messages (or misinformation or disinformation), ethical use of such online applications and user perceptions about the credibility of messages that spread on these diverse online social networks. Accordingly, the following research questions are formulated:

RQ1: What are the levels of awareness of users about social media issues (such as misinformation or disinformation and ethical usage of social media)?
RQ2: What are the perceived levels of credibility of messages circulated on social media?
RQ3: Are awareness and credibility related?
RQ4: Are awareness and credibility related to the extent of usage of social media?
RQ5: Are demographic variables related to the extent of usage of social media, awareness and credibility?

PAST STUDIES AND THEORETICAL UNDERPINNINGS

A handful of research works have studied the phenomena of misinformation involving social media in India (Bali & Desai, 2019; Banaji et al., 2019; Garimella & Eckles, 2020; Kadam & Atre, 2020; Talwar et al., 2019; 2020; Tasnim et al., 2020; Vasudeva & Barkdull, 2020). Garimella and Eckles (2020) quantitatively investigated images from thousands of public WhatsApp groups in India in the run-up to the 2019 Parliamentary elections to observe a high prevalence of image misinformation, accounting for 13 per cent, highlighting the problem. Talwar et al. (2020) used the rationale of third-person effect and the honeycomb framework to understand the motives to share fake news on social media and investigate such sharing behaviour. Their findings suggested that the need to share information instantaneously resulted in the sharing of fake news, as there was no time or religiosity to verify before sharing, and those who intended to authenticate information before sharing and thus maintain a reputation desisted from sharing.

While the users are motivated to use social media platforms and share information for several reasons, it has been unclear why users tend to share unverified critical information on these platforms despite the issues related to misinformation and disinformation that are highlighted in the mainstream media.

Talwar et al. (2019) also related the dark side of social media use with fake news sharing behaviour, formulating a model that employs the social comparison theory, self-determination theory and the rational choice theory. Studying the year 2018, when India was shocked by the WhatsApp-triggered lynchings, Vasudeva and Barkdull (2020) drew upon the theories related to racial and caste divides in India and combined them with understandings about techno-determinism to examine the case of lynchings triggered using social media. Bali and Desai (2019) studied the impact of fake news as disruption of the public sphere and looked for measures to control it. Several such studies have attempted to understand why users tend to share unverified information on social media platforms and have also raised several issues concerning fake information on social media. Popular issues also find space in mainstream media offering visibility to these issues. Despite this, misinformation and disinformation continue to circulate on social media applications. Is it ignorance or the lack of awareness about such misinformation and disinformation being circulated on the social media or do they fabricate a delusion of credibility to justify the use of such social networks that they are addicted to? This also becomes the primary premise for the current study.

To offer such justifications, the current study consults a few classical theories that are posited well before the appearance of the so-called people's media and that seem to explain such dissonant online behaviours. For one, the cognitive dissonance theory (Festinger 1957)—which posits that when there is a cognitive dissonance (a situation involving conflicting attitudes), an alteration is made in one of those attitudes to reduce the discomfort—is used to explain why the user would engage in sharing unverified information on social media. Despite the awareness about ethics and misinformation, the user may tend to share unverified information to justify the use of the medium that offers a plethora of benefits. It could also create an illusion of artificial credibility that the user may attach to social media that mostly circulates unverified information. The unmindful acts of sharing misinformation and disinformation on social media could also be viewed with the lens of the third-person effect theory (Davison, 1983). Users who generally recognize the problem of fake news on social media may consider themselves unaffected even when exposed. As proposed by Jost and van der Toorn (2012), the system justification theory also offers a valid explanation for active users continuing to circulate messages on social media. It posits that 'people are motivated (to varying degrees depending upon situational and dispositional factors) to defend and justify prevailing social arrangements (the status quo)'. It is logical to assume that awareness about social media issues such as misinformation that spread across social networks and ethical usage of social media could bring down the credibility that users attach to social media messages, bringing down their usages. That is, awareness could have a negative relationship with credibility and usage. But will this theory hold good for users who are addicted to social media? As discussed earlier and postulated by the theory of cognitive dissonance, highly active social media users may shun knowledge or awareness about misinformation and allied issues and continue to unmindfully trust and share social media messages. Accordingly, the following hypotheses are proposed.

H1: Awareness and credibility are negatively associated.

H2: Awareness and credibility are associated with the extent of usage of social media.

H3: Demographic variables are associated with the extent of usage of social media, awareness and credibility.

H4: Extent of usage of social media moderates the relationship between awareness and credibility of social media messages.

RESEARCH METHOD

In this quantitative survey, a sample of 2,500 social media users were selected from across the Indian state of Tamil Nadu, using a multistage cluster sampling procedure during January 2020–January 2021. Data was collected when India was reeling under the COVID-19 pandemic, which has since then been declared a worldwide pandemic.

In January 2020, India reported its first case of COVID-19. According to Dong et al. (2020) and GitHub (2021), the number of confirmed COVID-19 cases in India stood at over 10.5 million, with over 151,000 deaths, as of January 2021. The number of new cases peaked at over 97,000 a day around mid-September. After the first COVID-19-related lockdown was imposed nationwide during March 2020, a series of them followed with varying restrictions and were continuing even till January 2021.

Survey Instrument

The survey questionnaire used to measure the extent of usage of social media, awareness about ethical issues and misinformation spread on social media and credibility of social media was a part of a larger instrument that was created for a state-wide project funded by the Indian Council of Social Science Research (ICSSR) under the IMPRESS scheme. In this project, a range of variables are measured through a mixed methods research and the relationship that they share among them is examined to propose recommendations for the formation of policies to regulate the sprawling social media space.

First, the Indian state of Tamil Nadu was divided into five strata or zones: north, south, east, west and central. For each of these five zones, two or three districts were chosen as prime points for data collection, and respondents were chosen from each of these zones leading to a grand total of 2,500 respondents.

A pilot study was conducted using a survey instrument that had 135 items, under 16 sections. Based on the feedback of the respondents, the survey instrument was revised to finally have 98 items under 16 sections. In the final instrument, there were 13 questions operationalizing the three variables—extent of usage of social media, awareness and credibility—apart from demographic variables—age, education, gender, occupation and family monthly income. We used a five-point Likert scale with a response format of strongly agree to strongly disagree for the variables, awareness and credibility.

DATA ANALYSIS

Descriptive Statistics

A quantitative survey was used to measure usage, awareness and credibility—apart from demographic variables—age, education, gender, occupation and family monthly income. Their descriptive statistics are presented in Tables 3.1 and 3.2.

RQ1: What are the levels of awareness of users about social media issues (such as misinformation or disinformation and ethical usage of social media)?
RQ2: What are the perceived levels of credibility of messages circulated on social media?

Of the 2,500 samples studied for the quantitative analysis, about 50 per cent of them reported low levels of social media usage, 42.7 per cent moderate and 7.4 per cent high levels of usage. Similarly, 9.2 per cent had low levels of awareness about social media ethics and misinformation circulating on the online social networks, 44.5 per cent moderate and 46.3 per cent high levels of awareness. About 26.1 per cent of the social

Table 3.1 *Descriptive Statistics: Demographics*

		Frequencies			
Zone	Central	500	Gender	Male	1,320
	North	500		Female	1,144
	South	500	Location	Rural	1,015
	East	500		Urban	1,485
	West	500		Employed	810
Education	Plus two or below	587	Occupation	Unemployed	308
	Undergraduate	1,233		Retired	148
	Postgraduate	680		Homemaker	266
Income	Less than ₹15,000	1,007		Student	968
	₹15,001 to ₹30,000	772	Age	Less than 23 years	1,184
	₹30,001 to ₹45,000	434		23–30 years	788
	Above ₹45,000	287		Above 30 years	528

Table 3.2 *Descriptive Statistics: Usage, Awareness and Credibility*

		Frequencies	Percentage
Usage	Low	1,296	50
	Moderate	1,067	42.7
	High	184	7.4
Awareness	Low	229	9.2
	Moderate	1,113	44.5
	High	1,158	46.3
Credibility	Low	652	26.1
	Moderate	1,157	46.3
	High	691	27.6

media users attributed low levels of credibility to social media messages, while 46.3 per cent moderate and 27.6 per cent totally believed all that were circulated on these platforms (see Table 3.2).

About 76.4 per cent of the users used at least three social media platforms, while 59.1 per cent used four and 37.6 per cent used five or more social media platforms. Similarly, 83.8 per cent of the users spent at least 30 minutes a day on social media, while 57.7 per cent used social media for at least two hours a day, indicating high levels of addictive behaviour. About 15.2 per cent of the users used social media for 6–10 hours a day, and 3.6 per cent used it for more than 10 hours. About 35 per cent of the users thought only credible information was circulated on social media. About 16.7 per cent of the users disagreed that fake messages are spread on social media platforms, and about 14.7 per cent do not verify information before trusting them, while 27.5 per cent would or wouldn't verify information before trusting them.

Hypothesis Testing

H1: Awareness and credibility are negatively associated.
H2: Awareness and credibility are associated with the extent of usage of social media.

To test these hypotheses and the relationships among these variables, the data are analysed using quadratic regression to find out the best-fitting arithmetic model.

The R-Square value for the quadratic curve is 0.048, which indicates a fit and is validated by the F-test (significance value is less than 0.0005). In the model, the constant value is 18.538, indicating that people with zero awareness attach high values of credibility to social media messages and the slope is negative (-0.707), which means credibility wanes as awareness increases. However, those with very high levels of awareness tend to attach some credibility to social media messages as the $b2$ value indicates (0.018).

However, this trend is just a minimal rise. Analysis of the coefficients infers that credibility decreases as awareness increases (see Table 3.3 and Figure 3.1).

Table 3.3 *Model Summary and Parameter Estimates: Awareness vs Credibility*

	Dependent Variable: Credibility							
Equation	Model Summary					Parameter Estimates		
	R-Squared	F	df1	df2	Sig.	Constant	b1	b2
Quadratic	0.048	62.479	2	2497	0	18.538	−0.707	0.018
	The independent variable is Awareness.							

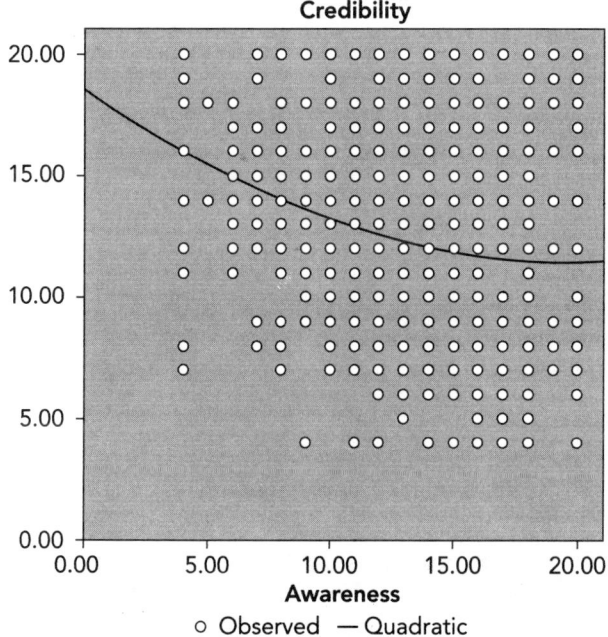

○ Observed — Quadratic

Figure 3.1 *Plot for Awareness vs Credibility*

Correlation test also showed a negative relationship ($R = -0.208$, significant at the 0.01 level, 2-tailed). Hence, the hypothesis *H1* is accepted.

Even among those with high levels of awareness (1,158), about 29.8 per cent (345) attached moderate credibility to social media messages and 26.9 per cent (312) attached high levels of credibility to the messages on social media.

The R-Square value for the quadratic curve is 0.024, which indicates a fit and is validated by the F-test (significance value is less than 0.0005). In the model, the constant value is 16.008, indicating that people with zero usage attach high values of credibility to social media messages and the slope is negative (−0.731), which means credibility wanes as usage increases. However, those with very high levels of usage tend to attach more credibility to social media messages as the $b2$ value indicates (0.032). Analysis of the coefficients shows that credibility decreases when the usage increases from low to moderate, but then as the usage increases further users tend to start attaching more credibility to social media messages (see Table 3.4 and Figure 3.2).

It could also be interpreted as moderate social media users are the ones that attach the lowest levels of credibility to messages circulated on social media.

The R-Square value for the quadratic curve is 0.072, which indicates a fit and is validated by the F-test (significance value is less than 0.0005). In the model, the constant value is 10.121, indicating that people with zero usage held moderate levels of awareness about ethics and misinformation spread on social media and the slope is positive (0.922), which means the awareness increased as usage increases.

Table 3.4 *Model Summary and Parameter Estimates: Usage vs Credibility*

Dependent Variable: Credibility							
Equation	Model Summary					Parameter Estimates	
	R-Squared	F	df1	df2	Sig.	Constant	b1	b2
Quadratic	0.024	31.183	2	2,497	0	16.008	−0.731	0.032
The independent variable is Usage.								

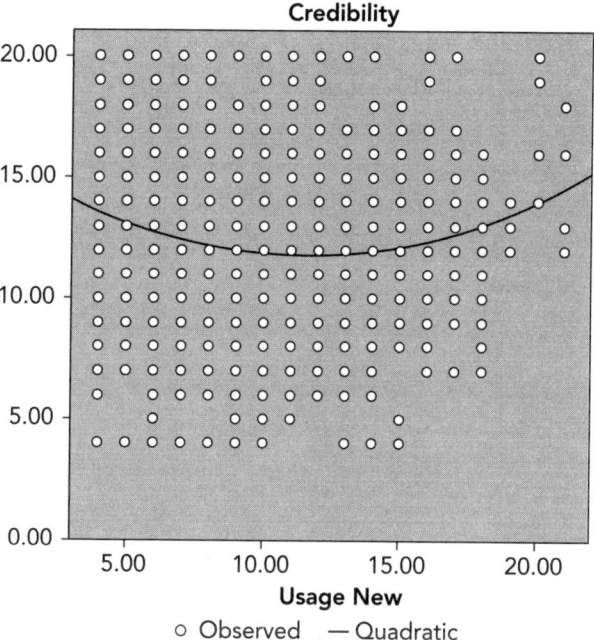

Figure 3.2 *Plot for Usage vs Credibility*

However, those with very high levels of usage tend to have the least awareness as the $b2$ value indicates (-0.049) (see Table 3.5 and Figure 3.3).

Table 3.5 *Model Summary and Parameter Estimates: Usage vs Awareness*

	Dependent Variable: Awareness							
Equation	Model Summary					Parameter Estimates		
	R-Squared	F	df1	df2	Sig.	Constant	b1	b2
Quadratic	0.075	101.924	2	2,497	0	10.121	0.922	−0.049
	The independent variable is Usage.							

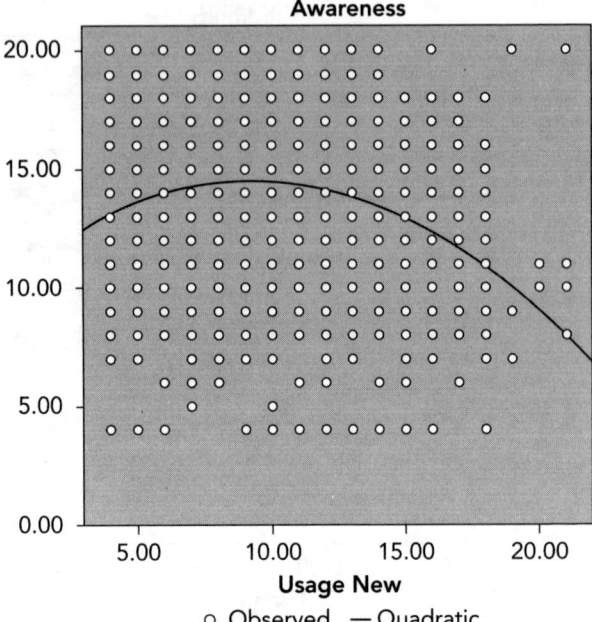

Figure 3.3 *Plot for Usage vs Awareness*

Analysis of the coefficients shows that awareness increases when the usage increases from low to moderate, but then as the usage increases further users tend to start having lesser awareness about social media happenings.

It could also be interpreted as moderate social media users having the highest levels of awareness about social media ethics and misinformation on social media. Or those with high awareness levels tend to use social media moderately and those who use social media a lot are the ones with low levels of awareness. As the quadratic regression models for both usage vs awareness and usage vs credibility have significant F-test scores, the hypothesis *H2* is also accepted.

H3: Demographic variables are associated with the extent of usage of social media, awareness and credibility.

To test this proposed hypothesis, one-way ANOVA and t-test were conducted and the results are presented in Table 3.6.

Table 3.6 ANOVA and t-Test Results: Demographic Variables

	Results	Usage	Awareness	Credibility
Age	ANOVA (p)	0.000	Not Sig.	0.000
	Highest	23–30	23–30	>30
	Lowest	<23	>30	23–30
Gender	t-test (p)	0.000	0.000	0.000
	Highest	Male	Male	Female
	Lowest	Female	Female	Male
Education	ANOVA (p)	0.000	0.000	0.000
	Highest	PG	+2	PG
	Lowest	+2	PG	+2
Occupation	ANOVA (p)	0.000	0.000	0.000
	Highest	Retired	Employed	Student
	Lowest	Student	Retired	Employed
Income	ANOVA (p)	0.000	0.001	0.000
	Highest	30–45K	15–30K	>45K
	Lowest	<15K	30–45K	<15K
Location	t-test	0.000	0.000	0.000
	Highest	Urban	Urban	Rural
	Lowest	Rural	Rural	Urban

One-way ANOVA results indicated association between age and usage and credibility. While those belonging to the age group of 23–30 years tend to use social media the most, those belonging to the age group of less than 23 years used it the least. Male users were reported to have high awareness levels and low credibility, but they were, ironically, inclined to use social media more than their female counterparts. Female users were low on awareness and high on credibility. Similarly, postgraduates had low awareness levels and attached higher credibility to social media messages, and they made use of social media the most. Young students were most aware of the circulation of misinformation on social media and attached least credibility to messages. Also, they have minimized social media use during the COVID-19 period. While the retired were the least aware of social media threats, they were also the ones who made the most of social media platforms. The employed were the most aware group attaching least levels of credibility to social media messages. Students believed social media messages the most but used the platforms the least. Those belonging to the income group of ₹30,001 to ₹45,000 had the least awareness and used social media the most. Those earning below ₹15,000 attached least credibility to social media messages and used the platforms the least. While those belonging to the income group of ₹15,000 to ₹30,000 were the most aware; those earning more than ₹45,000 attached the highest level of credibility to social media messages. Ironically, highly aware urbanities also made the most of social media applications.

H4: Extent of usage of social media moderates the relationship between awareness and credibility of social media messages.

To test this hypothesis, linear regressions were run between user awareness and credibility for different extents of usage of social media groups and the regressions scores were compared. Test results and the findings are presented in Table 3.7 and Figure 3.4.

Table 3.7 *Linear Regression for Awareness vs Credibility for Social Media Usage Groups*

Usage_Nominal		Unstandardized Coefficients		Standard Coefficients		
		B	Standard Error	Beta	t	Sig.
Low usage	Awareness	−0.274	0.034	−0.216	−7.96	0
	(Constant)	16.279	0.493		33.044	0
Moderate usage	Awareness	−0.234	0.035	−0.2	−6.716	0
	(Constant)	15.336	0.496		30.91	0
High usage	Awareness	−0.128	0.085	−0.141	−1.518	0.132
	(Constant)	14.578	1.018		14.313	0

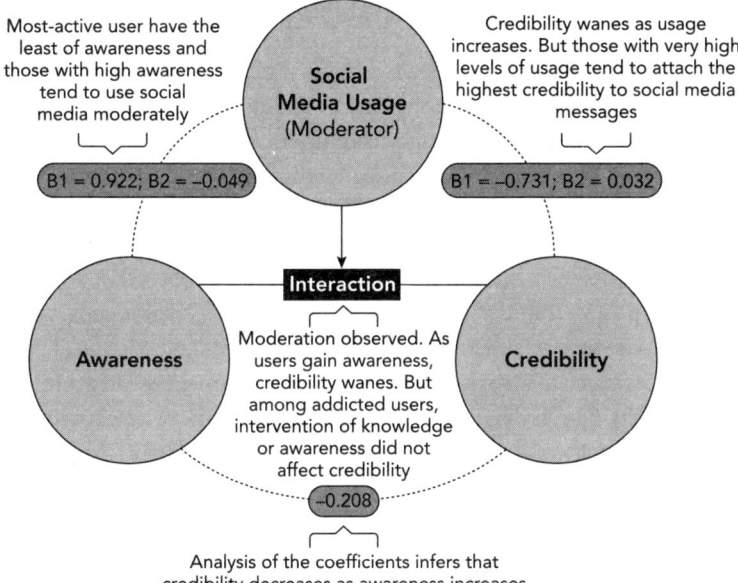

Figure 3.4 *Conceptual Model and Study Findings*

Regression tests show that the beta coefficients for awareness vs credibility are different for the different usage groups, and hence, the hypothesis that (*H4*) extent of usage of social media moderates the relationship between awareness and credibility of social media messages is accepted. Among those who have low social media usage, awareness and credibility have a negative association (−0.216) which is significant, which implies that as they gain knowledge and awareness about social media issues such as fake news and misinformation, their perceived trustworthiness of social media messages goes down. Similar was the case with the moderate users as well but with a slight difference of −0.200. But in the case of highly active or addicted users of social media, the intervention of knowledge or awareness about fake news on social media did not affect the credibility that they attach to social media messages. That is, even after knowledge about fake news, they continue to blindly trust social media messages. This anomaly is also reflected in the relationship between awareness and usage.

DISCUSSION

Study results indicate that even though users are well aware of the spread of misinformation on social media and ethical use, they tended to use such applications, attaching credibility to messages spread on those platforms. Evidence suggests that, generally, as awareness increases the credibility of social media decreases. Even among those with high levels of awareness (1,158), however, 29.8 per cent (345) attached moderate credibility to social media messages and 26.9 per cent (312) attached high levels of credibility to messages circulated on social media. This anomaly can be explained by the increase in social media usage. Those who understand that social media messages are unverified tend to use social media moderately, while those who attach more credibility use the platforms the most. Similarly, well-aware users kept their social media usage at moderate levels, while users with little awareness were addicted to the social networks.

It could also be interpreted as moderate social media users have the highest levels of awareness about social media ethics and misinformation on social media. Or those with high awareness levels tend to use social media moderately and those who use social media a lot are the ones with low levels of awareness. About 67 per cent of moderate social media users attached moderate-to-high levels of credibility to social media messages. Similarly, among the addictive users of social media, 57.1 per cent attached moderate credibility and 26.1 per cent high levels of credibility. Similarly, among those with high levels of awareness (1,158), over 50 per cent of the users had moderate-to-high levels of awareness.

Urban, male postgraduates aged 23–30 years and with moderate family earnings tend to use social media the most, while young, rural females belonging to low-income groups tend to use social media the least. Similarly, urban males belonging to the age group of 23–30 years tend to have more awareness about social media fake information. Females, students, those belonging to the age group of over 30 years, the highly educated, rural dwellers and those belonging to the high-income groups thought the social media messages were highly credible information.

In line with the past studies (Bali & Desai, 2019; Banaji et al., 2019; Garimella & Eckles, 2020; Kadam & Atre, 2020; Talwar et al., 2019; 2020; Tasnim et al., 2020; Vasudeva & Barkdull, 2020), this study, too, identifies social media misinformation as a problem, with still a large section of the population lacking awareness.

Despite the observations of researchers such as Garimella and Eckles (2020), who identified high prevalence of misinformation, still a major section of social media users think information circulated on online social media is trustworthy. While lack of awareness about such misinformation and disinformation being circulated on social media is a major reason, as supported by the study findings, among the most active users, there is a high tendency to blindly believe what goes around social media. It could be a fabricated delusion of credibility to justify the use of such social networks that they are addicted to due to various reasons, from communication, companionship and identity creation to political deliberation, awareness creation and opinion exchange. This thought is also supported by the theories consulted such as cognitive dissonance theory (Festinger, 1957), third-person effect theory (Davison, 1983) and system justification theory (Jost & van der Toorn, 2012).

Examining the Indian scenario, social media has a role in the transformation and cohesion of societies. As the social media landscape gets denser, more complex and more participatory, the networked population is gaining greater access to information and an enhanced ability to undertake collective action (Shirky, 2011). Rapid adoption of social media in India has, however, outpaced the regulatory framework, while media information literacy is still at a low. Mass sharing of messages and fake article links without concerns about credibility and posting of inaccurate messages have become a major issue. At least 31 people were killed in 2017 and 2018 as a result of mob attacks fuelled by rumours on WhatsApp (Nazmi et al., 2018). Alarmed by the rise of this fake news distemper and in a bid to tackle this issue, efforts came from all sides, including the government (Jayaswal, 2019; PTI, 2018), search engines such as Google, fact-checking websites and even social media applications such as WhatsApp that limited its chat group size and message forwarding, apart from launching public education campaigns in India (Gupta, 2018). But in 2019, fake news brought two nuclear-armed neighbours (India and Pakistan) close to fighting a war (Bagri, 2019). On 14 February 2019, a car bomb attacked a convoy of Indian paramilitary police officers in Kashmir and claimed 40 officers. Soon, Indian social media accounts were rife with gory images and videos, mostly fake (Bagri, 2019), generating public outcry and forcing the Indian government to retaliate.

In the same year, the Indian Ministry of External Affairs slammed Pakistan Prime Minister Imran Khan for peddling 'fake news' after he tweeted a video of what he claimed was police action in Uttar Pradesh, but it turned out to be an incident in Bangladesh (Press Trust of India, 2020). Spread of fake news hit a new high in 2019 with every major event (Chaturvedi, 2019), from general elections (Ponniah, 2019) and Pulwama attack to the scrapping of Article 370 and Citizenship (Amendment) Act, 2019. About 95 per cent of protesters felt CAA would take away their citizenship, thanks to fake news (PTI, 2019).

This fake news trend continued in 2020 and 2021 as well, despite government efforts (BT, 2021) and renewed social media campaigns (IANS, 2020).

Notwithstanding the plethora of issues related to social media in India, Indian social media users continue to attach moderate-to-high amounts of credibility to messages circulating on such social media with moderate-to-low awareness on social media issues, especially among those active on those applications. Another issue is the lack of clarity both among the scholarly preview and the users on the ethical use of social media.

Misuse of social media tools for political propaganda has raised significant national security and privacy considerations that remain unaddressed. A horde of ethical issues from privacy invasion and data misuse to pornography, cyberbullying and fake news are also plaguing social media, despite efforts from several fronts to fight them.

It is now evident that, supported by the study findings, more rigorous efforts are needed from all stakeholders to increase media information literacy and awareness about fake news and the other ethical issues related to social media by inventing newer methodologies strong enough to break the knowledge resistance of highly active social media users, who continue to attach high levels of credibility to and share unverified social media messages to avoid dissonance. It is also understood that not just awareness generation, the intervention of regulation is needed for the highly active or addicted group of social media users.

CONCLUSION

Though the study findings identified moderate-to-high levels of awareness about misinformation and disinformation on social media among a majority of the users, they tended to believe messages circulated on these unregulated networks to a large extent. They were also found to be highly active on social media, amounting to addiction. Awareness had a deterring effect on social media credibility. Highly active users, however, tended to attach high credibility to social media messages. Users with low awareness and high credibility also tended to use the popular social media networks the most.

Consulting the theoretical frameworks reviewed, from cognitive dissonance (Festinger, 1957) and third-person effect hypothesis (Davison, 1983) to system justification theory, the all-embracing premise that emerges is that users overuse social media mainly because of ignorance and their tendency to believe in this medium that they are addicted to despite issues regarding its credibility raised from several quarters. From the study findings, the archetype of a highly active social media user who has low awareness and attaches high credibility to social media messages emerges to be female postgraduates, who are above 30 years of age, belonging to high-income groups and from rural settings. Among the addictive users of social media, 57.1 per cent attached moderate credibility and 26.1 per cent high levels of credibility. Similarly, among those with high levels of awareness (1,158), over 50 per cent of the users had moderate-to-high levels of awareness. While the data collection period coincided with the outbreak of the worldwide COVID-19 pandemic, which resulted in a series of lockdowns, home confinement and media applications being the window to the outside world, the study findings are relevant otherwise as well, as there is still a need to raise awareness about the untrustworthiness of social media messages that are blindly circulated from sources that are hard to identify. As the study findings indicate, a combination of both awareness generation and regulation (especially for the addicted users) would be necessary to moderate the misinformation enervation and other ethical concerns.

REFERENCES

Allcott, H., Gentzkow, M., & Yu, C. (2019). Trends in the diffusion of misinformation on social media. *Research & Politics*, *6*(2), 2053168019848554.

Bagri, N. T. (2019, March 15). When India and Pakistan clashed, fake news won. *Los Angeles Times*. https://www.latimes.com/world/la-fg-india-pakistan-fake-news-20190315-story.html

Bali, A., & Desai, P. (2019). Fake news and social media: Indian perspective. *Media Watch*, *10*(3), 737–750.

Banaji, S., Bhat, R., Agarwal, A., Passanha, N., & Sadhana Pravin, M. (2019). WhatsApp vigilantes: An exploration of citizen reception and circulation of WhatsApp misinformation linked to mob violence in India. Report published by the Department of Media and Communications, London School of Economics and Political Science, London, UK. Retrieved from https://www.lse.ac.uk/media-and-communications/assets/documents/research/projects/WhatsApp-Misinformation-Report.pdf

Barclay, F. P. (2017). Media effect on media: Progression of political news and tweets during India 2014. *Journal of Media and Communication*, *1*(1), 1–28.

Barclay, F. P., Chinnasamy, P., & Pichandy, P. (2014). Political opinion expressed in social media and election outcomes—US presidential elections 2012. *GSTF International Journal on Media & Communications*, *1*(2), 15–22.

Barclay, F. P., Pichandy, C., Venkat, A., & Sudhakaran, S. (2015). India 2014: Facebook 'like' as a predictor of election outcomes. *Asian Journal of Political Science*, *23*(2), 134–160.

Barclay, F. P., Pichandy, C., Venkat, A., & Sudhakaran, S. (2016). Twitter sentiments: Pattern recognition and poll prediction. In *Communication and Information Technologies Annual*. Emerald Group Publishing Limited.

Bode, L., & Vraga, E. K. (2018). See something, say something: Correction of global health misinformation on social media. *Health Communication*, *33*(9), 1131–1140.

Bradshaw, S., & Howard, P. N. (2018). The global organization of social media disinformation campaigns. *Journal of International Affairs*, *71*(1.5), 23–32.

BT. (2021, May 8). Centre asks social media platforms to check COVID-19 misinformation. *BusinessToday*. Retrieved from https://www.businesstoday. in/current/economy-politics/centre-asks-social-media-platforms-to-check-covid-19-misinformation/story/438578.html

Bursztyn, L., Rao, A., Roth, C. P., & Yanagizawa-Drott, D. H. (2020). *Misinformation during a pandemic* (No. w27417). National Bureau of Economic Research.

Chadwick, A., & Vaccari, C. (2019). *News sharing on UK social media: Misinformation, disinformation, and correction*. Loughborough University.

Chaturvedi, A. (2019, December 20). 2019—The year of fake news. *The Economic Times*. Retrieved from https://economictimes.indiatimes.com/news/politics-and-nation/fake-news-still-a-menace-despite-government-crackdown-fact-checkers/articleshow/72895472.cms?from=mdr

Chou, W. Y. S., Oh, A., & Klein, W. M. (2018). Addressing health-related misinformation on social media. *Jama, 320*(23), 2417–2418.

Colliander, J. (2019). 'This is fake news': Investigating the role of conformity to other users' views when commenting on and spreading disinformation in social media. *Computers in Human Behavior, 97*, 202–215.

Dasgupta, Victor. (2021, January 25). WhatsApp fact check: Beware! This fake message is getting viral on social media, *India.com*. Retrieved from https:// www.india.com/technology/whatsapp-message-fact-check-beware-this-fake-message-is-getting-viral-on-social-mediawhatsapp-message-fact-check-beware-this-fake-message-is-getting-viral-on-social-media-4354001/

Davison, W. P. (1983). The third-person effect in communication. *Public Opinion Quarterly, 47*(1), 1–15.

Del Vicario, M., Bessi, A., Zollo, F., Petroni, F., Scala, A., Caldarelli, G., Stanley, H. E., & Quattrociocchi, W. (2016). The spreading of misinformation online. *Proceedings of the National Academy of Sciences, 113*(3), 554–559.

Dong, Ensheng, Hongru Du & Lauren Gardner. (2020). An interactive web-based dashboard to track COVID-19 in real time. *The Lancet Infectious Diseases, 20*(5), 533–534.

Fact Check Bureau. (2019, November 26). Clip, flip and photoshop: Anatomy of fakes in Indian elections, *India Today*. Retrieved from https://www.indiato-day.in/elections/story/india-lok-sabha-elections-fake-news-photoshop-lie-truth-1537053-2019-05-28

Festinger, L. (1957). *A theory of cognitive dissonance* (Vol. 2). Stanford University Press.

Fox, C. (1983). Information and misinformation. An investigation of the notions of information, misinformation, informing, and misinforming. Westport. Greenwood Publishing Group.

Garimella, K. & Eckles, D. (2020). Images and misinformation in political groups: Evidence from WhatsApp in India. arXiv preprint arXiv:2005.09784.

GitHub. (2021). COVID-19 Data Repository by the Center for Systems Science and Engineering (CSSE) at Johns Hopkins University. GitHub.com, retrieved from https://github.com/CSSEGISandData/COVID-19

Godfrey-Smith, P. (1989). Misinformation. *Canadian Journal of Philosophy*, *19*(4), 533–550.

Gottlieb, M., & Dyer, S. (2020). Information and disinformation: Social media in the COVID-19 crisis. *Academic Emergency Medicine*, *27*(7), 640–641.

Gupta, K. (2018, August 29). WhatsApp ramps up user education drive to curb fake news. *Mint*. Retrieved from https://www.livemint.com/Companies/If4LwADEG6yWpNFYxEMnwN/WhatsApp-ramps-up-user-education-drive-to-curb-fake-news.html

IANS. (2020, May 15). Coronavirus: WhatsApp launches new campaign to curb fake news. *The Tribune*. Retrieved from https://www.tribuneindia.com/news/sciencetechnology/coronavirus-whatsapp-launches-new-campaign-to-curb-fake-news-85209

Jayaswal, R. (2019, January 21). Government to sensitise schoolkids to combat fake news. *Hindustan Times*. Retrieved from https://www.hindustantimes.com/india-news/government-to-sensitise-schoolkids-to-combat-fake-news/story-tElDI3HPNsW2757ElT6g3N.html

Jost, J. T., & van der Toorn, J. (2012). System justification theory. In P. A. M. Van Lange, A. W. Kruglanski, & E. T. Higgins (Eds.), *Handbook of theories of social psychology* (pp. 313–343). SAGE Publications. https://doi.org/10.4135/9781446249222.n42

Kadam, A. B., & Atre, S. R. (2020). Negative impact of social media panic during the COVID-19 outbreak in India. *Journal of Travel Medicine*, *27*(3), taaa057.

Krishnan, Murali. (2018, June 27). Fake social media messages fuel latest mob lynchings in India, *National Herald India*. Retrieved from https://www.nationalheraldindia.com/opinion/fake-social-media-messages-fuel-latest-mob-lynchings-in-india

Kuklinski, J. H., Quirk, P. J., Jerit, J., Schwieder, D., & Rich, R. F. (2000). Misinformation and the currency of democratic citizenship. *The Journal of Politics*, *62*(3), 790–816.

Nair, Parvathy S., & Barclay., Francis P. (2017). Twitter usage patterns as a predictor of user gender. *Journal of Media and Communication*, *1*(2), 1–23.

Napoli, P. M. (2019). *Social media and the public interest: Media regulation in the disinformation age*. Columbia University Press.

Nazmi, S., Nenwani, D., & Narhe, G. (2018, November 13). Social media rumours in India: Counting the dead. *BBC News*. Retrieved from https://www.bbc.co.uk/news/resources/idt-e5043092-f7f0-42e9-9848-5274ac896e6d#:%7E:text=Across%20India%20mob%20attacks%20are,years%20and%20dozens%20more%20injured

Ponniah, B. K. (2019, April 6). WhatsApp: The 'black hole' of fake news in India's election. *BBC News*. Retrieved from https://www.bbc.com/news/world-asia-india-47797151

Press Trust of India. (2020, January 3). Tweet fake news, get caught, delete tweet: MEA on Imran Khan's 'UP video'. *India Today*. Retrieved from https://www.indiatoday.in/india/story/tweet-fake-news-get-caught-delete-tweet-mea-on-imran-khan-s-up-video-1633800-2020-01-03

PTI. (2018, August 15). Fake news issue: Government portal starts advocacy on WhatsApp safety for students, others. *The Economic Times.* Retrieved from https://economictimes.indiatimes.com/news/politics-and-nation/fake-news-issue-government-portal-starts-advocacy-on-whatsapp-safety-for-students-others/articleshow/65415158.cms?from=mdr

PTI. (2019, December 18). Supreme Court asks Centre to consider publicising info about CAA to curb circulation of fake news. *The Economic Times.* Retrieved from https://economictimes.indiatimes.com/news/politics-and-nation/supreme-court-asks-centre-to-consider-publicising-info-about-caa-to-curb-circulation-of-fake-news/articleshow/72871637.cms?from=mdr

Sahoo, Niranjan. (2020, January 30). How fake news is complicating India's war against COVID-19. *Observer Research Foundation.* Retrieved from https://www.orfonline.org/expert-speak/how-fake-news-complicating-india-war-against-covid19-66052/

Saurwein, F., & Spencer-Smith, C. (2020). Combating disinformation on social media: Multilevel governance and distributed accountability in Europe. *Digital Journalism, 8*(6), 820–841.

Sharon (2018, January 24). Advantages and misuse of social media during disasters and crisis. Webtraffic.Agency. Retrieved from http://www.webtraffic.agency/2018/01/advantages-and-misuse-social-media-disasters-crisis/

Shirky, Clay. (2011). The political power of social media; technology, the public sphere, and political change. *Foreign Affairs*, Published by the Council of Foreign Relations. https://www.cc.gatech.edu/~beki/cs4001/Shirky.pdf

Shu, K., Bhattacharjee, A., Alatawi, F., Nazer, T. H., Ding, K., Karami, M., & Liu, H. (2020). Combating disinformation in a social media age. *Wiley Interdisciplinary Reviews: Data Mining and Knowledge Discovery, 10*(6), e1385.

Statista. (2021a). Number of internet users in India from 2015 to 2020 with a forecast until 2025. Statista.com. Retrieved from https://www.statista.com/statistics/255146/number-of-internet-users-in-india/

Statista. (2021b). Number of social network users in India from 2015 to 2018 with a forecast until 2023. Statista.com. Retrieved from https://www.statista.com/statistics/278407/number-of-social-network-users-in-india/

Talwar, S., Dhir, A., Kaur, P., Zafar, N., & Alrasheedy, M. (2019). Why do people share fake news? Associations between the dark side of social media use and fake news sharing behavior. *Journal of Retailing and Consumer Services, 51*, 72–82.

Talwar, S., Dhir, A., Singh, D., Virk, G. S., & Salo, J. (2020). Sharing of fake news on social media: Application of the honeycomb framework and the third-person effect hypothesis. *Journal of Retailing and Consumer Services, 57*, 102197.

Tandoc Jr, E. C., Lim, D., & Ling, R. (2020). Diffusion of disinformation: How social media users respond to fake news and why. *Journalism, 21*(3), 381–398.

Tasnim, S., Hossain, M. M., & Mazumder, H. (2020). Impact of rumors and misinformation on COVID-19 in social media. *Journal of Preventive Medicine and Public Health, 53*(3), 171–174.

Tucker, J. A., Guess, A., Barberá, P., Vaccari, C., Siegel, A., Sanovich, S., Stukal, D., & Nyhan, B. (2018). Social media, political polarization, and political disinformation: A review of the scientific literature. (March 19, 2018). http://dx.doi.org/10.2139/ssrn.3144139

United Nations. (2021). India: General information. UNData App. Retrieved from http://data.un.org/en/iso/in.html

Valenzuela, S., Halpern, D., Katz, J. E., & Miranda, J. P. (2019). The paradox of participation versus misinformation: Social media, political engagement, and the spread of misinformation. *Digital Journalism, 7*(6), 802–823.

Vasudeva, F., & Barkdull, N. (2020). WhatsApp in India? A case study of social media related lynchings. *Social Identities, 26*(5), 574–589.

Wang, Y., McKee, M., Torbica, A., & Stuckler, D. (2019). Systematic literature review on the spread of health-related misinformation on social media. *Social Science & Medicine, 240*, 112552.

Wu, L., Morstatter, F., Carley, K. M., & Liu, H. (2019). Misinformation in social media: definition, manipulation, and detection. *ACM SIGKDD Explorations Newsletter, 21*(2), 80–90.

PART II

Use and Misuse of Social Media

Chapter 4

Twitter for Political Propaganda
An Analysis of Literary-Rhetorical Devices

Akhila S. and Francis P. Barclay

INTRODUCTION

Having become an entwined and integral part of people's daily routine, online social media is serving several purposes including social communication, civic engagement and political participation (Gil de Zúñiga et al., 2012), advertising and promotion (Chu, 2011), sharing of public opinion (Barclay et al., 2015; 2016), as a news media (Alarifi et al., 2016; Kwak et al., 2010; Lee & Ma, 2012), for mining of public sentiments, poll prediction and scholarly research (Barclay et al., 2015a). Primarily, on these online social media platforms, users create social networks for communication through messages and reactions. Several social media applications provide open spaces for people to share their ideas, opinions and feelings to the world, about issues that concern them (Kaur & Verma, 2018).

A subset of the social media sphere, microblogging, has also captivated the masses, aiding quick exchange of opinion and thoughts (Bose et al., 2019; Larsson & Moe, 2012). Among a multitude of microblogging platforms, Twitter stands out (Carpenter & Krutka, 2014; Hu et al., 2013), where users broadcast short messages called 'tweets' to a potentially global audience (Conover et al., 2014), and it is available publicly and is instantly accessible. Twitter users post, on an average day, about 500 million tweets (Crannell et al., 2016) and about 80 per cent of them are sent from mobile devices (Carley et al., 2016). Twitter, as a platform open for public content creation and consumption, serves as a venue for public debates and discourse (Kim, 2011). This microblogging platform could be used also for mass opinion and real-time sentiment mining (Gokulakrishnan et al., 2012).

TWITTER AND POLITICS

Created in March 2006, by Jack Dorsey, Noah Glass, Biz Stone and Evan Williams and based in San Francisco, California, this popular microblogging website had about 11.5 million users in India in 2013 (Statista, 2015), and it is estimated to be over 34 million in 2019. Initially, the tweets were restricted to 140 characters, but later that limit was doubled. Twitter claims to have 126 million daily active users and this number is rising (Shaban, 2019). As a popular information-sharing tool, Twitter has varied political applications and is seen as influential, both in engaging the electorate and in altering their political thoughts and actions (Barclay et al., 2015). Hence, it isn't surprising that social media campaigns contributed to a major share of the Parliamentary poll budgeting in 2019 in India (Joy, 2019). Similar is the political importance accorded to social media across the world (Kaur & Verma, 2018). During the recent 2019 Lok Sabha elections in India, Twitter users posted a torrent of political messages on social media platforms.

Online and social media presence had become a must-have for politicos contesting the polls. As stated by Twitter, about 396 million tweets were sent during the Indian parliamentary elections during January–May 2019 (Alawadhi, 2019). Popular Indian politicians on Twitter were Narendra Modi (47.3 million followers), Aravind Kejriwal (14.9 million), Amit Shah (13.5 million), Arun Jaitley (14.8 million), Sushma Swaraj (12.7 million), Rahul Gandhi (9.5 million), Shashi Tharoor (6.88 million), Piyush Goyal (5.5 million), Nitish Kumar (4.85 million) Yogi Adithyanath (4.02 million), Mamata Banarjee (3.31 million), Manmohan Singh (112,000), Sonia Gandhi

(96,500) and Mayawati (27,900). Conversations around elections kept Twitter buzzing over the last one month in the run-up to the elections, with over 45 million tweets being shared and Prime Minister Modi emerging as the 'most mentioned figure' during this first phase (Business Today, 2019).

Several past studies and observations have indicated that the so-called people's media is a crucial platform for sociopolitical development, propagating political participation, and hence, the kind of political communication on these social networks has to be examined, critically. To investigate the nature of political communication happening on this platform, the following variables are considered in the current study: political polarity, source type, topic, form, frame, device and response.

Several latest studies have measured political polarity towards a party as positive, neutral and negative or favourable, neutral and unfavourable (Barclay et al., 2014; 2017); that is, the variable measures whether a tweet is posted in support of a party, opposing it or without any clear political polarity. Regarding source type, the tweet can come from sources such as political, media, government, corporate or the public. Depending on the source of information, the response to the tweet can also vary. For instance, a message from an established media source could be viewed as more credible than from a political source or an unverified individual. Also, the choice of topic could affect political communication as the users may be interested in some topics while a few other topics may not be of their interest.

On Twitter, short messages of up to 140 characters can be posted as tweets. Pictures or videos can be attached to a tweet or even a web link can be embedded in it. Since a tweet can take varied forms, the kind of responses could also vary depending on its form. For instance, a simple text tweet may not draw the kind of attention that a tweet with a colourful photograph draws. It also becomes crucial to study the literary–rhetorical devices used in tweets to frame political ideas. Measuring which political frame or device used draws what kind of response could help and understand their uses and help to develop efficient political communication formulae for online social media.

Accordingly, the following research questions are proposed:

RQ1: What is the polarity of political tweets?
RQ2: Who are the sources?
RQ3: Are the sources verified?
RQ4: In what forms are these messages sent?
RQ5: What topics are the political tweets about?
RQ6: Which are the frames used in political tweets?
RQ7: Which are the rhetorical and literary devices used for those political arguments?
RQ8: What is the response to political tweets?
RQ9: What are the relationships among these variables?

Several studies have measured these variables and tested the relationships among them. Several studies have gauged political opinion using social media messages (Boatwright et al., 2019; Calderon et al., 2015; Tumasjan et al., 2010; Yaqub et al., 2017) and used political polarity to predict election results (Baid & Chaplot, 2019; Barclay et al., 2016). Teran and Mancera (2019) demonstrate that Twitter could offer valuable results and provide insights into the connection between voters and political candidates. Employing the theory of media framing, several studies have analysed media content to examine the use of frames in political communication. Joseph and Barclay (2018) performed a content analysis to analyse news reports under six popular conflict-based news frames: conflict, attribution of responsibility, human interest, morality, economic and diagnostic/prognostic frame.

A handful have studied the role of Twitter in political communication, especially in the context of the Indian elections. During the 2014 Indian Lok Sabha elections, several studies were conducted on Twitter political campaigns (Ahmed et al., 2016; 2017), the use of Twitter by political leaders (Rajput, 2014) and how political parties used the microblogging website to create and frame agendas (Bajaj, 2017). A study on the 2014 Indian general elections and the changing political traditions (Jaidka & Ahmed, 2015) found that the most successful parties used Twitter to provide regular updates and feedback to their followers on both virtual and offline campaign activity. Through effective political campaigns, Twitter can transform not only political parties but even political leaders into big brands and rebrand them (Antil & Verma, 2019; Pal et al., 2016; Rajadesingan et al., 2020). Pal et al. (2016) found that Narendra Modi has become a strong online brand through strategic content creation on Twitter. Many topics, frames and devices are used for that purpose.

Tayal et al., (2014) demonstrated that political sentiments expressed could be used to gauge the extent of inclination or the amount of dissatisfaction of the masses with regard to a party, leader, candidate or the government, and also thereby, help in poll prediction. Hemphill et al. (2013) observed that political entities use social media platforms to their advantage to frame political issues by concentrating on specific topics that support them and promoting hashtags related to those topics. Further, they identified that divisive and negative issues drew the most framing efforts and that voting patterns generally align with tweeting patterns. Twitter sentiment analysis and opinion mining have wide and varied usage in several domains, including research, politics and governance, from understanding people's opinion on important issues, gauge resentment against or reactions to government policies to measuring public mood and predicting poll results (Yaqub et al., 2017). Of late, there have also been counterarguments questioning the efficacy of Twitter sentiment analysis, courtesy paid promotions, manipulations and the proliferation of fake accounts (Gayo-Avello et al., 2011, Metaxas et al., 2011). Somani (2020) observed that Narendra Modi used ancient communication strategies of classical rhetoric, such as pathos, ethos and logos.

A study on 'populist style and antagonistic messaging' in the Twitter feeds of Donald Trump, Narendra Modi, Nigel Farage and Geert Wilders by Pal et al., (2018) found that Trump was a 'consistent outlier in terms of using critical language on Twitter' when compared to the other three, but all of these political leaders engaged in 'antagonistic messaging', including personal insults, sarcasm and labelling and that these were rewarded online with high likes and retweets.

Reyes et al. (2013) identified irony, satire, parody and sarcasm as 'overlapping figurative phenomena' on this microblogging website, whose differences are a 'matter of usage, tone, and obviousness'. While sarcasm is a mocking strategy, irony, more often not, is a sophisticated and subtle version of ridicule. Mourão et al. (2016) content analysed

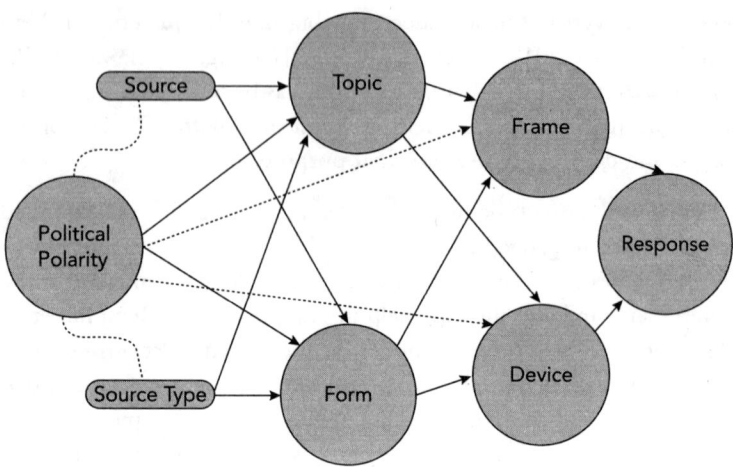

Figure 4.1 *Initial Model*

hundreds of political tweets and observed humour as a predominant device used by journalists on Twitter. Such humorous tweets garnered the most retweets. About 20 per cent of the tweets posted by journalists on Twitter employed humour and those jokes were mostly aimed at politicians, whereas satire was pointed at news outlets. Based on the review of the past studies, the following hypotheses are generated:

H_a1: Political Polarity is associated with Topic, Form, Frame and Device.
H_a2: Political Polarity is associated with Source and Source Type.
H_a3: Source and Source Type are associated with Topic and Form.
H_a4: Topic and Form are associated with Frame and Device.
H_a5: Frame and Device are associated with Response.

These hypotheses are presented in a graphical form in Figure 4.1.

METHODOLOGY

In the current study, to measure the chosen variables, a manual content analysis was employed with a tweet as the unit of analysis. Tweets were mined using the Search API of Twitter and the search terms that were employed were 'bjp' and 'cong'. Tweets were mined from 10 October

2018 to 20 October 2018. In total, 268 tweets were mined (134 tweets each for the two terms) and sentiment and other analyses were performed on them. Sample analysis was conducted by mining tweets using a list of political search terms related to the two top parties contesting the Lok Sabha elections, including 'modi', 'narendra', 'rahul', 'gandhi', 'sonia', 'congress' and 'bharatiya janata party'. However, the terms 'bjp' and 'cong' were found to garner the most number of mentions and also the most relevant tweets related to the parties. The window of examination for the study was 10 October to 20 October.

For tweets with the mention of both terms, three categories were chosen for categorization—BJP positive, Cong positive and neutral. While dealing with an issue or controversy, if a tweet contained a view or statement of a party or its candidate, then the tweet was classified as positive for that political party. The dominant view was taken into consideration in the case of multiple views. If a tweet was observed to be hurting the political party or a candidate belonging to that party, it was rated as positive for the opposing party. If a tweet favoured the political campaign of that party, then it was classified as positive for that party. Positive and negative sentiments were tracked to also decide the polarity. A tweet that did not exhibit a perceivable political polarity was categorized as neutral. The measured variables and their groups are presented in Table 4.1.

Table 4.1 List of Variables

Variable	Groups	Remarks
Political polarity	BJP positive Neutral Congress positive	Manual sentiment analysis
Source type	Verified Unverified	The blue verified badge on Twitter lets people know that an account of public interest is authentic
Source	Political Media Government Corporate People	Sources are determined using the descriptions publicly available in the Twitter user's profile

(Table 4.1 Continued)

(Table 4.1 Continued)

Variable	Groups	Remarks
Form	Article/link Memes Picture Video	Analysed by the coder according to the elements present in the tweet
Topic	Corruption Policy/ Governance Employment Election Economy Personal attacks	A pilot study was conducted to determine the categories for topics; all the topics discussed in the tweet are coded by expert coders
Frame	Morality	Basing a political argument on moral values
	Efficiency	Basing a political argument on efficiency
	Convention	Referring to tradition or standard practice
	Logic	Portraying as a logical explanation
	People	Denoting as for or about the people
	Rights	Discussing rights and privileges
	Law	Referring to the rulebook
Devices	Humour	Using humour
	Hyperbole	Using exaggerated statements or claims not meant to be taken literally
	Sarcasm	Using irony to mock or convey contempt
	Metaphor	Using a thing regarded as representative or symbolic of something else
	Simile	Comparing one thing with another thing of a different kind, used to make a description more emphatic or vivid
	Ridicule	Making mockery out of somebody or something
	Anaphora	Repeating a word or phrase at the beginning of successive clauses

Variable	Groups	Remarks
	Personification	Attributing human characteristics to something not human
	Alliteration	Repetition of the same letter at the beginning of words or syllables
	Understatement	Makes a person or idea seem less important
	Pleonasm	Use of superfluous words
	Oxymoron	Use of an apparent contradiction
Response	Likes Retweets Comments	Measured as numbers, as displayed below the tweets, at the time of mining. Using these three measurements, a single variable response (with eigenvalues over 1) was extracted using factor analysis employing the principal components method without extraction. Kaiser–Meyer–Olkin measure of sampling adequacy was 0.73, above the commonly recommended value of 0.6, and Bartlett's test of sphericity was significant (χ^2 (153) = 840.26, $p < 0.05$). The regression values of the factor response were saved for further analysis.

A common formula was applied to each of the tweets in this study to mitigate any inherent bias in the data analysis. Categories of the variables chosen were determined during a sample study of 50 tweets. Content analysis was performed by expert coders.

FINDINGS

RQ1: What is the polarity of political tweets?

Of the 268 tweets that were analysed, as many as 120 were in favour of the BJP, while 101 tweets supported the Congress and the remaining 47 did not have an apparent bias.

RQ2: Who are the sources?

A majority of the tweets (128) came from ordinary people, 79 tweets from political sources, 54 tweets from media sources, four tweets from corporate sources and three tweets from government sources.

RQ3: Are the sources verified?

As many as 153 were from verified Twitter accounts, while 115 came from unverified accounts.

RQ4: In what forms are these messages sent?

A majority of them (136) carried pictures, followed by 101 tweets with article links, 26 with memes and the remaining 23 with videos.

RQ5: What topics are the political tweets about?

As many as 108 tweets were about policy or governance, 85 tweets discussed personal attacks, 42 tweets were about the election, 25 tweets discussed development, four tweets were about the economy and three tweets were about employment.

RQ6: Which are the frames used in political tweets?

A total of 163 tweets used morality frame, 110 tweets had efficiency frame, 44 tweets used people' frame, 16 tweets used law frame, eight tweets used logic as frame, six tweets had convention as frame and five tweets used right as a frame.

RQ7: Which are the rhetorical and literary devices used for those political arguments?

A total of 155 tweets used the literary-rhetorical device sarcasm, 56 tweets used hyperbole, 47 tweets used ridicule, 23 tweets used anaphora, 12 tweets used simile, nine tweets used alliteration, eight tweets used humour and understatement, every two tweets used metaphor and one tweet used oxymoron.

RQ8: What's the response to political tweets?

Using three components—likes, comments and retweets—responses were for the tweets. On an average, the tweets secured 607 likes, 246 retweets and 46 comments.

Hypothesis Testing

Testing the Initial model

H_a1: *Political Polarity is associated with Topic, Form, Frame and Device.*

To test the relationship between variables political polarity and topic, form, frame and device, a one-way ANOVA test was performed, and the results are presented in Table 4.2.

Table 4.2 *ANOVA Results: Political Polarity vs Topic, Form, Frame and Device*

Variables	F	Sig.	Finding
Topics	—	—	No significant association was observed between political polarity and the topics corruption, policy/governance, development, employment, election, economy and personal attacks.
Form: article/link	6.122	0.003	There is a significant association between political polarity and form article/link. Neutral tweets had the most number of article links (60%) in them, while, among the politically inclined tweets, those support-ing the BJP had more tweets with article links.
Other forms	—	—	No significant association was found between political polarity and forms picture, video and memes.
Frames	—	—	No significant association was found between political polarity and frames morality, efficiency, conven-tion, logic, people, rights and law.
Device: sarcasm	11.465	0.000	There is a significant association between political polarity and device sarcasm. Tweets supporting BJP party used sarcasm the most (65%).

(Table 4.2 Continued)

(Table 4.2 Continued)

Variables	F	Sig.	Finding
Device: ridicule	7.266	0.001	There is a significant association between political polarity and device ridicule. Tweets supporting BJP party used ridicule the most (26%).
Other devices	—	—	No significant association was found between political polarity and devices hyperbole, metaphor, simili, anaphora and personification.

H_a2: *Political Polarity is associated with Source and Source Type.*

To test the relationship between political polarity and source and source type, a chi-square test was performed, and the results are presented in Tables 4.3, 4.4 and 4.5.

H_a3: *Source and Source Type are associated with Topic and Form.*

To test the relationship among source, source type, topic and form, one-way ANOVA test was performed, and the results are presented in Table 4.6.

Table 4.3 *Chi-square Results: Political Polarity vs Source and Source Type*

Variables	Sig.	Finding
Political polarity vs source	0.000	There is a significant association between political polarity and source. Congress was favoured the most in political circles (38 tweets), while the BJP had more support among government, corporates and the people (62 tweets).
Political polarity vs source type	0.000	There is a significant association between political polarity and source type. A majority of BJP supporters were unverified (66), while the Congress party had more verified Twitter users (62).

Table 4.4 *Political Polarity vs Source: Frequency Distribution*

Source	Political	Media	Government	Corporate	People	Total
BJP positive	34	18	3	3	62	120
Neutral	7	22	0	0	18	47
Congress positive	38	14	0	1	48	101

Table 4.5 *Political Polarity vs Source Type: Frequency Distribution*

Source Type	Verified	Unverified	Total
BJP positive	54	66	120
Neutral	37	10	47
Congress positive	62	39	101

Table 4.6 *ANOVA Results: Source vs Topic and Form*

Variables	F	Sig.	Finding
Source vs topics	—	—	No significant association between source and topics corruption, policy/governance, development, employment, election, economy and personal attacks.
Source vs forms: article/link	10.523	0.000	There is a significant association between source and form article/link. Tweets from media sources contained the most number of article links (70%).
Source vs forms: meme	4.092	0.003	There is a significant association between source and form meme. Tweets from corporate sources (25%) and people (16%) carried more memes.

(Table 4.6 Continued)

(Table 4.6 Continued)

Variables	F	Sig.	Finding
Source vs other forms	—	—	No significant association between source and forms picture and video.
Source type vs topic: corruption	16.585	0.000	There is a significant association between source type and topic corruption. A majority of tweets from verified sources (40%) discussed the topic corruption.
Source type vs topic: election	14.539	0.000	There is a significant association between source type and topic election. A majority of tweets that came from unverified sources discussed the election topic (25%).
Source type vs other topics	—	—	No significant association between source type and topic policy/governance, development, personal attacks, employment and economy.
Source type vs form: article/link	44.520	0.000	There is a significant association between source type and form article/link. A majority of tweets from verified sources used article links (54%).
Source type vs form: meme	17.842	0.000	There is a significant association between source type and form meme. A majority of tweets that came from unverified sources used memes (18%).
Source type vs other forms	—	—	No significant association between source type and forms picture and video.

H_a4: *Topic and Form are associated with Frame and Device.*

To test the relationship among variables topic, form, frame and device, Pearson's product–moment correlation test was run, and the results are presented in Tables 4.7, 4.8, 4.9 and 4.10. The study results indicated that morality and logic were used to frame the corruption-based tweets.

Table 4.7 Correlation Results: Topic and Form vs Frame

Correlation	Morality	Efficiency	Convention	Logic	People	Rights	Law
Corruption	0.262**	-0.202**		0.171**	-0.138*		
Policy governance	-0.135*				0.334**		0.210**
Development		0.228**			0.170**		
Employment							
Election	-0.222**	0.329**					
Economy							
Personal attacks	0.202**	-0.161**					
Picture			-0.154*				
Video				0.181**			
Article/link						0.120*	
Memes							

**Correlation is significant at the 0.01 level (2-tailed).
*Correlation is significant at the 0.05 level (2-tailed).

Table 4.8 *Correlation Results: Topic and Form vs Device*

Correlation	Humour	Hyperbole	Sarcasm	Metaphor	Simile	Ridicule	Anaphora	Pleonasm
Corruption		-0.218**	0.216**					
Policy governance		-0.142*						
Emp.			-0.125*					
Election		0.435**	-0.297**				0.124*	0.132*
Economy			-0.144*		0.122*			
Personal attacks		-0.212**	0.241**	0.127*		.192**		
Picture	0.129*							
Video			-0.143*					0.151*
Article/link						-0.156*		
Memes	0.165**		0.152*			0.247**		

**Correlation is significant at the 0.01 level (2-tailed).
*Correlation is significant at the 0.05 level (2-tailed).

Table 4.9 *Correlation Results: Topic vs Form*

Correlation	Picture	Video	Article/link	Meme
Corruption	–.164**			–0.161**
Policy governance	0.140*			
Election			–0.123*	
Economy	0.121*			

**Correlation is significant at the 0.01 level (2-tailed).
*Correlation is significant at the 0.05 level (2-tailed).

Table 4.10 *Correlation Results: Frame vs Devices*

Correlation	Hyperbole	Sarcasm	Under-statement	Ridicule	Oxy-moron
Morality	–0.170**	0.367**		0.209**	
Efficiency	0.243**	–0.194**	0.166**	–0.145*	
Logic		–0.161**			
People		–0.132*			0.138*
Law	–0.130*				0.243**

**Correlation is significant at the 0.01 level (2-tailed).
*Correlation is significant at the 0.05 level (2-tailed).

The people and law frames were used in tweets on policy and governance. For discussing the topic development, efficiency and people frames were used.

Those who engaged in personal attacks on Twitter used the morality frame the most. Similarly, when the forms of tweets and the frames were related, associations were found between picture tweets and convention ($R = -0.154$); video and logic frame ($R = 0.181$); and article links and the rights frame ($R = 0.120$).

While tweeting about corruption, users use sarcasm ($R = 0.216$), avoiding hyperbole ($R = -0.218$). Meanwhile, on the subject of policy or governance, an association was found with hyperbole ($R = -0.142$). Similarly, employment and sarcasm are correlated ($R = -0.125$), implying the absence of the use of sarcasm. For discussing election-related topics, hyperbole ($R = 0.435$), anaphora ($R = 0.124$) and pleonasm ($R = 0.132$) are used, while sarcasm ($R = 0.297$) is not employed. Though simile ($R = 0.122$) is made use of to tweet economy-based topics, sarcasm ($R = 0.144$) is not applied. While employing tweets to attack people personally, sarcasm ($R = 0.241$), metaphor ($R = 0.127$) and ridicule ($R = 0.192$) are often resorted to in contrast with the avoidance of hyperbole ($R = -0.212$). The study also found associations between form, picture and device, humour ($R = 0.129$). Moreover, sarcasm is employed in video ($R = -0.143$), though pleonasm ($R = 0.151$) is never used. On the other hand, article or link never makes use of ridicule ($R = -0.156$). In the case of memes, the devices, humour ($R = 0.165$), sarcasm ($R = 0.152$) and ridicule ($R = 0.247$) are used.

Correlations were found between topic and form. Corruption is associated with forms picture ($R = -0.164$) and meme ($R = -0.161$). Moreover, policy or governance is also associated with picture ($R = 0.140$). However, election is correlated with article or link ($R = -0.123$). Furthermore, economy is also associated with picture ($R = 0.121$).

While employing the frame morality, sarcasm ($R = 0.367$) and ridicule ($R = 0.209$) are found to be used in contrast to the absence of the device hyperbole ($R = -0.170$). The devices hyperbole ($R = 0.243$) and understatement ($R = 0.166$) are used with frame efficiency. But on the other hand, sarcasm ($R = -0.194$) and ridicule ($R = -0.145$) are absent. Logic is also associated with sarcasm ($R = -0.161$). While sarcasm ($R = -0.132$) is avoided in the case of the frame, people, there is a usage of the device oxymoron ($R = 0.243$). Considering the case of the frame, law, hyperbole ($R = -0.130$) is never used, although oxymoron ($R = 0.243$) is employed.

H_a5: *Frame and Device are associated with Response.*

To test the relationship among variables topic, form, frame and device, Pearson's product–moment correlation test was run, and the results are presented in Table 4.11.

Table 4.11 *Correlation Results: Frame and Device vs Response*

Correlations	Response
Morality	–0.086
Efficiency	–0.041
Convention	0.123*
Logic	0.194**
People	0.095
Rights	–0.026
Law	–0.033
Humour	–0.013
Hyperbole	0.078
Alliteration	–0.018
Sarcasm	–0.03
Metaphor	–0.03
Simile	0.055
Understatement	–0.063
Ridicule	–0.075
Anaphora	–0.012
Pleonasm	-0.033
Oxymoron	–0.022

The study results found that there is a positive correlation between the frames convention ($R = 0.123$) and logic ($R = 0.194$) with response. Correlations were not found between the other variables.

Based on the study results, the final model is presented in Figure 4.2.

Based on the final model (Figure 4.2) the important findings are given in Table 4.12.

DISCUSSION

As the study results have indicated, political polarity of the tweets (that has the categories of BJP positive, Congress positive and neutral)

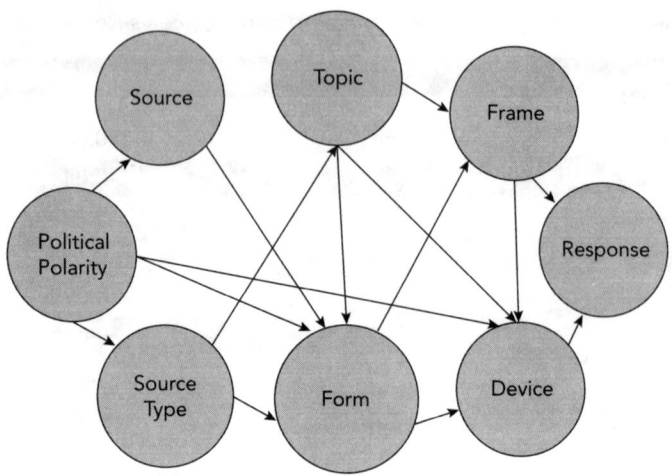

Figure 4.2 *Final Model*

Table 4.12 *Study Findings*

Congress Positive	BJP Positive	Neutral
Favoured the most among the political circles.	BJP had more support among government sources, corporates and the people.	Majority of media sources sent neutral tweets.
More verified Twitter users offered support to Congress.	Majority of BJP supporters were unverified.	Neutral tweets had mostly verified users.
Verified sources discussed corruption the most.	Unverified sources discussed election the most.	Discussed all topics without much difference.
Used more of article links.	Used memes a lot.	Used mostly article links.
Tweets on corruption used mostly the morality and logic frames.	Tweets on election used the efficiency frame to base their arguments.	Article/links used the rights frame the most.
Used mostly sarcasm and ridicule.	Relied heavily on hyperbole and understatement.	Desisted using ridicule.

was associated with the sources of the tweets (government, political, media, corporate and people), source types (verified and unverified), certain forms of the tweets (article links and memes) and a few literary-rhetorical devices used in the tweets (hyperbole, sarcasm, ridicule, etc.). Neutral tweets carried the most number of tweets with article links, followed by tweets supporting Congress. Similarly, tweets supporting the Congress party used hyperbole the most. As Barclay et al. (2016, 2017) have stated political polarities are identified within tweets and can be measured with a great deal of accuracy. That is, in the current study, the variable political polarity measured whether a tweet was posted in support of the BJP, Congress or found to be not exhibiting an apparent political favourability. Using the methodology, the data analysis identified 120 tweets supporting the BJP, while 101 were in favour of the Indian National Congress. As many as 47 tweets were identified with no political polarity as the operationalization of the political favourability in the current study. A majority of the tweets (128) came from ordinary people, 79 tweets from political sources, 54 tweets from media sources, four tweets from corporate sources and three tweets were from government sources. Of the 268 tweets content analysed, as many as 153 were from verified Twitter accounts, while 115 came from unverified accounts. Teran and Mancera (2019) found that Twitter offered meaningful results and new insights into the relationship between voters and candidates.

Employing the theory of media framing, several studies have ana-lysed media content to examine the use of frames in political commu-nication. The current study results indicate that using different types of frames can accelerate the effectiveness of political tweets. The major frames used for tweeting political messages are morality, efficiency, people, rights and law. Several studies have examined the news frames used in conflict reporting (Joseph & Barclay, 2018) and identified attribution of responsibility and human interest as the most popular. In the current study, which uses self-devised political frames to study tweets, the frames morality and efficiency were found to be the most popular. But it is the frame logic that draws the best responses—likes, comments and retweets.

Hemphill et al. (2014) found that politicians actively use social media to frame issues by choosing hot topics, divisive issues and specific hashtags within those topics. Voting patterns generally align with tweeting patterns. Twitter sentiment analysis is also used in a vast array of areas related to governance and public trust ranging from predicting resentment against government policies to predict general election results (Yaqub et al., 2017). Of the 268 tweets analysed, 40.3 per cent tweets were on policy and governance, 31.7 per cent tweets were personal attacks on politicians, 30.2 per cent of the tweets spoke about the corruption, 15.7 per cent tweets were on the forthcoming elections, 9.3 per cent tweets were about development, 1.5 per cent tweets were on economy and 1.1 per cent tweets were on the topic of employment. From these numbers, it is concluded that policy governance is the most discussed political topic on twitter during this study period.

A study on populist style and antagonistic messaging in the tweets of Donald Trump, Narendra Modi, Nigel Farage and Geert Wilders by Pal et al. (2018) found that Trump is a consistent outlier in terms of using critical language on Twitter when compared to the other three, but that all four leaders showed investment in various forms of antagonistic messaging, including personal insults, sarcasm and labelling and that these were rewarded online by higher retweet rates. Similarly, the current study results found that Twitter users use several devices in political tweets. Sarcasm and hyperbole were the most popular devices used in the political tweets mined and governance was the most popular topic discussed. While sarcasm was used to ridicule the corrupt, hyperboles were used to exaggerate poll issues. Reyes et al. (2013) found that irony, satire, parody and sarcasm are overlapping figurative phenomena in Twitter, whose differences are a matter of usage, tone and obviousness. For instance, sarcasm has an obviously mocking tone that is used against another, while irony is often more sophisticated, more subtle and ambiguous and even self-deprecating. Mourão et al. (2016) content analysed tweets posted by 430 political journalists during the debate found widespread use of humour by journalists on Twitter, especially associated with the retweet function.

About one-fifth of the journalists' tweets included jokes, suggesting a growing acceptance of the rhetorical device on Twitter. Overall, political journalists tended to avoid humour as a means of criticism. Similarly, the current study results pointed out that in political tweets, humour is not a popular literary-rhetorical device compared to sarcasm and hyperbole.

For criticizing, sarcasm and ridicule were used mostly. Most of the relationships suggested by the initial model were tested to be accepted: political polarity, source and source type were associated with the form of the tweets; topic and form determined the frame and devices used in the tweets, which had an influence on the responses.

CONCLUSION

Twitter has been widely used for political propaganda by all stakeholders, from politicians and people to the government, media and corporate fraternities. The most popular frames used in political tweets are morality and efficiency. But it is logic that draws the best response—likes, comments and retweets. Among the literary–rhetorical devices, sarcasm and hyperbole are popular devices used in political tweets. Governance was the most discussed on Twitter during this election, although the Twitter space was loaded with personal attacks. The rhetorical device sarcasm was mostly used for ridiculing the corrupt through political tweets. Similarly, hyperbole was used to exaggerate poll issues.

REFERENCES

Ahmed, S., Cho, J., & Jaidka, K. (2017). Leveling the playing field: The use of Twitter by politicians during the 2014 Indian general election campaign'. *Telematics and Informatics, 34*(7), 1377–1386.

Ahmed, S., Jaidka, K., & Cho, J. (2016). The 2014 Indian elections on Twitter: A comparison of campaign strategies of political parties *Telematics and Informatics, 33*(4), 1071–1087.

Alarifi, A., Alsaleh, M., & Al-Salman, A. (2016). Twitter Turing test: Identifying social machines. *Information Sciences, 372*, 332–346.

Alawadhi, Neha. (2019, May 24). Twitter sees record election-related activity with 396 million tweets. Retrieved from https://www.business-standard. com/article/elections/twitter-sees-record-election-related-activity-with-396-million-tweets-119052301866_1.html

Antil, A., & Verma, H. V. (2019). Rahul Gandhi on Twitter: An analysis of brand building through Twitter by the leader of the main opposition party in India. *Global Business Review.* doi:10.1177/0972150919833514

Baid, P., & Chaplot, N. (2019). Sentiment analysis of live tweets after elections. In Rathore V., Worring M., Mishra D., Joshi A., & Maheshwari S. (Eds.), *Emerging Trends in Expert Applications and Security,* Advances in Intelligent Systems and Computing, vol 841 (pp. 307–314). Springer, Singapore.

Bajaj, S. G. (2017). The use of Twitter during the 2014 Indian general elections: Framing, agenda-setting, and the personalization of politics. *Asian Survey, 57*(2), 249–270.

Barclay, F. P. (2017). Media effect on media: Progression of political news and tweets during India 2014. *Journal of Media and Communication, 1*(1), 1–28.

Barclay, F. P., Chinnasamy, P., & Pichandy, P. (2014). Political opinion expressed in social media and election outcomes–US presidential elections 2012. *GSTF Journal on Media and Communications, 1*(2), 15–22.

Barclay, F. P., Pichandy, C., and Venkat, A. (2015). India elections 2014: Time-lagged correlation between media bias and Facebook trend. *Global Journal of Human-Social Science Research, 15*(2). 0975-587X

Barclay, F. P., Pichandy, C., Venkat, A., & Sudhakaran, S. (2015). India 2014: Facebook like as a predictor of election outcomes. *Asian Journal of Political Science, 23*(2), 134–160.

Barclay, F. P., Pichandy, C., Venkat, A., and Sudhakaran, S. 2016. Twitter sentiments: Pattern recognition and poll prediction. *Communication and Information Technologies Annual: [New] Media Cultures* (pp. 141–167). Emerald Group Publishing Limited.

Boatwright, B., Mazer, J. P., & Beach, S. (2019). The 2016 US presidential election and transition events: A social media volume and sentiment analysis. *Southern Communication Journal, 84*(3), 196–209.

Bose, R., Dey, R. K., Roy, S., & Sarddar, D. (2019). Analyzing political sentiment using Twitter data. *Information and Communication Technology for Intelligent Systems, 107*, 427–436.

Business Today. (2019). PM Modi most talked about figure on Twitter; Indian election sees near 46 million tweets. Retrieved from https://www.business-today.in/latest/economy-politics/story/pm-modi-most-talked-about-figure-on-twitter-indian-election-sees-near-46-million-tweets-188134-2019-04-12

Calderon, N. A., Fisher, B., Hemsley, J., Ceskavich, B., Jansen, G., Marciano, R., & Lemieux, V. L. (2015). Mixed-initiative social media analytics at the World Bank: Observations of citizen sentiment in Twitter data to explore 'trust' of political actors and state institutions and its relationship to social protest. In F. Luo, K. Ogan, M. J. Zaki, L. Haas, B. C. Ooi, V. Kumar, S. Rachuri, S. Pyne, H. Ho, X. Hu, S. Yu, M. H-I. Hsiao, & J. Li (Eds.), *Proceedings—2015 IEEE International Conference on Big Data, IEEE Big Data 2015* (pp. 1678–1687). Institute of Electrical and Electronics Engineers Inc. https://doi.org/10.1109/BigData.2015.7363939

Carley, K. M., Malik, M., Landwehr, P. M., Pfeffer, J., & Kowalchuck, M. (2016). Crowdsourcing disaster management: The complex nature of Twitter usage in Padang Indonesia. *Safety Science, 90*, 48–61.

Carpenter, J. P., & Krutka, D. G. (2014). How and why educators use Twitter: A survey of the field. *Journal of Research on Technology in Education, 46*(4), 414–434.

Crannell, W. C., Clark, E., Jones, C., James, T. A., & Moore, J. (2016). A pattern-matched Twitter analysis of US cancer-patient sentiments. *Journal of Surgical Research, 206*(2), 536–542.

Chu, S. C. (2011). Viral advertising in social media: Participation in Facebook groups and responses among college-aged users. *Journal of Interactive Advertising, 12*(1), 30–43.

Conover, M. D., Gonçalves, B., Ratkiewicz, J., Flammini, A., & Menczer, F. (2011). Predicting the political alignment of Twitter users. In *2011 IEEE Third International Conference on Privacy, Security, Risk and Trust and 2011 IEEE Third International Conference on Social Computing* (pp. 192–199). IEEE.

Gayo-Avello, D., Metaxas, P., & Mustafaraj, E. (2011). Limits of electoral predictions using Twitter. *Proceedings of the International AAAI Conference on Web and Social Media, 5*(1), 490–493. Retrieved from https://ojs.aaai.org/index.php/ICWSM/article/view/14189

Gil de Zúñiga, H., Jung, N., & Valenzuela, S. (2012). Social media use for news and individuals' social capital, civic engagement and political participation. *Journal of Computer-mediated Communication, 17*(3), 319–336.

Gokulakrishnan, B., Priyanthan, P., Ragavan, T., Prasath, N., & Perera, A. (2012, December). Opinion mining and sentiment analysis on a Twitter data stream. In *International Conference on Advances in ICT for Emerging Regions (ICTer2012)* (pp. 182–188). IEEE.

Hemphill, L., Culotta, A., & Heston, M. (2013). Framing in social media: How the US Congress uses Twitter hashtags to frame political issues. Available at *SSRN 2317335.*

Hu, X., Tang, L., Tang, J., & Liu, H. (2013). Exploiting social relations for sentiment analysis in microblogging. In *Proceedings of the sixth ACM international conference on Web search and data mining* (pp. 537–546). ACM in Twitter. *Language Resources and Evaluation, 47*(1), 239–268.

Jaidka, K., & Ahmed, S. (2015). The 2014 Indian general election on Twitter: An analysis of changing political traditions. In *Proceedings of the Seventh International Conference on Information and Communication Technologies and Development, 43,* 1–5. https://doi.org/10.1145/2737856.2737889

Joseph, N., & Barclay, F.P. (2018). Media framing: A comparative newspaper analysis of Kashmir conflict 2016. *Journal of Media and Communication, 2*(2), 1–24

Joy, S. (2019, June 3). Rs 60,000 crore spent during LS Polls 2019: Report. *Deccan Herald*. Retrieved from https://www.deccanherald.com/national/national-politics/rs-60000-crore-spent-during-ls-polls-2019-report-737840.html

Kaur, M., & Verma, R. (2018). Social media: An emerging tool for political participation. In *Media Influence: Breakthroughs in Research and Practice, 1*–8. IGI Global. https://doi.dx.org/10.4018/978-1-5225-3929-2.ch001

Kim, Y. (2011). The contribution of social network sites to exposure to political difference: The relationships among SNSs, online political messaging, and exposure to cross-cutting perspectives. *Computers in Human Behavior, 27*(2), 971–977.

Kwak, H., Lee, C., Park, H., & Moon, S. (2010). What is Twitter, a social network or a news media?. In *Proceedings of the 19th International Conference on the World Wide Web,* (pp. 591–600). ACM. https://doi.org/10.1145/1772690.1772751

Larsson, A. O., & Moe, H. (2012). Studying political microblogging: Twitter users in the 2010 Swedish election campaign. *New Media & Society, 14*(5), 729–747.

Lee, C. S., & Ma, L. (2012). News sharing in social media: The effect of gratifications and prior experience. *Computers in Human Behavior, 28*(2), 331–339.

Metaxas, P. T., Mustafaraj, E., & Gayo-Avello, D. (2011, October). How (not) to predict elections. In *2011 IEEE Third International Conference on Privacy, Security, Risk and Trust and 2011 IEEE Third International Conference on Social Computing* (pp. 165–171). IEEE. doi:10.1109/PASSAT/SocialCom.2011.98

Mourão, R., Diehl, T., & Vasudevan, K. (2016). I love Big Bird: How journalists tweeted humor during the 2012 presidential debates. *Digital Journalism, 4*(2), 211–228.

Pal, J., Chandra, P., & Vydiswaran, V. V. (2016). Twitter and the rebranding of Narendra Modi. *Economic & Political Weekly, 51*(8), 52–60.

Pal, J., Thawani, U., Van Der Vlugt, E., Out, W., and Chandra, P. (2018). Speaking their mind: Populist style and antagonistic messaging in the tweets of Donald Trump, Narendra Modi, Nigel Farage, and Geert Wilders. *Computer Supported Cooperative Work, 27*(3–6), 293–326.

Rajadesingan, A., Panda, A., and Pal, J. (2020). 'Leader or Party? Personalization in Twitter Political Campaigns during the 2019 Indian Elections'. *International Conference on Social Media and Society* (pp. 174–183).

Rajput, H. (2014). Social media and politics in India: A study on Twitter usage among Indian political leaders. *Asian Journal of Multidisciplinary Studies, 2*(1), 63–69.

Reyes, A., Rosso, P., & Veale, T. (2013). A multidimensional approach for detecting irony in Twitter. *Language Resources and Evaluation, 47*(1), 239–268.

Shaban, Hamza (2019). 'Twitter reveals its daily active user numbers for the first time'. Available at https://www.washingtonpost.com/technology/2019/02/07/twitter-reveals-its-daily-active-user-numbers-first-time/ (accessed on 26 June 2021).

Somani, A. (2020). Why Aristotle would be proud of Prime Minister Modi. LinkedIn. Posted May 13, retrieved Oct 10, 2021, from https://www.linkedin.com/pulse/why-aristotle-would-proud-prime-minister-modi-amit-somani

Statista. (2015). Number of Twitter users in India from 2013 to 2019 (in millions). Retrieved from https://www.statista.com/statistics/381832/twitter-users-india

Tayal, D. K., Yadav, S., Gupta, K., Rajput, B., & Kumari, K. (2014). Polarity detection of sarcastic political tweets. *International Conference on Computing for Sustainable Global Development (INDIACom),* 625–628. IEEE.

Tumasjan, A., Sprenger, T., Sandner, P., & Welpe, I. (2010). Predicting elections with Twitter: What 140 characters reveal about political sentiment. In *Proceedings of the International AAAI Conference on Web and Social Media, 4*(1), 178–185.

Teran, L., & Mancera, J. (2019). Dynamic profiles using sentiment analysis and Twitter data for voting advice applications. *Government Information Quarterly, 36*(3), 520–535.

Yaqub, U., Chun, S. A., Atluri, V., & Vaidya, J. (2017). Analysis of political discourse on twitter in the context of the 2016 US presidential elections. *Government Information Quarterly, 34*(4), 613–626.

Chapter 5

Social Media Exposure and Religious Intolerance

Malini Srinivasan and Francis P. Barclay

INTRODUCTION

Thanks to media convergence and the pervasive smartphone, people are connected to diverse media platforms—both traditional and new—round the clock. Such indulgence, especially among the wired younger generation, could lead to dependency, affecting facets of their lives (Brooks, 2015) and attitudes (Venkat, 2017; Zhou & Moy, 2007). Millennials—those reaching young adulthood in the early 21st century—are more fascinated with gadgets and internet applications—particularly when compared with broadcast and print alternatives (Hutto et al., 2016). Online interaction has become an integral aspect of their social activities (Duffett & Wakeham, 2016). Moving beyond communication with friends and family, social media platforms like Facebook and Twitter influence people in many aspects of their public life (Auer, 2011; Romero et al., 2011). Their online social media usage could be used to study their moods, opinion and traits (Golbeck et al., 2011) and predict behaviours (Barclay et al., 2014, 2015, 2015a, 2015b, 2016). Perrin (2015) observed that social media platforms have altered communication patterns across the globe

(Gulyàs, 2015), changing people's involvement in politics and religious deliberation. Barclay (2017) observed that both the traditional and new media have strong effects.

While the developed world has a well-known ageing population problem, several South and South-East Asian countries are majorly millennial and witnessing rising levels of disposable income (Ahluwalia, 2018). The choices and behaviours of these digital natives could have a profound effect on the future and development (Ahluwalia, 2018). In the current study, the media usage patterns of this demographic group are mapped and related with their levels of religious intolerance, narcissism and pessimism by choosing a sample from India. According to a Pew Research Center analysis involving 198 countries, India was ranked as the fourth worst in religious intolerance (Bhattacharya, 2017). Bergman et al. (2011) suspected a connection between social media usage and narcissism and found that the latter offered several motivations to use social media. Online social media had gained prominence (Lewis, 2009) and social media discourse was a constitutive part of online news consumption and distribution (Kümpel et al., 2015). Aosved and Long (2006) studied the co-occurrence of rape myth acceptance and several other oppressive belief systems such as ageism, classism, racism, homophobia, sexism and religious intolerance. Several researchers have studied religious discourse in both traditional and online social media (Awan, 2014), but the association between diverse media usage and religious intolerance, especially among the millennials has not been explored in depth. Another important question to ponder over is whether social media usage is related to narcissistic and pessimistic attitudes with the reasoning that social media platforms, which they are hooked to, induce alienation among its users who tend to reduce offline social interaction due to their smartphone engagement and negativity is thronging on these social platforms.

Religious intolerance is a topical issue in India, gaining widespread coverage in traditional media (Ali, 2020; Boorstein, 2020; PTI, 2021) and being a talking point on social media, with religion also being a critical political issue (Dutta 2021; PTI, 2019, 2020). From reviewing the studies, it is evident that media exposure can affect religious beliefs and a host of other attitudes. With this understanding, the following research questions are proposed:

RQ1: What is the media usage pattern of the millennials?

RQ2: Is media exposure related to religious intolerance, narcissism and pessimism?

RQ3: Are religious intolerance, narcissism and pessimism related?

Online social media surge could mean increased capabilities of information and opinion sharing. While, potentially, it could lead to an explosion of diverse—and an eruption of supposedly suppressed—viewpoints, popular beliefs could still sway social media conversations, deepening inherent discrimination and intolerance. We, hence, propose the theory of escalation, where an increase in interpersonal communication, triggered by technological intervention, could impregnate and escalate existing opinion and beliefs.

To examine the media usage patterns among millennials, demographic variables such as age and location are taken into consideration. In the current study, the usages of newspapers, magazines, radio, television, mobile phones, cinema, the internet and social media are analysed. Content related to religions in the mainstream media and discussions on the topic in online social media can potentially alter the opinion of the media users. Such public groups can be termed as the discursive community, which Turner and Killian (1957) defined as 'a dispersed group of people interested in and divided about an issue, engaged in a discussion of that issue, with a view to registering a collective opinion which is expected to affect the course of action of some decision-making group or individual'.

Chang et al. (2006) argued that the legitimacy of interpretation and definition of political actions, issues and situations is based on the remarkable implications of the conventions that govern political discourse, and here, the media plays a pivotal role.

Karaflogka (2002) observed that online social media discourse, otherwise called cyberspatial discourse, whether it is based on 'religion or not, cannot be specifically confined within restricted boundaries' and it should be perceived as 'unforeseen changeable structure, having the capacity to adapt itself according to the visions, fantasies, ingenuities and inventiveness of the users'. Despite the 'rhizomatic' construction of cyberspace, news and information posted and consumed through numerous religious websites can be construed as a 'logical' formation. Millennials recognize social networking sites as a source of information and news (Baumgartner et al., 2010) and a platform for democratic discourse (Boulianne, 2015). For the millennials, multitasking in the media has also become a common, simple and easy task (Bardhi et al., 2010). Diehl (2016) observed that social media news-seeking behaviour and interaction increases political deliberation and has the potential to change political views.

Alloway et al. (2014) found some aspects such as photo features in Facebook to be linked with narcissism. Narcissism was also used to predict features that are presented through user-generated content like the frequency of status updates (Ong et al., 2011).

Further, Gerbaudo (2018) observed that social media, especially Facebook, acts as a training ground for politically inexperienced media-savvy youth, and it also functions as a launching pad for protests. Nelson et al. (2017) posited that individual behaviour, attitude, views and decisions are influenced by religiosity and spirituality. Baum et al. (2008) showed that mass media plays a significant role in shaping the public attitude and influence. Gunther (1998) stated that press coverage of the news is used by the people to estimate public opinion—an indirect effect that can have significant consequences on mass media. Barclay et al. (2014) viewed traditional and online media in both humanist and behavioural traditions. Online social media also enables effective two-way communication that traditional media restrict. Shanahan et al. (2011) posited that public opinion is influenced by media policy in two ways: first, by strengthening 'congruent reader opinions, and second, they "convert" when read by audiences with divergent opinions'. Conover et al. (2011) investigated how social media helped communication between communities with different political orientations and how it shaped the networked public sphere. De Vreese et al. (2006) found that 'one-sided message flow' could affect 'politically-less-sophisticated individuals' and also trigger discussions among the so-called politically sophisticated. Social media chatter is a reflection of prevailing moods and opinions that could also influence others (Barclay et al., 2015).

Loader and Mercea (2011) asserted that the major aspects of social media such as open and collaborative networking are used as a democratic renewal of new technological optimism and it is a replacement of the early conception of 'digital democracy as a virtual public sphere'. Based on a review of literature, it can be assumed that media exposure can affect religious intolerance, narcissism and pessimism. Accordingly, the following hypotheses are proposed:

> H1: Demographic variables such as Gender, Age and Location have an association with the extent of usage of Media (Newspaper/Magazine, Radio, Television, Mobile Phone, Cinema, Internet and Social Media), Religious Intolerance, Narcissism and Pessimism.
>
> H2: Extent of usage of Media (Newspaper/Magazine, Radio, Television, Mobile Phone, Cinema, Internet and Social Media) is associated with Religious Intolerance, Narcissism and Pessimism.
>
> H3: Religious Intolerance, Narcissism and Pessimism are interrelated.

Based on the proposed hypotheses, the initial model is developed (see Figure. 5.1).

RESEARCH METHOD

In the current study, the demographic variables used are age, gender and area of residence (location). As many as 215 respondents were chosen for the study from the Indian state of Tamil Nadu using a multi-stage stratified random sampling procedure. The distribution of the respondents based on these demographic variables is presented in Table 5.1. The data collection period was from 20 March 2018 to 18 April 2018.

The extent of the usages of traditional and new media was measured along with the levels of religious intolerance, narcissism and pessimism, using a questionnaire. The extent of usages of newspapers and magazines, radio, television, cinema, internet, mobile phones and social media were measured using self-reported data received through

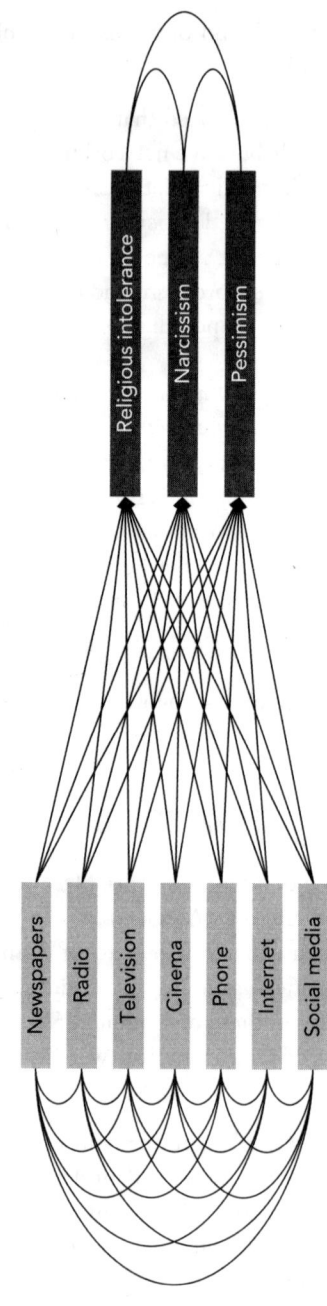

Figure 5.1 *Initial Model*

Table 5.1 *Distribution of Respondents According to Demographic Variables*

Age	Frequency	%
Less than 20 years	33	15.3
20–25 years	137	63.7
Above 25 years	45	20.9
Total	215	100
Gender	**Frequency**	**%**
Male	89	41.4
Female	126	58.6
Total	215	100
Location	**Frequency**	**%**
Rural	88	40.9
Urban	127	59.1
Total	215	100

a questionnaire. The final questionnaire which was refined after a pilot study had 83 questions.

To measure pessimism, a revised Life Orientation Test scale was used (Scheier et al., 1994). Of the 10 questions offered by this scale, seven were chosen. A Likert five-option scale was used for these seven questions (I agree a lot, I agree a little, I neither agree nor disagree, I disagree a little and I disagree a lot). An abbreviated version of the Narcissistic Personality Inventory that is offered by the Open Source Psychometrics Project was used to measure narcissism. Of the 40 questions offered in the inventory, 10 were chosen. Each of them had two options to choose from with a common question: choose the one that you most identify with. To measure religious intolerance, a modified version of the Godfrey–Richman ISM Scale as prescribed by Godfrey et al. (2000) was used. The 25-item modified scale used a three-option scale to measure the level of religious intolerance (Yes, Maybe and No).

FINDINGS

In the current study, the extent of usage of diverse media and the dependent variables were measured and the levels of usage for each of the medium chosen are presented in Table 5.2.

Of the respondents surveyed, a majority of them (54%) were moderate users of newspapers, television, cinema, smartphones, the internet and online social media. However, they were light users of radio. When it comes to religious intolerance, a majority of them belonged to the high category. It was the same case with regard to pessimism as well. However, a majority of them were moderately narcissistic in nature, as shown by study results.

Hypothesis Testing

H1: Demographic variables such as Gender, Age and Location have an association with the extent of usage of Media (Newspaper–Magazine, Radio, Television, Mobile Phone, Cinema, Internet and Social Media), Religious Intolerance, Narcissism and Pessimism.

To test the relationship between the demographic variables—age, gender and location and the dependent variables—newspaper, radio, television, cinema, mobile phone, internet, social media, religious intolerance, narcissism and pessimism one-way ANOVA/t-test was conducted and presented in Table 5.3.

Analysis shows that there is a statistically significant association between age and internet usage and social media usage and between location and mobile phone usage.

Those belonging to the age group less than 20 years were highly active users of online social media, compared to others (see Table 5.4).

Similarly, those from urban areas used phones more than the rural people.

Table 5.2 *Extent of Media Usage: Percentages*

	NP	Radio	TV	Cinema	Phone	Int	SM	RI	Narcissism	Pessimism
Low	22.8	42.8	22.8	27.9	9.3	18.1	27.9	0.5	27	25.1
Moderate	54	38.6	54	55.8	46.5	41.4	49.8	31.6	61.9	36.7
High	23.3	18.6	23.3	16.3	44.2	40.5	22.3	67.9	11.2	38.1

Table 5.3 One-way ANOVA/t-test Results: Demographic Variables vs Dependent Variables

Independent Variable	Dependent Variable	F Value	p Value
Age	Newspaper	1.505	0.202
	Radio	0.355	0.841
	TV	0.409	0.802
	Cinema	1.059	0.378
	Phone	1.372	0.245
	Internet	2.716	0.031
	Social media	4.623	0.001
	Religious intolerance	1.120	0.348
	Narcissism	1.492	0.206
	Pessimism	2.100	0.082
Gender	Newspaper	1.732	0.190
	Radio	3.798	0.053
	TV	0.614	0.434
	Cinema	0.546	0.461
	Phone	2.103	0.148
	Internet	1.690	0.195
	Social media	0.035	0.852
	Religious intolerance	0.597	0.441
	Narcissism	2.274	0.133
	Pessimism	1.712	0.192
Location	Newspaper	0.128	0.721
	Radio	0.193	0.661
	TV	0.312	0.577
	Cinema	0.029	0.866
	Phone	7.274	0.008
	Internet	0.039	0.844
	Social media	2.350	0.127
	Religious intolerance	0.618	0.433
	Narcissism	0.217	0.642
	Pessimism	0.912	0.341

Table 5.4 *Table of Means*

DV	Age Groups	N	Mean	Std Deviation	Std Error
Social media	Less than 20 years	33	0.3935145	0.95845884	0.16684627
	20–25 years	137	–0.1660725	0.72579097	0.06200851
	Above 25 years	45	0.2170211	0.90906508	0.13551542

Location vs Smartphone Usage	N	Mean	Std Deviation	Std Error
Rural	88	2.306	0.68372	0.07288
Urban	127	2.545	0.60594	0.05377

RQ1: What is the media usage pattern of the millennials?

To check the patterns of usage of newspaper/magazine, radio, television, cinema, mobile phone, internet and social media, factor analysis was conducted and the results are presented in Table 5.5 and Figure 5.2. An examination of the Kaiser–Meyer–Olkin measure of sampling adequacy suggested that the sample was just factorable (KMO = 0.626) and Bartlett's test of sphericity was significant (χ^2 =167.045, $p < 0.0005$).

The default principal component method without rotation was employed to extract the common factors from the media usage variables. Results of the factor analysis showed that three factors contributed to 61.511 per cent of the total variance in the seven variables (see Table 5.5). The three factors had eigenvalues of 2.123, 1.177 and 1.005 (see Figure 5.2). It shows that three factors majorly contributed to the variance in the seven media usage variables.

Study results indicated three major media usage patterns: millennials using mainly radio, television, cinema, phone and the internet; those using mainly newspapers, magazines, radio, television and social media and those using mainly phone and social media.

Table 5.5 *Factor Analysis Results*

		Radio	TV	Cinema	Phone	Internet	SM
Correlation	NP–Magazines	0.195	0.024	0.018	-0.050	0.088	0.130
	Radio		0.274	0.193	0.151	0.152	0.011
	Television			0.343	0.140	0.207	0.146
	Cinema				0.359	0.371	0.077
	Phone					0.451	0.139
	Internet						0.009
Sig. (1-tailed)	NP–Magazines	0.002	0.361	0.399	0.231	0.100	0.029
	Radio		0.000	0.002	0.013	0.013	0.434
	Television			0.000	0.020	0.001	0.016
	Cinema				0.000	0.000	0.130
	Phone					0.000	0.021
	Internet						0.445

a. Determinant = 0.453.

KMO and Bartlett's Test

Kaiser–Meyer–Olkin measure of sampling adequacy	0.626	
Bartlett's test of sphericity	Approx. chi-square	167.045
	df	21
	Sig.	0.000

Communalities

	Initial	Extraction
NP–Magazines	1.000	0.596
Radio	1.000	0.662
Television	1.000	0.389
Cinema	1.000	0.555
Phone	1.000	0.629
Internet	1.000	0.555
Social media	1.000	0.920

Extraction method: principal component analysis

H2: Extent of usage of Media (Newspaper–Magazine, Radio, Television, Mobile Phone, Cinema, Internet and Social Media) is associated with Religious Intolerance, Narcissism and Pessimism.
H3: Religious Intolerance, Narcissism and Pessimism are interrelated.

To test the relationships among media exposure, religious intolerance, narcissism and pessimism, an SEM analysis was conducted on the initial model.

SEM Analysis results
Minimum was achieved
Chi-square = 37.157
Degrees of freedom = 29
Probability level = 0.142

Total Variance Explained

Component	Initial Eigenvalues	Extraction Sums of Squared Loadings					
	Total	% of variance	Cumulative %	Total	% of variance	Cumulative %
1	2.123	30.332	30.332	2.123	30.332	30.332
2	1.177	16.819	47.152	1.177	16.819	47.152
3	1.005	14.359	61.511	1.005	14.359	61.511
4	0.936	13.370	74.881			
5	0.711	10.161	85.042			
6	0.582	8.310	93.351			
7	0.465	6.649	100.000			

Extraction method: principal component analysis

	Group 1	Group 2	Group 3
NP–Magazines	0.16	0.754	–0.043
Radio	0.483	0.451	–0.475
Television	0.586	0.2	–0.075
Cinema	0.726	–0.164	–0.028
Phone	0.672	–0.365	0.208
Internet	0.697	–0.258	–0.06
Social media	0.239	0.372	0.851

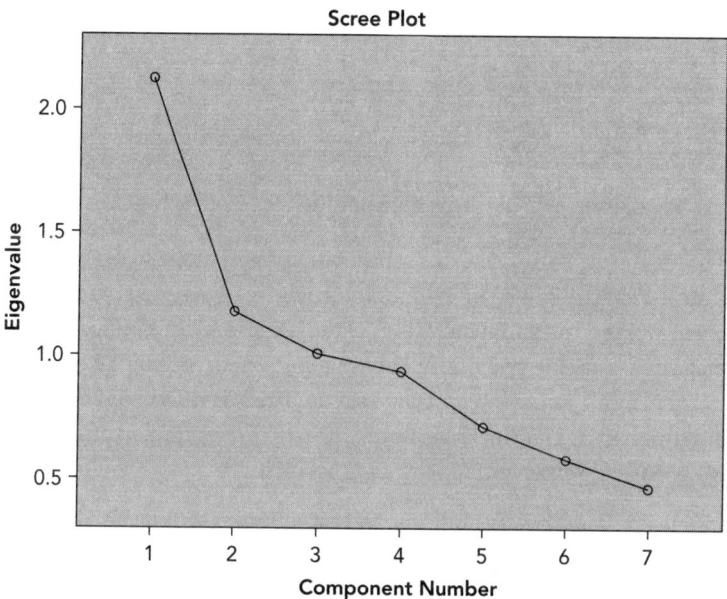

Figure 5.2 *Scree Plot*

The final model (Figure 5.3) was identified with an excellent fit. All the relationships proposed in the final model had statistically significant regressions. The extent of usage of newspapers and magazines and mobile phone had a positive relationship with pessimism, while the extent of usage of social media had a positive relationship with religious intolerance. similarly, the variable extent of usage of social media was negatively associated with both pessimism and narcissism.

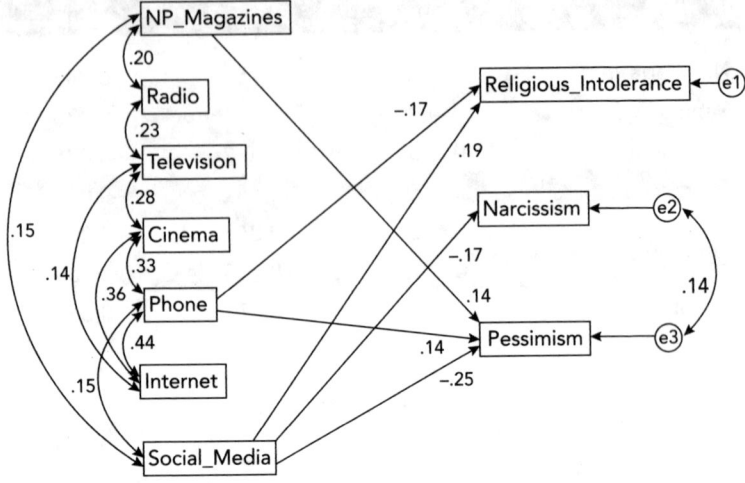

Figure 5.3 *Final Model*

DISCUSSION

The extent of the usages of traditional and new media was measured along with the levels of religious intolerance, narcissism and pessimism using a questionnaire. The extent of usages of newspapers and magazines, radio, television, cinema, internet, mobile phones and social media was measured using self-reported data received through a questionnaire. The final questionnaire which was refined after a pilot study had 83 questions.

One-way ANOVA result shows that there is a statistically significant association between age and internet usage and social media usage, which implies that persons who use the internet also access social media. There is a statistically significant association between location and mobile phone usage. To check the patterns of usage of newspaper–magazine, radio, television, cinema, mobile phone, internet and social media, factor analysis was conducted. It shows that three factors majorly contributed to the variance in the seven media usage variables. Perrin (2015) observed that social media platforms have altered communication patterns across the globe. The current study results indicated three major media usage patterns: millennials mainly using radio, television, cinema, phone and the internet; those using mainly newspapers, magazines, radio, television and social media and those using mainly the phone and social media. It can be inferred that millennials who use mobile phone also access the internet and they are also exposed to radio, television and cinema; those who are exposed to newspaper, magazine, radio, television also access social media; people who use mobile phone more also access social media. SEM analysis was conducted to test the relationships among media exposure, religious intolerance, narcissism and pessimism.

All the relationships proposed in the final model had statistically significant regressions. The extent of usage of newspapers and magazines and mobile phone had a positive relationship with pessimism, while the extent of usage of social media also had a positive relationship with religious intolerance. Similarly, the variable extent of usage of social media was negatively associated with both pessimism and narcissism.

Duffett and Wakeham (2016) had observed the integration of online interaction and social media activities. Results of the current study also indicate relationships among the usages of mobile phone, the internet and online social media platforms. Golbeck (2011) had observed that online social media acts as a key to predict the moods and opinions of the users. Bergman et al. (2011) suspected a connection between social media usage and narcissism and found that the latter offered several motivations to use social media. Interestingly, the current study result states that the people's extent of usage of social media has a positive relationship with religious intolerance, but it is negatively associated with pessimism and narcissism.

According to a Pew Research Center analysis of 198 countries, India ranked as the fourth worst for religious intolerance (Bhattacharya, 2017). Awan (2014) also referred to several studies on religious discourse in both traditional and online social media. The findings state that people who access social media more also have high levels of religious intolerance.

Positive associations were observed among the usages of the different communication media, indicating that when a user uses one kind of media, there is also a tendency to use the others as well. A positive correlation was observed between narcissism and pessimism.

As the study results have indicated, there is a surge in the usage of mobile applications and online social media. Religious intolerance has been a hot topic in India. Continuous and increased exposure to content that propagates or reinforce intolerance through online social media applications could be a reason why social media users exhibit higher levels of intolerance. That millennials who are hooked to their smartphones and with lesser offline social interactions are exhibiting higher and alarming levels of religious intolerance is a shocking indication that new media technologies can reinforce existing ideologies and attitudes.

As Barclay (2016) and Barclay et al. (2014, 2015, 2015a, 2015b, 2016, 2016a, 2017) have observed positive media effects and the resurgence of the strong–effects paradigm in the digital era, the current study also reiterates the effects on traditional and new media on the audience.

CONCLUSION

Indian millennials are avid users of communication media. These digital natives were found to be hooked to their smartphones accessing the internet, movies, television content and social media. Study results indicate three major media usage patterns among the millennials: millennials mainly using radio, television, cinema, phone and the internet; those mainly using newspapers, magazines, radio, television and social media and those mainly using the phone and social media. Social media usage is positively associated with religious intolerance, while the usages of diverse media are interrelated. Further research is needed to explore deeper into the association between social media usage and religious intolerance, ascertaining which aspects of social media are causing the correlation. Similarly, newspaper usage is increasing pessimism among the readers, the study results indicate. The inclination of the Indian media to prefer and cover negative news over positive ones could be the reason for such an increase in pessimism among newspaper readers.

REFERENCES

Ahluwalia, Harveen. (2018, February 20). Millennials to redefine India's consumption story: Report. *Live Mint*. Retrieved from https://www.livemint.com/Consumer/vj5e3v3uGyQR9KRwcvNBvN/Millennials-to-redefine-Indias-consumption-story-report.html?utm_source=scroll&utm_medium=referral&utm_campaign=scroll

Ali, S. M. (2020, May 8). India's religious intolerance. *The Express Tribune*. Retrieved from https://tribune.com.pk/story/2216434/indias-religious-intolerance

Alloway, T., Runac, R., Qureshi, M., & Kemp, G. (2014). Is Facebook linked to selfishness? Investigating the relationships among social media use, empathy, and narcissism. *Social Networking*, *3*(03), 150.

Aosved, A. C., & Long, P. J. (2006). Co-occurrence of rape myth acceptance, sexism, racism, homophobia, ageism, classism, and religious intolerance. *Sex Roles*, *55*(7–8), 481–492.

Auer, M. R. (2011). The policy sciences of social media. *Policy Studies Journal*, *39*(4), 709–736.

Awan, I. (2014). Islamophobia and Twitter: A typology of online hate against Muslims on social media. *Policy & Internet*, *6*(2), 133–150.

Barclay, F. P. (2016). Inter-media interaction and effects in an integrated model of political communication: India 2014. *Global Media Journal*, *13*(15),1–39.

Barclay, F. P. (2017). Media effect on media: Progression of political news and tweets during India 2014. *Journal of Media and Communication*, *1*(1), 1–28.

Barclay, F. P., Pichandy, C., & Venkat, A., Sudhakaran, S. (2015b). India 2014: Press trend as a predictor of election outcome. In K. M. Baharul Islam and Nandita Roy (Eds.), *New Directions in Media—Critical Practitioner's Series* (pp. 161–194), Bloomsbury Publications.

Barclay, F. P., Pichandy, C., & Venkat, A., Sudhakaran, S. (2016a). Twitter sentiments: Pattern recognition and poll prediction. *Studies in Media and Communications*, 11,141–167.

Barclay, F. P., Pichandy, C., & Venkat, A. (2014). Indian elections, 2014: Political orientation of English newspapers. *Asia Pacific Media Educator*, *24*(1), 7–22.

Barclay, F. P., Pichandy, C., & Venkat, A. (2015). India 2014: Facebook 'Like' as a predictor of election outcomes. *Asian Journal of Political Science*, *23*(2), 134–160. doi:10.1080/02185377.2015.1020319

Barclay, F. P., Pichandy, C., & Venkat, A. (2015a). Indian elections 2014: Time-lagged correlation between media bias and Facebook trend. *Global Journal of Human-Social Science*, *15*(2), 29–41.

Barclay, F. P., Pichandy, C. & Venkat, A. (2016). Media effect: Correlation between press trends and election results. *Media Asia*, *42*(3–4), 192–208.

Bardhi, F., Rohm, A. J., & Sultan, F. (2010). Tuning in and tuning out: Media multitasking among young consumers. *Journal of Consumer Behaviour*, *9*(4), 316–332.

Baum, M. A., & Potter, P. B. (2008). The relationships between mass media, public opinion, and foreign policy: Toward a theoretical synthesis. *Annual Review of Political Science, 11*, 39–65.

Baumgartner, J. C., & Morris, J. S. (2010). MyFaceTube politics: Social networking websites and political engagement of young adults. *Social Science Computer Review, 28*(1), 24–44.

Bergman, S. M., Fearrington, M. E., Davenport, S. W., & Bergman, J. Z. (2011). Millennials, narcissism, and social networking: What narcissists do on social networking sites and why. *Personality and Individual Differences, 50*(5), 706–711.

Bhattacharya, Ananya. (2017, April 14). India is the fourth-worst country in the world for religious violence. *Quartz India*. Retrieved from https://qz.com/959802/india-is-the-fourth-worst-country-in-the-world-for-religious-violence/

Boorstein, M. J. S. (2020, April 28). Religious freedoms in India deteriorated last year, U.S. government watchdog says. *Washington Post*. Retrieved from https://www.washingtonpost.com/religion/2020/04/28/india-receives-low-rating-us-government-watchdog-religious-freedom/

Boulianne, S. (2015). Social media use and participation: A meta-analysis of current research. *Information, Communication & Society, 18*(5), 524–538.

Brooks, S. (2015). Does personal social media usage affect efficiency and well-being? *Computers in Human Behavior, 46*, 26–37.

Chang, G. C., & Mehan, H. B. (2006). Discourse in a religious mode. *Pragmatics, 16*(1), 1–23.

Conover, M., Ratkiewicz, J., Francisco, M. R., Gonçalves, B., Menczer, F., & Flammini, A. (2011). Political polarization on Twitter. *ICWSM, 133*, 89–96.

De Vreese, C. H., & Boomgaarden, H. G. (2006). Media message flows and interpersonal communication: The conditional nature of effects on public opinion. *Communication Research, 33*(1), 19–37.

Diehl, T., Weeks, B. E., & Gil de Zuniga, H. (2016). Political persuasion on social media: Tracing direct and indirect effects of news use and social interaction. *New Media & Society, 18*(9), 1875–1895.

Duffett, R. G., & Wakeham, M. (2016). Social media marketing communications' effect on attitudes among millennials in South Africa. *The African Journal of Information Systems, 8*(3), 2.

Dutta, P. K. (2021, March 26). Not just CAA, even cow slaughter ban has forced BJP to play different tunes in polls. *India Today*. Retrieved from https://www.indiatoday.in/elections/story/bjp-caa-cow-slaughter-ban-different-tunes-assembly-elections-bengal-assam-1783810-2021-03-26

Gerbaudo, P. (2018). *Tweets and the streets: Social media and contemporary activism*. Pluto.

Godfrey, S., Richman, C. L., & Withers, T. N. (2000). Reliability and validity of a new scale to measure prejudice: The GRISMS. *Current Psychology, 19*(1), 3–20.

Golbeck, J., Robles, C., Edmondson, M., & Turner, K. (2011, October). Predicting personality from Twitter. In *2011 IEEE Third International Conference on Privacy,*

Security, Risk and Trust and 2011 IEEE Third International Conference on Social Computing (pp. 149–156). IEEE.

Gulyás, À. (2015). Millennials, news and social media: Is news engagement a thing of the past? *Digital Journalism. 3*(1), 132–133.

Gunther, A. C. (1998). The persuasive press inference: Effects of mass media on perceived public opinion. *Communication Research, 25*(5), 486–504.

Hutto, A., & Kassaye, W. W. (2016). Exploring millennials' motives in media class preferences: Advertising implications. *International Review of Business and Economics, 1*(2), 109–132.

Karaflogka, A. (2002). Religious discourse and cyberspace. *Religion, 32*(4), 279–291.

Kümpel, A. S., Karnowski, V., & Keyling, T. (2015). News sharing in social media: A review of current research on news sharing users, content, and networks. *Social Media + Society, 1*(2). https://doi.org/10.1177/2056305115610141.

Lewis, B. K. (2009). *Social media and strategic communication: Attitudes and perceptions among college students* [Doctoral dissertation, Oklahoma State University].

Loader, B. D., & Mercea, D. (2011). Networking democracy? Social media innovations and participatory politics. *Information, Communication & Society, 14*(6), 757–769.

Nelson, M. F., James, M. S., Miles, A., Morrell, D. L., & Sledge, S. (2017). Academic integrity of millennials: The impact of religion and spirituality. *Ethics & Behavior, 27*(5), 385–400.

Ong, E. Y., Ang, R. P., Ho, J. C., Lim, J. C., Goh, D. H., Lee, C. S., & Chua, A. Y. (2011). Narcissism, extraversion and adolescents' self-presentation on Facebook. *Personality and Individual Differences, 50*(2), 180–185.

Perrin, A. (2015, October 8). Social media usage: 2005–2015. Pew Research Center. Retrieved from https://www.pewresearch.org/internet/2015/10/08/social-networking-usage-2005-2015/

PTI. (2019, June 26). Lynching of youth an example of religious intolerance: TMC. *The Times of India.* Retrieved from https://timesofindia.indiatimes.com/city/kolkata/lynching-of-youth-an-example-of-religious-intolerance-tmc/articleshow/69958437.cms

PTI. (2020, February 26). US lawmakers condemn Delhi violence, express concern. NDTV.com. Retrieved from https://www.ndtv.com/india-news/us-lawmakers-condemn-delhi-violence-express-concern-2186324

PTI. (2021, May 8). Allowing religious intolerance not good for a secular country, says HC. *The Economic Times.* Retrieved from https://economictimes.indiatimes.com/news/india/allowing-religious-intolerance-not-good-for-a-secular-country-says-hc/articleshow/82482666.cms

Romero, D. M., Galuba, W., Asur, S., & Huberman, B. A. (2011, September). Influence and passivity in social media. In *Joint European Conference on Machine Learning and Knowledge Discovery in Databases* (pp. 18–33). Springer, Berlin, Heidelberg.

Scheier, M. F., Carver, C. S., & Bridges, M. W. (1994). Distinguishing optimism from neuroticism (and trait anxiety, self-mastery, and self-esteem): A re-evaluation of the life orientation test. *Journal of Personality and Social Psychology*, 67, 1063–1078.

Shanahan, E. A., McBeth, M. K., & Hathaway, P. L. (2011). Narrative policy framework: The influence of media policy narratives on public opinion. *Politics & Policy*, *39*(3), 373–400.

Turner, R. H., & Killian, L. M. (1957). *Collective Behavior*. Prentice-Hall.

Venkat, Anusha. (2017). A motivation-based perspective of Facebook addiction. *Journal of Media and Communication*, *1*(1): 49–71. CUTN.

Zhou, Y., & Moy, P. (2007). Parsing framing processes: The interplay between online public opinion and media coverage. *Journal of Communication*, *57*(1), 79–98.

Chapter 6

Framing Conflicts on Social Media

C. Pichandy, C. J. Ravikrishnan and Boobalakrishnan N.

INTRODUCTION

The Palk Bay conflict is not a sociological or intellectual construct arising from a hasty generalization of sporadic phenomena with vested interests but an empirical fact which one could perceive for oneself if he/she ventured to accompany the Indian Tamil fishermen on any fishing day to the Palk Bay or even to the rim of Indian sea borders. The plight of the Tamil fishermen of India in the context of the polemical offensive of the Sri Lankan Navy in the Palk Bay could be labelled as a peripheral phenomenon with reference to the Indian mainstream politics concerning the livelihood of a people of peripheral existence at the seashores of the Palk Bay. The repetitive nature of the polemic and of the fishing performance of the fishermen braving the odds has metamorphosed the episodes as conflicts and the performance plight as protests. From the empirical premises projecting the protest, one has to transcend the empirical structure into the semantics of deep-structure relationships and unearth the underlying dissent discourse. None could witness the episodes at the sea unless one braves to be a participant-observer. As such, the reliance on the print media reports has turned crucial and any research shall have to confront the implications of the media paradigm.

The alienated peripheral existence of the fishermen community causes perceptual problems. The mainstream politics has not been holistic in its comprehension and has been found to pursue a safer course of concern that lacks the conscientizing mission and vision. The onshore open protest actions of the fishermen have remained restricted to the shores. Communication with them itself causes hurdles.

As regards common perception, many fragmentations and obfuscations blur the vision of the people at large. Many observed facts remain unrelated. The authority of the Sethupathy of Ramnad; the British colonial dispensation and Katchatheevu strategy; the historical pre-colonial ties between the Tamil fishermen communities on both sides of the sea; the Katchatheevu transfer in post-independence India; the civil war in Sri Lanka and its bearing on the Palk Bay interactions; the allegations arising therefrom; the contrasting economic dispensation in both the countries after independence making a significant impact on the fisheries; the projection of polarity between territorial sovereignty and historicity; the alleged excesses of the Sri Lankan Navy; the break in the historical kinship ties of the Tamil fishermen of southern India and northern Sri Lanka; and continued arrest of the Tamil fishermen in Sri Lankan waters, their imprisonment, the Indian plea and the merciful release; all these are presented unrelated and non-holistically. It is imperative that research shall proceed on safer lines, judiciously combining empirics with historicity and political bilateral dynamics of contemporary political discourse with the view to comprehending the problem.

Scholars from India and across the world have studied the Palk Bay conflict between Indian Tamil fishermen and the Sri Lankan Navy in the context to analyse the issue and its impact amongst the fishermen community and bilateral relations between India and Sri Lanka. Most of the scholars who have written about the Palk Bay conflict agreed that before the Katchatheevu agreements (1974 and 1976) were signed between India and Sri Lanka to define their marine boundaries at Palk Bay, the fishermen communities from both countries had harvested sea resources without any conflict. Palk Bay has a rich and old fishing tradition. A large fishing population is spread out along the coasts of Palk Bay. The fishing population shares a common language Tamil and a history of interaction (Scholtens et al., 2012). According to V. Vivekanandan, the civil war in Sri Lanka has had a deep impact on the Palk Bay conflict. Till 1983, the fishermen from both the countries shared common resources, which were abundant in the shallow waters of Palk Bay. Due to the civil war in Sri Lanka, fishing operations from the Sri Lankan side drastically got reduced due to security reasons. The civil war displaced most of the fishermen from their native villages. On the Indian side, Indian Tamil fishermen faced many hardships inlcuding shooting and harassment for the last three decades. From Ramnad and Nagapattinam districts of Tamil Nadu state, 4,000 trawl boats operate currently; most of the boats depend upon fishing in Sri Lankan waters. Nearly, 1,000 trawl boats of Ramnad district totally depend on Sri Lankan waters in view of the proximity (just 7 km away) to the Sri Lankan borders (Vivekanandan, 2004).

The agreements between India and Sri Lanka regarding maritime boundary (1974 and 1976) did not reflect the actual sentiments of Indian Tamil fishermen. The agreements have given space for confusion among the fishermen from both the countries. Vivekanandan (2004) has viewed that the lack of proper navigation and location identifying equipment on board the Indian trawlers might have led to accidental crossing of international borders. Fishing vessels from both the countries did intentional border crossings at Palk Bay region and travelled deep into the sea. He stated that Palk Bay turned into a hotspot for trans-boundary fishing conflict at the global level. Before the 1970s, the fishermen from both countries, who have ethnic linkage, without any restrictions fished all over the Palk Bay (Vivekanandan, 2010).

The Indo-Sri Lankan maritime boundaries created by the Katchatheevu agreement in 1974 remain largely ignored by the Tamil fishermen of both the countries. As Sri Lanka witnessed civil war since 1983, the marine boundaries became a security concern for both the governments. Since then, hundreds of incidents of fishermen arrest and detention by the Sri Lankan Navy have taken place. Many Indian fishermen lost their lives to the bullets of Sri Lankan Navy personnel. With the help of multi-day vessels, Sri Lankan fishermen are also involved in cross-border fishing in the exclusive economic zone of India.

During the civil war, the Sri Lankan government said that Indian Tamil fishermen were aiding the Liberation Tigers of Tamil Eelam (LTTE) organization to have access to essential commodities and weapons. 'To curb the supply to LTTE, we have no option but to take strict action against Indian Tamil Fishermen', said Sri Lankan government officials. After the bitter end of the LTTE movement in 2009, Sri Lankan Navy has been using heavy weapons against the unarmed innocent Indian fishermen in the name of safeguarding their sea resources. Forced eviction from traditional regions, unsafe working conditions and personal security threats are considered as human rights violations by international rules and laws. Developing countries such as India, Philippines, Cambodia, and South Africa are witnessing such kinds of human rights violations. While accessing their fishing rights at sea regions (Ratner et al., 2014) the governments could have reduced the incidence of conflict among the fishing communities by adopting equitable fishing rights allocation and a scientific sea resource management system. Suryanarayan (2005) has viewed that the prolonged civil war fuelled the fishermen conflict at Palk Bay. For him, the Palk Bay witnessed 236 incidents of attack on Tamil Nadu fishermen by the Sri Lankan Navy during the civil war, resulting in 75 deaths.

There is a strong linkage between the civil war and fish production decline in Sri Lanka. Following the civil war in Sri Lanka, the country's total fish catch fell by 27 per cent. Just one decade before, Sri Lanka had attained its 1983 fish catch. Due to the civil war, most fishermen in the northern part of the country were involved in the civil war against the government forces. Besides fish production decline, many people belonging to fishing villages in Sri Lanka were internally displaced from their native villages.

According to the authors, poor and developing countries witnessed fishing conflicts which destroyed physical and human capital and frustrated capital investments, both within the conflict-affected country and in its neighbours. They also argued that post conflict society would concentrate more on development issues. The changed situation would attract more internal and foreign aids from governments and agencies, which would help them to reconstruct their lives. With the help of

NGO funding, Tamil fishermen from the northern part of Sri Lanka reinvested in fishing equipment and boats (Hendrix & Glaser, 2011).

Suryanarayan had argued that the agreements (1974 and 1976) crafted to result in morale relationship between the two neighbouring countries have severely affected the livelihood of thousands of Tamil fishermen from both the countries. The rich fishing resources at Palk Bay have made it a conflict zone between Indian Tamil fishermen and the Sri Lankan Navy. It was observed that the agreements did not reflect the ground realities of the livelihood concerned; instead, they were country-centric (Suryanarayan, 2005).

Stephen et al. observed that the current conflict situation which exists in the Palk Bay region must be understood from the political ecology perspective. Also, he has argued about the politics of the Tamil Nadu state government, Government of India and Government of Sri Lanka. He said politics played a vital role in the Palk Bay conflict rather than the science of Palk Bay. The conflict between India and Sri Lankan fishermen in the Palk Bay remained unsolved due to political reasons. Norms and priorities for the governance of fisheries aren't being entirely established based on logic, needs and scientific method-ologies, courtesy the influence of politically-motivated decisions taken by the State and Central governments on fisheries governance. But it is being debated in the public domain. Trawl fishing by Tamil Nadu fishermen is causing hardship for small-scale fishermen of northern Sri Lanka. It is also fuelling political tension between India and Sri Lanka (Stephen et al., 2013).

Tamil Nadu government, Indian Central government and the Sri Lankan government are playing crucial and critical roles in the Palk Bay conflict by taking different stands. The Tamil Nadu government took a stand that Katchatheevu islet has to be considered as part of Tamil Nadu. But the governments of both India (Central government) and Sri Lanka took a stand that Katchatheevu is part of Sri Lanka. Due to opinion differences between the Tamil Nadu state government and the Central government, the AIADMK General Secretary and the then-Chief Minister J. Jayalalithaa filed a case against the Central government in the Supreme Court over the Katchatheevu islet problem seeking the retrieval of the right of access to the islet and Tamil Nadu fishermen's fishing rights. Till date, this case is pending before the Apex Court.

The plight of the Palk Bay Indian Tamil fishermen takes place in the micro sphere, whereas its solution lies within the macro sphere of inter-country interactions and bilateral relations. There is even the scope of a third country to intervene in view of its hegemonic designs. However, and paradoxically enough, the missing link in the Palk Bay issue has been its internalization in Indian polity. Why should the issue find its least expression in the political agenda of even the regional parties in the state of Tamil Nadu? Why not the fishermen take the issue beyond the source to the Tamils at large? Why should they not follow the peasants and invade the capital? These are perplexing questions in social science and communication research. The media paradigm has exposed all dimensions of the issue, though unrelated. But the media impact does not synchronize with the media coverage. As far as the people of Tamil Nadu are concerned, the plight has aroused mere sympathy on humanitarian grounds. For them, the innocent Tamil fishermen engaged in cross-border fishing in Sri Lankan waters are being inhumanly dealt with by the Sri Lankan Navy. The arrest in doses; pleas in doses and release in doses have become unrelated 'news' every day. The sympathy might turn barren in course of time with the routinization of all these practices.

Does it mean that there remains a total consensus of oneness with the mainstream politics and relegation of the issue to the intensities of the country's global political interactions and foreign policy manoeuvres? Do all the media and the powers that be at various levels function from the vantage point of adherence to mainstream State politics? Research will have to throw light on this aspect. The Palk Bay conflict has inevitably to be conceived in the present tense. The researcher cannot reconstruct the past and arrive at the present from the preconception since all the crucial documents relating to the Palk Bay have been appropriated by the Central government and are being preserved zealously as classified documents. As such, the historicity of the problem has to be presented only as the introductory space being shaped from the fragments of information available in the work in print.

The print media offers the largest hope for any researchers to seize the issue and grasp its roots. The mass print media (newspapers), both English and vernacular, have been providing coverage of the Palk Bay conflict as a continuum. The presentation has been in the form of news coverage, special articles and write-ups and editorial notes. Research works on the problem written and published by scholars of both the countries bear certain authentic information, but they have originated from the vantage points of the partisanship of their authors. Critical insight is needed to unearth the fact from the discourses.

Writings on the ethnicity of the Tamils, Sri Lankans, Sri Lankan Tamils and fishermen of both the countries are available. The social media has been reacting to the developments though not in a massive and decisive way. The specific feature of the social media response has been that it is largely the replication of the print media. However, social media has provided the opportunity to perceive its production as a media effect in response to the media paradigm. It has been a measure of popular response.

In the last one decade, the popularity of social media has been increasing day by day. Even major newspapers in India and Tamil Nadu state are disseminating news through social media such as Facebook and Twitter. Every day, the number of users of social media is increasing. As of now, Twitter micro-blogging service has 335 million active users (StatistaPortal, 2019) and Facebook has 1.74 million users.

Due to their policy, Facebook do not share their user data with third parties (Fortune, 2018), whereas Twitter is open source in nature and shares the content and information about users and even their geographical information with third parties. The conflict between Tamil Nadu fishermen and Sri Lankan Navy has been widely debated on Twitter.

The purpose of this chapter is to study the role of social media in carrying the message into the mainland with or without the mainstream political overtones. As such, this media effects analysis proceeds into the domain of the framing methodology and social construct approach. The objective of this chapter is to investigate how the print and social media portrayed the Palk Bay conflict by applying frame analysis.

Framing has roots in many disciplines ranging from sociology (Goffman, 1974), psychology (Tversky & Kahneman, 2000) and media and communication (Entman, 1993). This thesis is concerned with the print and social media framing in the context of communication. It is also more attentive on conflict framing which is constructed by the print and social media. According to Tuchman (1978), news is a window and its frames control the perception of reality. The frames of the window limit the perception of different realities by focusing on the specific issues. Due to this limitation in the perception process, some issues of the reality perceived through news will be more salient than the other issues (Tuchman, 1978).

According to Entman, framing is a scattered conceptualization. We can feel its omnipresence across the social sciences and humanities as it is embedded within media content and makes itself manifest in a text and has power to influence the thinking process. Framing describes the power of communication within the text, and analysis of these frames leads to the emergence of the way in which influence over a human is exerted by the transfer of communication from one location such as media content to that of consciousness.

The goal of framing is to identify and make explicit the common tendencies among the various uses of the term and to suggest a more precise understanding of it. Framing process involves selection and salience. Frame is to select some aspects of a perceived reality and make them more salient in a communication process. It promotes a particular issue or problem to give causal interpretation, evaluate and finally give suggestions to the issue or problem. Framing has the working nature of making a piece of information more noticeable, meaningful and memorable for the audience. An increase in salience improves the probability that receivers will perceive the reality and store it in their memory (Entman, 1993). While pursuing the literature related to the framing methodology (Iyengar, 1991; Neuman et al., 1992; Semetko & Valkenburg, 2000), researchers in the field have detected four commonly observed frames by which journalists presented the news. They have also identified the fifth, the morality frame. Thus, the study has adopted five types of major frames which are: (a) conflict frame; (b) human interest frame; (c) responsibility frame; (d) economic consequences frame and (e) morality frame.

Here, framing analysis is adopted to examine how the mainstream media (print) and social media viewed the Palk Bay conflict during the rule of Congress and BJP, before and after the transfer of power at the Centre respectively. The print media selected for the study are the national daily *The Hindu*, the vernacular daily *Dinamani* and the social media platform, Twitter.

The primary sources are the coverage of all kinds of news pertaining to Palk Bay conflict and consequent plight of Indian Tamil fishermen presented in *The Hindu* (national English daily), *Dinamani* (Tamil regional daily) and Twitter (social media) covering the period from May 2013 to May 2015. The secondary sources include the accessible official documents, other media coverages, written works on the issue, works on Sri Lankan and Indian economic and political history, works on the Eelam movement and Indian South East coast and research works on India's foreign policy orientation and diplomatic dispensation.

Media content are textual structures built around a central axis of thought on particular perspectives by media persons, who will provide an interpretive frame for the audience. From this angle, we can define a frame as a certain process in which some aspects of reality are identified and given more importance, so that the problem or issue gets defined, its causes diagnosed. Sometimes, even moral judgements are suggested and appropriate solutions proposed. Framing is present in the minds of media persons, who develop the media content that reaches the readers through a decoding process that is necessary to understand the media content. Ardevol and Weaver argued that a media frame is 'the central organizing idea for news content and it suggests what the issue is through the use of selection, emphasis, exclusion and elaboration' (Ardevol, 2015; Weaver, 2007).

The term frame can be applied to many different aspects of media content and messages. The latter can also be studied by means of systematic content analysis or more interpretive textual analysis. Framing is very much similar to the second-level agenda setting (Weaver, 2007). Examples are the Vreese, Peter, Semetko framing research works on the introduction of the Euro monetary unit. Their study defined the media frames which laid more emphasis on the quantum of conflict over the introduction of the Euro's economic consequences in four countries (De Vreese et al., 2001). Communication professionals in general and journalists in particular have to tell a story within certain time and space constraints and make it accessible to a broad and often heterogeneous public.

The only way to do this is by structuring the information and creating an interpretive framework that allows the comprehension of the message. In the making of texts, journalists use frames to give meaning to and simplify reality, in some way, and to maintain the interest of the public (Valkenburg et al., 1999).

Media professionals have also to tell the story within time and space. Media content is also to be made accessible to a broad and heterogeneous public. To make media content comprehensive, media professionals structure the content and create their own interpretive frameworks. They use the frames in their own way to simplify the information and make the media content interesting to the heterogeneous public. The endeavours of both are similar, but their patterns are different as also the nature of their chosen frames.

When media persons make news and build the description of reality with the help of words and images, they are selecting the frames. The journalists have a choice to select other frames by using another angle of construction, as well as other photographs. The objective of this process is to give prominence to one part of information and omitting others. All the news stories have omissions whether it may be deliberate or not (Ardèvol-Abreu, 2015).

According to Van Gorp, a frame is an invitation and an incentive to read a story in a certain way. As the frames form part of the culture, they are overlooked and so the construction process is hidden (Gorp, 2007). Scheufele and Tewksbury argued that frames used by media are macro constructs. They are used to reduce the complexity of the issue or problem and to adapt them to suit the needs and constraints of the media. In the minds of individuals, the frames become micro constructs which allow the receiver to use the received information to form his own perception and impression of reality (Scheufele & Tewksbury, 2007).

Media frames are constructed by use of media's own resources (media content). It may be a definition of a problem, an interpretation of causes, a moral assessment and recommended solution to the problem or issue. On the other hand, frames of individuals are the frames of interpretation of reality and schemata in which new information is associated. They do not have a physical manifestation like in media frames. But these frames have influence over the attitudes, perception and behaviour of the individuals. They are psychological processes which are influenced by sociological factors such as culture.

To identify the conflict frames of Tamil Nadu fishermen, the researchers decided to analyse a major national newspaper and a regional vernacular newspaper. The national English newspaper *The Hindu* has given a broad representation of Tamil Nadu fishermen conflict, whereas regional Tamil language newspaper *Dinamani* has dealt with the issue against the backdrop of the cultural and linguistic traditions of Tamil Nadu. According to Indian Readership Survey 2017, *The Hindu* had a readership of 38.5 lakhs all over India. This is 30 per cent more than other English major newspapers like *Times of India* and *Deccan Chronicle* (Hindu, 2018). *Dinamani* the regional Tamil daily has a readership of 4.76 lakhs within Tamil Nadu. The New Indian Express Group has been publishing this newspaper since 11 September 1933 (Info, 2011). Both the newspapers have their own traditions and values, which has widely covered the Tamil Nadu fishermen–Sri Lankan Navy conflict at Palk Bay for the last three decades. Both are well-respected newspapers for their sensitivity and history of being published from Tamil Nadu even from the pre-independence era.

METHODOLOGY

Considering the nature of the current study, *Dinamani*, *The Hindu* and Twitter have been discerned as independent variables and human rights violations, governments' stand, political parties' stand and fishermen's stand as dependent variables.

From May 2013 to May 2015 *Dinamani* has published 753 articles regarding the conflict. It has covered this conflict for more than three decades. Moreover, it reflects the state's and Tamil fishermens' senti-ments in their own context. *The Hindu* has published 330 articles regarding the conflict. It has also covered this conflict from its origin. Because it is a national newspaper of wider circulation, it has given comparatively less space to this conflict. It has covered this conflict from the nationalism perspective.

Twitter has been the most popular social media widely used by the public for political debate. Basically, it is an open source social media platform which provides access to anyone. Totally, 810 tweets were posted from this platform regarding the fishermen's conflicts.

While perusing the literature related to framing methodology (Iyengar, 1991; Neuman et al., 1992; Semetko & Valkenburg, 2000), researchers in the field have detected four commonly observed frames by which journalists presented the news. They have also identified the fifth, the morality frame

- By emphasizing conflict between parties or individuals (conflict frame)
- By focusing on an individual as an example or emphasizing emotions (human interest frame)
- By attributing responsibility, crediting or blaming certain political institutions or individuals (responsibility frame)
- By focusing on the economic consequence for the audience (economic consequence frame)
- By focusing on morality angle of issues (morality frame)

Thus, the study has adopted five types of major frames which are: (a) conflict frame; (b) human interest frame; (c) responsibility frame; (d) economic consequences frame and (e) morality frame. These frames and their corresponding consequences in journalistic assumption are based on the perception of the audience.

Based on this premise, news published in the selected print media publications, *The Hindu* and *Dinamani*, are content analysed to identify the key frames used. This apart, tweets are content analysed for major frames as detailed earlier, barring the economic consequences frame which is considered as not so relevant to the current study.

- Human rights violation (conflict frame)
- Governments' stand (responsibility frame)
- Political parties' stand (responsibility frame)
- Fishermen's stand (morality)

To measure the consequences of these news items for the current study, certain questions related to news items and opinions expressed in Twitter have been developed. Under each category of frames selected for the study, ideas in the analysed items that reflect the constructs (frames) are identified. This framing analysis was applied to all the chosen items from the print publications *The Hindu* and *Dinamani* and Twitter.

We adopted a five-point Likert scale to quantify the data, which were extracted from print media. According to the tone of the articles, they quantified data with the help of the five-point Likert scale (Strongly pro—5, Pro—4, Neutral—3, Anti—2, Strongly anti—1). The following research questions were raised to address the current study:

> *RQ1. Are we justified in calling the print media depiction as the media frames and that of social media as individual frames?*
> *RQ2. How far are the media frames or individual frames dependent or independent in themselves and in interaction?*
> *RQ3. What is the relative strength of the frames in terms of strong frames?*
> *RQ4. When predefined frames are used in comparative analysis with deductive method, what type of generic frames gain predominance?*
> *RQ5. Is there any difference in perception among various media (Hindu, Dinamani, Twitter) towards the human right violation frame?*
> *RQ6. Is there any difference in perception among various media towards government's stand?*
> *RQ7. Is there any difference in perception among various media towards overall political parties' stand?*
> *RQ8. Is there any difference in perception among various media towards Tamil Nadu fishermen's stand?*

ANALYSIS AND FINDINGS

RQ1. Are we justified in calling the print media depiction as the media frames and that of social media as individual frames?

The current investigation deals with the fishermen's conflict in Palk Bay with the Sri Lankan Navy as reflected in the mainstream print media and digital social media Twitter. In the construction of the major variables investigated as 'frames', the researcher relied on Scheufele and Tewlesbury (2007) who considered media frames as macro constructs, which make even the complex issues taller, making it made to appeal and arrest the attention of the audience in the simplest form possible (Scheufele & Tewksbury, 2007). This phenomena of media frames was also defined by Entman (1993) as a centrality of a storyline unfolding an issue meaningfully, in order to help the audience to understand, assimilate and interpret the event or issue reported (Entman, 1993). Relying on these theoretical notions, the present study explores the media frames deconstructed from the selected mainstream print media, *The Hindu,* with a national outlook and *Dinamani* with regional focus.

The Palk Bay conflict with a three-cornered multilateral geopolitical interest between two governments—India and Sri Lanka—and the state government of Tamil Nadu with a multi-tier conflict at Bay of Bengal, involving the fishermen from Tamil Nadu and Sri Lanka, the naval forces of India and Sri Lanka has gained currency and attracted national and international attention. Hence, both the mainstream print media widely covered the various facets of the conflict that took place in the waters and on the soil of both the countries. While deconstructing the contents based on the generic frames advocated by Valkenburg (2000), the researcher defined and identified four major frames—human rights violation, governments' stand, political parties' stand and fishermen's stand, which justify the print media depiction as major media frames. Further, the researcher sets out to explore the reaction to these major frames among the audience (Semetko & Valkenburg, 2000). While exploring the reflections, Entman, Ardevol Abreu and Scheufle have collectively structured the reflections as stored clusters of ideas in the minds of individuals and elaborated the information based on which was processed accordingly (Ardevol, 2015; Entman, 1993; Scheufele, 1999; Scheufele & Tewksbury, 2007).

Besides, these are considered individual frames intertwined in the minds of the audience, which are schema in nature and processed and interpreted accordingly. It is often said that 'Meaning is in the minds of the people'. Thus, while media frames are attributes of news, individual frames concern the cognitive construct which influences the attitude and behaviour of individuals. In this context, the researcher thought it appropriate to investigate the digital media Twitter as the platform of the reflection of the mainstream print media as it provided immediate feedback that was much sharper while focusing on these issues. These reflections were cognitive schema that assimilated, processed, interpreted and accordingly reflected in Twitter media platforms. Hence, these tweets from social media are feedback from the mainstream media and perceptions of micro constructs in the minds of Twitter users, thus justifying these micro constructs in social media Twitter as individual frames.

There is a dialectical relationship between the two media frames striking a polarity between institutional and individual presentation. One could not miss the contradiction between media paradigm and media effect. However, what ultimately counts is striking a balance between the two has been the value system of the reporters themselves and the middle-class orientation of the readers. Empirical analysis must throw light on this aspect. The dependence of social media on the knowledge of the episodes occurring offshore has been a crucial topological backdrop.

RQ2. How far are the media frames or individual frames dependent or independent in themselves and in interaction?

It is often debated while using framing methodologies as to how the media and individual frames are interdependent so as to infer meaningful influence on each other. Social scientists Valkenburg and Semetko attempted to understand these relationships and observed that often media persons are left with no choice but to structure news frames keeping in mind a very large heterogeneous audience. Since every frame is an attempted structure from the perspective of the respective audience, both the players have strong dependence both in reporting and receiving the news frames. So there is a strong relationship between media frames and individual frames (Holli & Valkenburg, 2000).

In order to understand this phenomenon in the current investigation, the researcher subjected the empirical data of both print and social media to a correlation test. The results of the test are given in Table 6.1.

Table 6.1 *Correlations*

Correlations between Social Media and Print Media		
	Print Media	Social Media
Print media	1	0.225**
Social media	0.225**	1

The data from Table 6.1 reveals that there is a strong correlation between the main frames of mainstream print media and individual frames of social media Twitter with a Pearson correlation value of 0.225 at 0.001 level of significance. The result shows a strong correlation and existence of mutual contributory relationship between selected media frames and individual frames of print and social media. Hence, dependence or independence is ultimately decided by the sway of a media polity. Under the given conditions, the research question is suitably answered.

RQ3. What is the relative strength of the frames in terms of strong frames?
RQ4. When predefined frames are used in comparative analysis with deductive methods, what type of generic frames gain predominance?

While attempting to uncover media countenance, the researcher often employed a comparative analytic frame of reference based on certain predetermined or defined frames as 'constructs' applying a deductive methodology. In the process, the frames that emerge are considered equal in importance and also in treatment. So it is very difficult to argue certain frames as strong and others weak. The complexity of news storylines makes it difficult to measure them as strong or weak. However, researchers Chong and Druckman advocated that the relative strength of frames can be measured in terms of the frequency, research and the contextual relevance of frames. Pragmatically, the researchers have widely applied a five-point or seven-point Likert interval scale in order to allow subjectivity and evolve reliable measures to empirically analyse the chosen subject investigated (Chong & Druckman, 2007).

Based on these premises, the current investigation set out to explore the major frames relying on instruments constructed based on a five-point Likert scale. In order to measure the relative importance and predominance of the generic frames adopted in this study, the investigator subjected the empirical data to mean difference study. The mean value of the aforementioned frames reveals that the human rights violation evolved as the strong frame among other frames with a mean value of 4.271, followed by fishermen's stand with a mean value of 3.785, political parties' stand with a mean value 2.966 and governments' stand with a mean value 2.7. The print (*Hindu* and *Dinamani*) and social media (Twitter) had given great importance to the human rights violation frame as against the other frames. One has to understand the human rights violation frame from a historical perspective.

Tamil fishermen from India and Sri Lanka have an umbilical cord bondage and cultural oneness. The fishermen from both the sides of the Palk Bay lived happily and harvested marine resources to mutual benefit for many generations. However, the ethnic conflict that erupted between Sri Lankan Tamils and Sinhalese during the 1980s has changed the attitude towards sharing of resources in the Palk Bay region. The LTTE played an important role in support of Indian fishermen to explore and establish their fishing in the conflict zone, with a mutual understanding till the end of Eelam War IV and ethnic conflict in 2009 (Krishnan et al., 2014). The LTTE helped the Indian fishermen as *naishkarmya karmics* (that is, without expecting anything in return from them) but their struggle against the Sri Lankan government could have been an influence. Meanwhile, at the onset of the Blue Revolution, the Indian government helped to equip Indian fishermen, which resulted in the swift advancement in their fishing pattern. At the end of the war, the Palk Bay zone went under the control of Sri Lankan Navy, the conflict between the Indian fishermen and the Sri Lankan Navy became a regular event, by torturing them, seizing their boats and even killing them. These incidents totally disheartened the fishing communities who lost hopes of their livelihood.

Whenever the Sri Lankan Navy attacked Tamil fishermen at sea, the Tamil Nadu government and the public around the world strongly reacted and condemned those inhuman acts, which were only reflected in the print and the social media. The national daily *The Hindu* and *Dinamani* had provided space and coverage and debated the issue in various levels as news stories, editorials and columns. Although Twitter offered a forum for not only sharing and reflecting the reality but also appealing to other media to notice and thus forming part of the investigation. Hence, human rights violation emerged as a strong frame among other frames, followed by the fishermen's stand.

RQ5. Is there any difference in perception among various media (Hindu, Dinamani, Twitter) towards the human rights violation frame?

The result of one-way ANOVA reflects a very significant existence of difference between variables studied. The F value of 5.956 is significant at 0.003 level indicating a significant difference in perception between print and social media. Here, the native language newspaper *Dinamani* is vocal and gives wider coverage on every incident of conflict. Relatively similar reflection has been observed in Twitter, where in, tweeters deliberate more on conflict and its implications. However, *The Hindu* with its moderate policies had given moderate coverage of conflicting situations. Thus, it is inferred that regional print media *Dinamani* is more vocal in its coverage followed by the Twitter and *The Hindu* indicating a difference in coverage of human rights violations between print media and social media. News stories that are related to human rights violations at Palk Bay region between the Tamil Nadu fishermen and Sri Lankan Navy at Palk Bay region, especially after the Eelam war and the subsequent media coverage of print and social media deliberations were analysed.

The result shows that between the print media *The Hindu* and *Dinamani* there is a vast difference in terms of the number of items published for the news frame 'human rights violations'. However, subsequent reflection in the social media, Twitter, is comparatively better with 60 tweets for human rights violation, compared to that in the print media, *The Hindu*.

In order to understand a holistic perception of the print media (*The Hindu and Dinamani*) and social media (Twitter) towards the coverage given to the Palk Bay fishermen conflict, the following research question has been raised:

RQ6. Is there any difference in perception among various media towards government's stand?

The result of one-way ANOVA for the print media (*The Hindu* and *Dinamani*) and social media (Twitter) reveals a significant difference in total perception in terms of pro and anti towards their coverage with an F value of 6.854 and the level of significance is at 0.001 exhibiting significant variability in terms of difference in perception.

The data revealed that *The Hindu* had given a total number of 131 items over the period of two years (June 2013 to May 2015). *Dinamani* had given 312 items during the same period, whereas there were 341 items in Twitter during this period on this subject. Thus, it can be inferred that both *Dinamani* and Twitter were more vibrant and dynamic in terms of news coverage and *The Hindu* remains moderate in its views. In order to understand, the print media coverage and social media representation in terms of the news and views as pro and anti, the data which were taken at a five-point Likert scale was subjected to a one-way ANOVA in order to understand the difference in perception. Similar tendencies of positively resolving the issue by all three governments were reflected in Twitter, whereas *Dinamani* continued to express its reservation and scepticism over all the three governments resolving the Palk Bay conflict.

Hence, the result reveals that *The Hindu* as a newspaper reported more news items on governments' stand. It has given more importance to governments' opinions. It has also given positive coverage for both the Congress and the BJP governments. Twitter users also circulated more government-supported tweets and they retweeted positive news items. When compared to other media, *Dinamani* had given less importance to coverage of the government's stand and took a pro Tamil Nadu fishermen stand in its coverage and their views.

RQ7. Is there any difference in perception among various media towards overall political parties' stand?

The result of one-way ANOVA for various media (*The Hindu*, *Dinamani*, Twitter), as seen in Table 6.1 reveals that there is a significant difference among the media groups towards political parties' stand as the F ratio (F = 3.054) pertaining to the various media is significant at 0.049 level. Hence, the results reveal that Twitter has given more space to political parties' opinion regarding the Tamil Nadu fishermen conflict. When compared to the national daily *The Hindu*, the regional Tamil language daily *Dinamani* has given more importance to the political parties' opinion.

RQ8. Is there any difference in perception among various media towards Tamil Nadu fishermen's stand?

The results of ANOVA for various media (*Hindu, Dinamani,* Twitter) reveal that there is no significant difference between the print and the social media on overall coverage of fishermen's stand of both the countries. It may be concluded that both the print and the social media had given equal importance to the fishermen's conflict at Palk Bay.

DISCUSSION AND CONCLUSION

Print media has largely served the purpose compared to social media for two reasons. First, there has been no confrontation between the fishermen and the government at the Centre. Second, the impact through social media has been constrained by the peripheral existence of the fishermen. Hence, the mass media had to take the lead in terms of reach. Without prejudice to the analysis part of this study, the empirical observations are correlated with the critical conceptualizations here.

- Framing effect has been observable from the influence being exercised on the release of the fishermen from Sri Lankan prisons on a regular basis. Media has linked politics with the public in this regard (Chong & Druckman 2007).
- The media coverage of the Palk Bay conflict has contributed to generate a regional-/ national-level collective identity uniting the alienated intellectuals, urban middle class and the fishermen at large as was the case in the Tunisian revolution (Breuer, 2012).
- Repeated presentation of the plight of fishermen in the sea has generated a kind of emotional integration. 'Our right! Our right!', the cry of the fishermen has been reported as parallel to the 'Beladi! Beladi' (my country, my country) cry of the people during the Egyptian revolution (Eltantawy & Wiest, 2011).
- The media coverages have to be perceived as strategic efforts to polarize individual actions into collective actions (Edwards & Mcarthy, 2004). The continuous framing of similar episodes develops a predictable pattern of reality (Scheufele, 1999) and promotes organizational solidarity (Tusa, 2013).

- The human rights violation frame has gained qualitative precedence over the other frames in the portrayal of the Palk Bay conflict in both the print and social media. Generally, across the globe and especially in the West, human rights have become the focal point of social action dynamics. This approach negated the adherence to political dogmas and sectarian class war theorizations and generated the path for the issue to be universalized in status, cutting across any bias as well as the scope for the emergence of an offline social movement. One has to comprehend the parallelism between the mass media's preferred and institutionalized political ethos and the middle-class backdrop of the social media users who invariably pursue an apolitical perception. As a result of this correlation, the human rights violation frame became predominant in the media handling of the Palk Bay conflict.

- The Twitterites and most of the print media including *The Hindu* reflected a mainstream view that the BJP government can solve the conflict and it will be resolved amicably. The exception was *Dinamani*, which had been cautious and advocated the need for a much more aggressive posture and direct involvement of the Central government in resolving the conflict.

- The print and social media have expressed views in unison supporting Tamil Nadu fishermen of their rights to fish in Palk Bay with *The Hindu* being critical of certain aspects of Tamil Nadu fishermen's fishing mechanism.

- The Palk Bay conflict has two significant areas of interaction. At the macro level, mainstream politics reigns supreme. The unilateral transfer of Katchatheevu to Sri Lanka affected with least care to preserve the inalienable rights of the Tamil fishermen of the Palk Bay shores paved the way for the perennial plight of the latter in the sea.

- The inhuman acts of the Sri Lankan Navy being unleashed on a day-to-day basis have been a material act of ascendancy coupled to their diplomatic act of manipulative hegemony. India under the emergency sphere exercised its authoritarian power to affect the Katchatheevu transfer and silenced the voice of all the democratic forces in the country against any possible revolt.

- Sri Lanka could put an end to the civil war with the Indian government's support and later on develop the tactics of crushing the

Indian Tamil fishermen's hold over the Bay as part of their overall strategy of subdividing the Tamils both internally and in the sea. The assassination of former Prime Minister Rajiv Gandhi contributed to the Sri Lankan stand with the consequent sentimental backdrop against the LTTE. The rising hegemonic power of China has contributed to push India further to uphold Sri Lankan stand and adhere to a policy of appeasement of the fishermen by securing their release from Sri Lankan prisons as a routine exercise.

- The Tamil Nadu state government's polemical intervention in the matter demanding the cancellation of the agreement and the political implications of the rising Sinhala Buddhist hegemony in Sri Lanka have been significant intervening factors in the conflict. To not go to fish in the deep sea and avoid the conflict would cause serious economic problems and smack of a total surrender of the Tamil fishermen's right in the Palk Bay.

- In both countries mainstream politics has marginalized the peripheral fishermen community as a historical causality. It is clear that no visionary pragmatism prevails in political dispensation. At the micro level, the empirical premises of the conflict or the local processes that shape everyday fishing have to be identified and attended. Though these are advocated mainly by the scholars, who are in defense of the Sri Lankan stand, they are very crucial in terms of resolution of the conflict. Any creative solution must answer these issues too.

- At the fishing level, it is Indian bottom tracing trawl operation vis-a-vis traditional gill net fishers of Sri Lankan fishermen feared as greater exploitation of the sea resources by the former, leading to a resource crunch and causing damages to Sri Lankan nets. After 20 years of nomadic life owing to the civil war, the Sri Lankan fishermen returning to their shores were handicapped by the lack of adequate support from their country and had to face unhealthy competition with their Indian counterparts, who are empowered with the benefits of the Blue Revolution in India. The Sri Lankan government, indifferent to their plight, has seized the opportunity to whip up sentiments against the Tamil fishermen.

- Both the governments have resorted to define the conflict as one between the fishermen of both the shores. The uncontrolled expansion of trawls fishing in India occurs under patronage. Fishing companies have entered into the space and monopolized control over fishers in the Indian south-eastern coast. Capital expansion at one end and poverty increase at another is being witnessed. The Tamil fishermen have been left with no other option than to serve corporate interests. Deep sea fishing would not serve the interest of the companies for they are for the maximum exploitation with least expenditure. Inadequate spread or extension of fishers in Palk Bay and Gulf of Mannar indicates the corporate sway and government policy. The conflict exposes the contradiction between the export factor and consumption factor. Even among the Tamil fishermen the disputes of the traditional boat owning fishermen with those of trawlsmen are to be amicably settled.

The researcher now proceeds to correlate the findings of the empirical analysis with these ground realities to arrive at a pragmatic solution to the Palk Bay conflict.

• The print and social media frames have uniformly upheld the Tamil fishermen's cause. They are categorical in affirming the latter's historical rights in the Palk Bay and access to Katchatheevu. They are vociferous in their support to the fishermen in their plight in the sea. The frames have been uniformly impressive as to prevail upon the powers that be to secure the release of the arrested fishermen and generate mechanisms to provide them adequate security in fishing. The fishing mechanism being adopted by the Tamil fishermen contributing to the conflict has not been spared throughout uniformly.

• The Tamil fishermen's co-share right in Palk Bay and sociocultural partnership right over Katchatheevu find positive handling by both the media. The media, by and large, are supportive of the Central government's stand over the Palk Bay conflict. The prevalent optimism has been that the BJP-led government at the Centre and Sri Lanka government would see the writing on the wall and settle the issue by resolving the conflict through negotiations. The reservations in some print media as formed expression in certain frames only raise the alarm for cautious handling as against bilateral naivety.

• The overall stand of the media is perceivable from the low-key portrayal of human rights violations at the all-India level and vociferous critiques in vernacular press. Quite clearly, the media appeases the people and applauds the government on the Palk Bay conflict. There evidently lies a pattern, which is also seen by the wide coverage given to all the political parties and their opinions in the local press and selective coverage at the all-India level marginalizing most of them.

All arguments converge and the following conclusions emerge:

1. Ultimately the conflict could be resolved only through the direct and committed bilateral negotiation between India and Sri Lanka involving their Parliaments and judiciary on a specific agenda;
2. Arranging negotiations between the fishermen from both sides shall only chalk out the problem areas for political and government resolution and not to precipitate the conflict to further dimensions;
3. Both the countries must agree on the scientific exploitation, management and sharing of the sea resources paying heed to historical aspects and contemporary issues;
4. Sri Lanka must be made to come to reason regarding the social consequences of human rights violations. They must be told in unequivocal terms that no military solution exists for the resolution of the Palk Bay conflict
5. The Indian government should not be complacent with the assertion that the Katchatheevu transfer is over and takes pleasure in oft repeating the chant that it is sovereign Sri Lankan territory not to be intruded by the Tamils.

The end has been the beginning and the past mistakes associated with the raw deal are only haunting the country in this regard. India shall firmly assert and secure the co-sharing right of Tamil fishermen over Katchatheevu and preserve their right to fish in the sea waters around Katchatheevu based on fresh agreements and with agreed joint patrolling. India shall strive for establishing a controlled and coordinated free zone involving the sea territories of both the countries with a view to ensuring permanent peace in the Palk Bay.

Most significantly, the Government of India has recently decided to constitute a separate Ministry for fisheries. This could even be constructed as the impact of the Palk Bay conflict. The success lies in the constitution and functional dynamics of the Ministry in the years to come. There shall be no denial of the fact that this is a significant departure towards resolving the issue on and off the shores.

REFERENCES

Ardèvol-Abreu, A. (2015). Framing theory in communication research. Origins, development and current situation in Spain. *Revista Latina de Comunicación Social, 70,* 423–450.

Breuer, A. (2012). The role of social media in mobilizing political protest: Evidence from the Tunisian Revolution. German Development Institute. Discussion paper no. 10/2012. ISSN 1860-0441

Chong, D., & Druckman, J. N. (2007). Framing public opinion in competitive democracies. *American Political Science Review, 101*(4), 637–655.

De Vreese, C. H., Peter, J., & Semetko, H. (2001). Framing politics at the launch of the Euro: A cross-national comparative study of frames in the news. *Political Communication, 18,* 107–122.

Edwards, B., & McCarthy, J. D. (2004). Resources and social movement mobilization. In *The Blackwell Companion to Social Movements,* (pp. 116–152). Blackwell Publishing Ltd. https://doi.org/10.1002/9780470999103.ch6

Eltantawy, N. & Wiest, J. B. (2011). Social media in the Egyptian Revolution: Reconsidering resource mobilizing theory. *International Journal of Communication, 5,* 1207–1224.

Entman, R. M. (1993). Framing: Towards clarification of a fractured paradigm. *Journal of Communication, 43*(4), 51–58.

Fortune. (2018, April 21). The 4 biggest takeaways from Facebook's new data policy. Fortune. Retrieved from http://fortune.com/2018/04/20/what-to-know-facebook-new-data-policy/

Goffman, E. (1974). *Frame Analysis: An essay on the organization of experience.* Northeastern University Press.

Gorp, B. V. (2007). The constructionist approach to framing: Bringing culture back. *Journal of Communication, 57*(1), 60–78.

Hendrix, C. S., & Glaser, S. M. (2011). Civil conflict and world fisheries, 1952–2004. *Journal of Peace Research, 48*(4), 481–495.

Hindu. (2018). The Hindu is the undisputed #1 English daily in South India: Indian Readership Survey. https://www.thehindu.com/news/national/the-hindu-is-the-undisputed-1-english-daily-in-south-india/article22492686.ece. Chennai: The Hindu.

Info, B. M. (2011, June 27). IRS Q1 2011: Top 10 dailies in Tamil Nadu. BestMediaInfo. Retrieved from https://bestmediainfo.com/2011/06/irs-q1-2011-top-10-dailies-in-tamil-nadu.

Iyengar, S. (1991). *Is anyone responsible? How television frames political issues.* University of Chicago Press.

Kahneman, D., Tversky, A. (2000). *Choices, values and frames.* Cambridge University Press.

Krishnan, C. J. R., Pichandy, C., & Barclay, F. (2014). Eelam war and its aftermath: Editorial analysis of Dinamani. *Media Watch, 5*(2), 235–244.

Neuman, W. R., Just, M. R., & Crigler, A. N. (1992). *Common knowledge: News and the construction of political meaning.* Chicago University Press.

Ratner, B. D., Åsgård, B., & Allison, E. H. (2014). Fishing for justice: Human rights, development, and fisheries sector reform. *Global Environmental Change,* 27, 120–130.

Scheufele, D. A. (1999). Framing as a theory of media effects. *International Communication Association, 49*(1), 103–122.

Scheufele, D. A., & Tewksbury, D. (2007). Framing, agenda setting, and priming. *Journal of Communication, 57*(2007), 9–20.

Scholtens, J., Bavinck, M., & Soosai, A. S. (2012). Fishing in dire straits: Transboundary incursions in the Palk Bay. *Economic and Political Weekly, 47*(25), 87–95.

Semetko, H. A., & Valkenburg, P. M. (2000). Framing European politics: A content analysis of press and television news. *Journal of Communication, 50*(2), 93–109.

StatistaPortal, T. (2019). Number of monthly active Twitter users worldwide from 1st quarter 2010 to 1st quarter 2019 (in millions). The Statista Portal. Retrieved from https://www.statista.com/statistics/282087/number-of-monthly-active-twitter-users/

Stephen, J., Menon, A., Scholtens, J., & Bavinck, M. (2013). Transboundary dialogues and the 'politics of scale' in Palk Bay fisheries: Brothers at sea?. *South Asia Research, 33*(2), 141–161.

Suryanarayan, V. (2005). *Conflict over fisheries in the Palk Bay region.* Lancer Publishers.

Tuchman, G. (1978). *Making news: A study in the construction of reality.* New York Free Press.

Tusa, F. (2013). How social media can shape a protest movement: The cases of Egypt in 2011 and Iran in 2009. *Arab Media and Society, 2*(17), 1–19.

Tversky, A., & Kahneman, D. (1981). The framing of decisions and the psychology of choice, Science 2111(4481), 453–458; see also Robert H. Mnookin, Scott R. Peppet, Andrew S. Tulumello, Beyond winning: Negotiating to create value in deals and disputes, 207–209.

Valkenburg, P. M., Semetko, H. A., & De Vreese, C. H. (1999). The effects of news frames on readers' thoughts and recall. *Communication Research, 26*(5), 550–569.

Vivekanandan, V. (2004). *Fishing for a favour, netting a lesson.* South Indian Federation of Fishermen Societies, Trivandrum, 68.

Vivekanandan, V. (2010). *Trawl brawl.* Samudra Report, 57, 24–27.

Weaver, D. (2007). Thoughts on agenda setting, framing, and priming. *Journal of Communication, 57*(1), 142–147.

Chapter 7

Social Media and Social Movements
A Review

C. Pichandy, S. Ramamurthy and V. Palaniappan

INTRODUCTION

In the recent past, the growth of active users in social media has been tremendous. This chapter points out the positive significance in the growing numbers of social media access across the world. The active internet and social media user status has been growing towards infinity. The active internet users across the world have now crossed (January 2021) 4.66 billion score, from 59.5 per cent of global population (Statista, 2021). Here, over 3.6 billion users are accessing social media platforms actively and three-quarters of them are accessing social media platforms through mobile phones (Statista, 2021a).

Social media with a wealth of information enables users to stay in contact, exchange updates and share knowledge. Particularly, it is a flexible and the fastest platform for promoting participation on issues via public posts and shares. Thus, it enables us to build relationships beyond boundaries. The internet-based people across the world unite through social media. With sociability and participation, people are progressively and inherently given space for collective actions to discuss and address common issues.

Social media facilitates the link between people and their mobilization on particular events. Plenty of social media platforms have emerged resulting in their access by millions of people in the cyber world, and whatever happened around the world have found place on social media platforms and are being received by people engaged online and are talked about to invoke mass attention, awareness and huge support. Social media serves the primary function of mobilization of people and it is happening without any intention. It reveals the public interest towards the common issue. These dynamics used by social activists, NGOs, political activists and also self-motivated individuals to spread awareness have gathered like-minded people to activate mass social movements in the real world. Social media became popular in the recent past significantly, since 2011. Among them, Facebook and Twitter are the most important platforms affecting mobilization of the masses towards entertainment issues to sociopolitical issues. It may be said that the year 2011 was the beginning of social media mobilization and revolution, and the world realized the impact of Facebook and Twitter by the remarkable revolutions such as Tunisia Protests, Occupy Wall Street, Anti-austerity Protests in Europe, Unrest in Chile, 'Black Tuesday' in South Africa, monks' defiance in Burma, rallies in Russia, uprisings in China's countryside and India's anti-corruption movement (Conover et al., 2013; Gainous et al., 2013; Stelzner, 2014; Swank, 2000).

ON SOCIAL MOVEMENTS AND PROTESTS: THE THEORIES

Lopes (2014) defines social movements as the 'Conscious concerted and sustained efforts by ordinary people to change some aspects of their society by using extra institutional means'. For the author, the grievances alone are not enough to create movements. Only when the underlying motives contend with social networks, the basis for movement recruitment and the path to popular mobilization emerges. Social movements are the vehicles for social and political change and have the potential to transform the systems of institutionalized politics in which they occur. They explain popular voluntary cooperation and mobilization. They are implicated in the spread of democracy and social change.

A social movement for Lopes is the effect for opportunity structures such as the economic, institutional and the social contexts of a country conditioned by its access to social media, the intervening variable or mobilizing structures.

The opportunity structures take into account the grievances that drive a social movement. These grievances can be derived from a change or deterioration of social, political and economic conditions. Mobilization structures are the social networks and all resources necessary for popular mobilization. Both are necessary. Mobilizing structures constituting the social networks and the media provide five key aspects to the formation of social movements which are: (a) communication; (b) organization; (c) mobilization; (d) validation; (e) scope enlargement. Cammaerts (2015) has defined the social movement as

[A] social process through which collective actors articulate their interests, voice grievances, and critique, and proposed solutions to identified problems by engaging in a variety of collective actions. For the author, the social movement has three features: (a) They are conflictual; (b) They are structured; (c) They are geared towards developing, sustaining and sharing collective identities.

Diani (1992) has defined social movements as the 'informal information exchanges networked between the groups, institutions and/or mass individuals emerged on the grounds of a common collective identity in a political or cultural conflict'.

Tilly (1984) has stated that the repertoire of collective action of social movements has been the 'distinctive constellations of tactics and strategies developed over time and used by protest groups to act collectively in order to make claims on individuals and groups'. According to Van Laer and Van Aelst (2009), the 'action repertoire of social movements is as broad as there are social movements and activists, goals and causes, clams and grievances'. The authors, therefore, rely on the unorthodox and unconventional political behaviour and concentrate on those actions and tactics that are performed on the non-institutional side of politics, outside the realm of conventional or orthodox political participation.

According to Seebaluck (2014), social protests, besides enabling to fight for freedom and democracy under authoritarian or tyrannical rule, have helped exert pressure to bring about regime change as in the Philippines (2001), Ukraine during the Orange Revolution and Egypt and Tunisia during the Arab Spring. He has observed that social protests are complex events involving mass action that seems to be 'coordinated within the crowds'. 'Consequently, it is vital to understand how crowds are pulled together and what mechanism they use during political upheaval and mass social protests.' The chapter explains why the rulers attempt to crush the social protests and how the police are unable to control them except by resorting to brutal violence.

Oliver et al. (2003) states that the study of protest and social movements has grown into a large speciality area of sociology matching significant ties with political organizational and cultural sociology as well as social psychology. The social movement theorists, according to the author, see protest as 'Politics by other means' during contemporary times. It is now well recognized that extra-institutional and institutional politics are interdependent. Protests must be studied in terms of events. Early in 1939, Blumer (1939) defined social movements as 'collective enterprises to establish a new order of life. They have their inception in the condition of unrest, and derive their motive power on one hand, from wishes and hopes for a new scheme of living'. This was applicable more to the traditional social movements as well as modern Western societies. Following this, Gerlach and Hine (1970) have identified five key factors for a collective to become a movement. These are: (a) a segmented cellular organization with units having various personal, structural and ideological ties, (b) face-to-face recruitment, (c) personal commitment to the new set of values, (d) an ideology codifying values, goals and conceptual framework and (e) real or perceived opposition from society at large or from the established order within which the movement has arisen.

The last factor is a negative explanation of a positive state of affairs. The resistance to change is a Western characteristic not applicable to the social movements of the developing and underdeveloped countries.

Hence these factors were found fully applicable to the Wall Street movement as evidenced by the evaluators of the same. Politics and its role remained obscure in this definition. Tarrow (1988) has observed that the research on social movements in both political science and sociology in Western Europe and America was radically renewed by the movements of the 1960s. The 1970s saw the growth of the resource mobilization approach in the United States and of the new movements approach in Western Europe.

Politics remained obscured in both. West (2004) has stated that these movements referred to a group of social movements which had played a significant and progressive role in Western societies from the late 1960s. After the effects of the Second World War and after the transition into the post-war era, these new movements began to occur in Western society. 'New' typically refers to the new concern with issues other than class. This occurred once the post-war stability became ingrained and stagnant that the Western societies began to look at issues beyond rooting out the axis powers and creating a democratic Europe for improvement of livelihood. The environmental, ecological, feminist and green movements resulted, but the role of political ideology was yet to be restored.

The New movements theory of Western Europe was followed by the resource mobilization theory of the United States. According to Coleman (1988), open and affluent societies provide more favourable conditions or contentious groups to thrive making protest more common. The existence of many non-governmental organizations and civil society groups provide the crucial variable linking dissatisfaction to political action and allowing the acquiring of social and organizational skills, raising funds, increasing membership and using communication and awareness-raising strategies to promote their goals. During times of political stress, larger cycles of protest result. Closed authoritarian societies have the presence of latent networks, proto organizations and community leaders and organizers who can provide the basis for social mobilization. The New Media compensates for the lack of resources in such cases. The study of social movements during the 1980s restored politics to its central role in the origins, dynamics and outcomes of these movements with the concepts of the political opportunity structure and cycles of protest. Quoting Paul Wilkinson, the author has stated that social movements are clearly different from historical movements, tendencies of trends. Such tendencies and trends and the influence of unconscious or irrational factors may be crucial in illuminating the problems of social movement. However, a social movement must evince a minimal degree of organization and commitment and active participation on the part of the members. Objectives, ideology, programmes, leadership and organization are important, but they vary from very unstructured Messianic and subaltern movements alongside the organized peasant movements.

SOCIAL MEDIA AND SOCIAL MOVEMENTS

McCaughey and Ayers (2003), in their editorial article, have stated that the activists 'not only incorporated the internet into the repertoire but also have changed substantially what counts as activism, what counts as community, collective identity, democratic space and political strategy'. According to Van Laer and Van Aelst (2010) two roles of the internet count. First, it facilitates existing action forms making it possible to reach more people more easily in a time span that was unthinkable before. Second, it creates or adopts new tools of activism. This double impact has provided improved opportunities to engage in social and political action. The internet makes it possible that the civic groups with little resources could mobilize support and public attention more easily and independently than in the past.

For Cammaerts (2015), the internet provides opportunities for disadvantaged groups to self-represent themselves, communicate independently and organize transregional and transnational. There are two types of internet-related social processes: (a) internet-based practices and (b) internet-supported practices.

For Seebaluck (2014), the social media prompts instantaneous participating dialogue, enables the dissemination of huge volumes of information, allows mobilization for participation, facilitates the reaching of larger crowds at relatively high speed, increases the potential for the social movement organizations to become more autonomous and influential, generates instant modes of mediated exchange, plays a crucial role in mitigating the in-group coordination and interaction problems and exhibiting a positive impact on the probability of conflict occurrence, causes regime change through the pressure of social protests leading to upheavals, shapes political action through the social network existing in the virtual world and accentuates, through its expansion, the potential for increased social conflict.

Clark (2012) has observed that the 'social movements occur in an age in which digital communication technologies have created new possibilities for the world to bear witness and for activists to connect and organise themselves'.

For the author what is particularly intriguing

is the ability citizens now have to act and enact change within their own world amidst their social 'bubbles'. These bubbles that many people paid themselves immersed in a daily range from their Facebook and Twitter accounts to the video library on YouTube, or the even expanding blog-sphere. Indeed the new tool of social media which has grown in relevance and worldwide popularity over the past few years has arguably helped people without a voice to get one.

Valenzuela (2013) has tested three explanations for the link between social media use and political participation:

1. Social media is a source for news (information).
2. Social Media expresses political opinions (opinion expression).
3. Social Media enables timing causes and finding mobilizing information (activism).

Social media, for the author, enables social movements to reach critical mass through online individual networks, provides group identity through multiple channels, facilitates 'newsfeed', generates common concerns and builds member trust. The use of social media for news consumption, opinion expression and activism mediates the relationship between frequency and social media and protest behaviour.

For Lopes (2014), social media counts as the fastest and cheapest way to mobilize the resources necessitated by the social movement.

According to Benford and Snow (2000), the internet and social media are tools for creating imaginary solidarities which magically aid real solidarity. A social movement is not simply an object, it is primarily a process and should be studied as a historical phenomenon in a span of time and as events. Social media is implicated in the making of strategies of political mobilization and the patterns of protest diffusion as well as in influencing individual protest engagement. However, rich empirical data are needed to establish the causal relationship between the new media and protest mobilization. This leads to the case studies.

Since the autocrats use persecution, repression and propaganda to silence opposition, the citizens in such cases face incomplete information about their fellow citizen's attitudes toward the regime and their disposition to revolt. Nevertheless, the civilian–led anti–government protests did occur under authoritarianism of all kinds and got spread even across state boundaries during the last three decades of the 20th century and the first decade of the current century in different regions of the globe. For Mc Faul, the fourth wave of democratization has commenced.

As part of the Arab Spring, the Tunisian uprising led to the ouster of President Zine el Abidine Ben Ali in January 2011. Breuer (2012) and Breuer et al. (2015) have correlated the stages of the revolution with those of the spread of the internet and social media and identified the significant causation of the latter. The said revolution was born out of a broad coalition of social forces that united an alienated intellectual elite with the rural poor and urban middle class in opposition to the extremely authoritarian regime, the contribution of the ICT had shown the following three dimensions:

1. It facilitated the formation of networks of digital activists who challenged the monopoly of the state control of the public sphere.
2. It disseminated censored information on human rights violations by the state on the one hand and the magnitude of anti-regime protests on the other. This information enabled the mobilization for collective action based on shared grievances and to overcome the barrier of fear associated with the protest under authoritarian.
3. It enabled the formation of a national collective identity by providing elements of emotional mobilization.

Eltantawy and Wiest (2011) have stressed how social media provided additional resources for the resource-poor actors who led social protest movements, like the one in Egypt, and, thereby, contributed to the sustainability of the latter distinctively. Beyond the widely accepted impact of the internet and social media, the specific factor centring around the new media found attested in the Egyptian protest were:

- The early Egyptian blogosphere first attracted a domestic audience and later paved the way for Facebook, Flicker, Twitter and cellular phones;
- The space provided by the social media for the activists within and outside Egypt to interact;
- The martyrdom of Khalid said and the consequent emergence of Facebook groups like 'we are all Khalid said';
- The inspiring role of the Nobel Peace Prize holder Baradei's Facebook pages coupled with those of the National Association for Change offering a fear erasing polemic against the regime;
- The Facebook movement of 6 April 6 2008, pioneering the way for January 2011 protest;
- The Cebeladi beladi (our country, our country) call of the women activists began;
- The multiple Facebook pages of young activists;
- The social media voice of the exiled revolutionary Omav Afifi;
- The social media guidance of the Tunisian revolutionaries and the success of the Tunisian revolution;
- The crucial messages of the social media communicated during the blackout internet days (25 Jan and 27 Feb 2011); and
- The videos and images of the first-day protest communicated through Facebook, Twitter and blogs promoting emotional integration. The Tahrir (Revolution) square protest could retain its revolutionary character owing to these specific factors.

Another enlightening contribution to this has been the study by Tufekci and Wilson (2012) reinforcing the contents of the first-mentioned one. How the connectivity infrastructure of the media offered a counter to the durable authoritarianism of Hosni Mubarak and resulted in his resignation on 25 January 2011 has been illustrated.

The comparative study of Tusa (2013) has been quite significant with respect to social media and its mediatory power to spur political protest through online platforms. The study has explored the effect of the social media and internet-based communication or computer-mediated communication (CMC) on social movements by looking at two major processes of social movements framing and organizing in the Egyptian protest of December 2010–January 2011, called the Facebook Revolution and Iranian protest of 2009 called the Twitter revolution. Both the protests witnessed the use of tweets, blogs and internet posts. The constant use of injustice framed by the Egyptians during the years leading to the protest in a narrative that depicted Mubarak as the source of all trouble was crucial for creating the revolutionary movement (Rane & Salem, 2012). On the other hand, the Iranians relied on CMC for organizational purposes and were engaged in far fewer framings. They relayed information, not emotion.

Twitter, being limited to 140 characters, was not a convenient medium for fitting the events into a narrative. Further, the Iranian government had blocked Facebook and the dissenting blogs during the period preceding the protest. The Egyptian movement was benefitted by contrast in the use of the internet and framing and in the final emergence of the persuasive master frame or prognostic frame. The Iranian protest failed because of the exclusive reliance on Twitter for resource mobilization, the insignificant number of Twitter users, their urban base and the limitations of Twitter itself. The local Arabic language texts and narratives in Egypt were a significant development.

Valenzuela (2013) observed that, during the 'Winter discontent' in Chile, the social media and internet garnered powerful popular support for different social issues like education, environment and rehabilitation reconstruction involving a variety of interest groups. It led to the Santiago protest for education and the `Patagonia without Dams' protest to halt the hydroelectric dams, which forced the government to introduce full-blown educational reforms, allocate billions in fresh public funds by putting the dam projects on standby. If the voices of the citizens were heard, then Facebook and Twitter had a crucial part to play.

Chowdhury (2008) observed that the role of the internet in Burma's Saffron Revolution has been quite significant on many counts. On the one hand, Burma has presented an interesting case of the role of the internet in the protest and transnational democracy movements and on the other hand failure of the protest to lead to political change in contrast to the protest movements elsewhere. Here was the case of a successful authoritarian regime whose sustenance demanded historical scrutiny. In September 2007, the Saffron Revolution took place. Widespread protests erupted in which the popularly revered Buddhist monks participated for which the latter was tied to the trees, beaten and disrobed. The All Burma Monks' Alliance then led the large peaceful street protests of citizens with the priests in saffron robes condemning the autocracy. Mass arrests, torture and murder resulted. This phase was marked by the emergence of the new media. Unlike the 8888 uprising, also known as the People Power Uprising and the 1988 uprising, the Saffron Revolution could catch global attention as bloggers and digital activists flooded cyberspace with grainy images and videos of the processions. Citizens took pictures and videos on their mobile phones and sent digital files across the border to be uploaded. The global impact of the new media could not be controlled even during the total information blockade for nearly two weeks.

But the uprising could not lead to political change. Two causes are generally attributed to the failure: the authoritarian control over the internet operation and the diplomatic relations of Burma with India, China and Thailand, which offered immunity against the UN restrictions. The geographical, locational and political climate in Burma provided the ground for testing the resource mobilization theory.

Harlow (2012) has provided a unique case of the social media organizing online activism and moving offline, encouraging civic and political participation in the context of an underdeveloped country with diverse communities. President Alvaro Colom had set into process his autocratic authoritarian regime with left postures like General Ne (of Myanmar). Afterthe video exposure of lawyer Rodrigo Rosenberg's murder, however, the Guatemalans turned to online social media like Facebook and Twitter and began, changing their homepage statuses to call for Colom's ouster and justice for Rosenberg. Through the Facebook pages, the users joined forces initiating an online movement that moved offline promoting a series of large-scale protests. The National Palace square protest occurred on 17 August 2009 with 50,000 protestors and continued for weeks. A petition-making campaign was organized through Facebook and Twitter. Rosenberg's murder was ultimately hushed up (President Colom was exonerated later), but Guatemala showed the way for an online movement creating offline activism.

Ferreira (2016) has studied the contrasting media role in three protests in Brazil. Under the military dictatorship, social mobilization occurred during the 1960s demanding freedom of speech. Mass media was the only source of communication and reporting on the issues. Against heavy odds, mass media contributed to putting an end to military rule. Later on, the 1992 protests were against corruption. Again, mass media played a crucial role in laying the ground for the impeachment of President Fernando Color de Mello. Then commenced the mass protest against state apathy, non-development, promotion of private interests and lack of funds for education, infrastructure and healthcare. The material demands of daily life were the major factor behind the Vinegar Movement of 2013 which commenced on 20 June 2013 with one million people taking over the streets of Rio de Janeiro. Vinegar was used as a safeguard against tear gas shelling. Then mass media was led by the fear that democratization might limit the powers of the media companies in political terms. Hence, it retreated and ultimately resorted to delegitimizing the movement. It exposed its vulnerability to political pressure. It was for social media to contribute to social mobilization and grassroots integration. It was the go-to means of communication for the protestors. Twitter carried the protest to a larger audience under the 'come to the street' and 'free Brazil' tweets.

Such social media-based protests should begin at a physical public place to organize ideas and action plans so that social media could aid in spreading. The 'black blocs' were responsible for violence and they alone were portrayed in the mass media. The resulting violent scenario forced the protestors to fall back. The social media aiding mass movements against relative deprivation even during periods of economic stability was vindicated. A similar case was that of Africa. According to liberation technology theory, the mobile phones and internet, thanks to the opportunity they offer for two-way multiway mass communication and their low cost and decentralized open-access nature have the potential to foster citizen's political activism especially when civic forms of political participation are de facto or lawfully prevented. The spectacular African riots of the first decade of the century fostered by social media were indicative of the grievance structure, even during periods of economic growth, over relative deprivation.

Occupy Wall Street Movement of the United States would ever inspire the social movement on the globe transcending national frontiers, cultures, social institutions and specificity of social protests. It is the guiding star for the globalization era.

On 17 September 2011, the social movement 'Occupy Wall Street' began. For Clark (2012), this became the core of a movement that would lead to the ubiquitous term 'occupy', a rallying call against corporate greed, economic disparity and political corruption (and in later stages police brutality). Zuccotti Park was the headquarters of the movement's encampment. This was outside the New York Stock Exchange. The years preceding the movement had become a dark period staging the worst financial crisis since the time of the Great Depression. The citizens had become fed up with the social and economic inequality and the relationship between the powerful corporations and government and their ability to sway political agenda. 'We are the 99%' was the title of the mobilization, for this was the proportion of the population on the back end of the economic growth ladder and was taxed unjustly in comparison to the upper echelons of the realizing per cent. The income inequality and distribution of wealth was a salient point that the activists made for their rallying call. The encampment followed the massive march of about 5,000 citizens from Times Square to Wall Street. There was no real teacher or spokesperson. The overall message was the dissatisfaction with the government, the elite and the power of corporations having a grasp over legislation and the plight of the 99 per cent. 'Occupy Wall Street' was a non-violent social movement set up outside the financial capital of America with voices of people wanting to be heard the outcry of their deprivation. The communication tools for a majority of the activists at the Occupy Wall Street Movement as well as those who had begun to champion the social movement were poured out via the social media platforms. The message from thence was that 'We need a media polis'. The interacting capacity of new media has been hailed as a new form of the public sphere. The Wall Street Movement is considered to be a media event that linked public sphere metropolis and movement relationship to media. 'All eyes are fixed at the ceremonial centre through which each nuclear cell is connected to all the rest. Social integration of the highest order is thus achieved via Mass communication.' One would be reminded of the 'We are all Khalid said' Facebook proclamation of Egyptian revolutionaries.

Padmanabhan (2015) had also summed up the global and native social media-related movements and dealt with their impact on the sociopolitical interactions and civic engagements, besides human rights and environmental protection.

THE CASE OF *JALLIKATTU*

Jallikattu—a traditional sport of taming the fierce bull by overcoming its resistance with physical arm power—is connected with the use of the animal for ploughing agricultural fields, as attested in Classical Tamil literature. In contemporary times, however, it is a ritual being conducted with the bulls zealously brought up and specially fed for the sport by peasant holds, even against the backdrop of their economic constraints, has become a religious and cultural stamp. This ritual cult has had its dynamic origin from the primitive pastoral ecotypic (*Mullai*—one of the landscapes mentioned in the sangam literature, adjoining forests) life of the Tamils which necessitated the domestication of animals caught alive in hunting. With the origin of plough cultivation, the importance of the bull became more evident and taming it turned into a ritual, imparting among the peasant youth the spirit of valour and confidence required for the conduct of plough agriculture.

This popular Tamil cultural tradition has contextualized the phenomena intrinsic to it as rituals often with religious overtones. The spheres of the festival, valour display, ceremonies and cult practices have been no exceptions. It is associated with 'Pongal' (harvest) festival and conducted with varying degrees of divine invocation, social gathering and exhibition of physical prowess. The polarity associated with the ritual has a historical significance explaining the historical synthesis of a proto content with historical form.

Jallikkattu has to be perceived not merely as a sport but as a community ritual observed by the peasants in their struggle against the odds with the magical belief of redemption. Its specificity in selected places remains accommodated within the generality of observance of the 'Pongal' festival as a thanksgiving occasion. Hence, it is associated with the joy of the festive mood of the Tamils as a whole. The British could understand it and allow it. To fragment it from the Pongal galore, identifying it as violent and branding it as animal torture, on any count, would only be a smack of a non-peasant and alien anti-people ideology imported from the West. Moreover, the *Jallikattu* ritual has a historical and sociocultural legacy.`

The striking difference between the bull-taming of early pastoral life and those of contemporaneity has been that earlier the bulls caught from the wild were ferocious while the contemporary bulls have inherited generations of domestication and humanization. The ferocity of the ancient animals was very offensive and antagonistic while that of the present-day bulls is quite defensive. They are let into the sports field by their masters and then they run speedily to reach their masters for security at the end place, only overcoming the pull to halt them with ferocious postures.

The taming valour of the ancient times was warrior-like making a contrast with the overcoming fervour of those engaged in modern 'Jallikattu'. Another difference has been discernible with respect to the incentives offered. The 'Aayar' girls of the ancient society would not prefer to marry one who had not participated in *Jallikattu*. The application of the term 'taming the bull' which one commonly observed in journalistic or periodical coverages does not explain the historicity, for 'overcoming the bull' (from running away) would be the correct contemporary register in 'Jallikattu' description. The Jallikattu Movement (2017) in Tamil Nadu has been a social movement as it could be broadly classified as a movement that primarily took the form of non-institutionalized collective political action striving for political or social change. The movement has also been social media-led activism. It originated as a peasant cultural movement and later on got metamorphosed into a mass democratic movement. It has been episodic with the transformation of the sectarian peasant cultural movement of rural Tamil Nadu into a mass movement with urbanized leadership, the movement has presented itself as a process in the real sense of the term.

Jallikattu protest of 2017, also known as the pro-Jallikattu movement or 'Thai puratchi', refers to the larger apolitical youth groups protesting in several locations across the state of Tamil Nadu during January 2017, with support from other parts of India by periodic protests and also from across the border of the country. The main vigour of the protest is against the Supreme Court's order to ban *Jallikattu*. It was banned by the Supreme Court of India based on the objection by the animal rights activists, People for the Ethical Treatment of Animals (PETA) citing cruelty to animals and the Animal Welfare Board of India for violating the Prevention of Cruelty to Animals Act (PCA). The climax of the protest started by occupying sit-ins at Marina Beach, Chennai, along with a large support from the ground across the state. The protests were spontaneous and had no specific organizers. It was apolitical, seemingly anarchic and messianic. The protest was initially started using social media apps. The memes played a very important role in spreading the message across the youth even with satire and humour.

To study the Jallikattu movement, one requires pre-exposure to the operation dynamic of contemporary social movements with reference to their grievance structures, organizational status, resource mobilization position and mobilizing structures. The question as to how a sporadic protest in a few pockets could gain momentum both in qualitative and quantitative terms cannot be answered without a critical perception of the literature concerning these four areas. Jallikattu and the movement associated with it have been widely and regularly featured in both the mass and social media, but critical and creative analyses have been quite lacking. The works in vernacular have simply narrated the protest in cultural terms and have been at least bothered to link the movement to the political economy of the country, not to speak of the global involvement of the cartels and their mouthpieces. Especially in the context of delegitimizing frames of the mass media presented at the climax has helped to demonize the movement and frustrate positive appraisals of the letter.

Raja and Velayutham (2017) stated that Jallikattu protests have shed light on the global diaspora identity of the Tamils expressed through the new media on the 'Jallikattu' movement. For them 'combining new two emerging trends of diaspora and New media with special reference to Jallikattu, the present study aims to find out as to how the Tamil Diaspora community intends to look at their identity through the new media, through the protest for Jallikattu'. Analysing selected studies of the new media, the authors have made explicit as to how the diaspora had sought identity through solidarity with the homeland Tamil cause and drawn global attention towards the delegitimizing state action against the people through police excesses during the peak hours. The second aspect becomes crucial in the context of the negative framing by the native mass media on that count.

Kalaiyarasan (2017) has stated that the movement had acquired an iconic place in the history of Tamil Nadu for many reasons. The protesters saw the Jallikattu ban as an attack on Tamil culture and identity. Thus, Jallikattu became a symbol of Tamil pride. The forced evident end was due to the ire of the political establishment both at the state and the Centre sensing sociopolitical repercussions in such mobilization. The movement symbolized vibrant social media-led activism. This vibrant social media movement needed an educated class, shared vocabularies and a cultural language to connect, communicate and mobilize the public.

The youth pioneered the Jallikattu movement, caused and motivated its spread everywhere throughout Tamil Nadu, across the country and transnational space carried it to its climax and finally clinched the issue. All these affected apolitically and without projecting anybody as the leader. For the first time in Tamil history, a mass movement was generated within a very short time and without seeking the cooperation of a political party or trade union or sociopolitical organization but forcing them all to react in order to avoid marginalization. This was a puzzle that the orthodox political pundits and social theorists suddenly had to confront in January 2017. There were many other related puzzles too which confronted them from many angles cumulatively.

First, the students did not conduct formal strikes and campus raids but simply sought the identity as youth, freely merged with all their counterparts cutting across age, literacy status, caste, community and the religion and mobilized at common points. Moreover, they did not schedule the mobilization as a leisure-time activity but were well turned for the sustained protracted struggle braving all odds. Third, they were well received by the general people and the usual apathy towards student struggle was gone. Finally, politicians were rudely puzzled and shocked to know that the youth were well within the social interaction with clear social awareness and disciplined praxis as against the farmer's cherished prejudices of indifference and ideological bankruptcy. When the struggle galloped, all of them could realize that social media had stepped in to fill in the vacuum created by the apathetic politics and the sectarian interests and democratize the communication network.

This movement can be studied and summed up under three heads: (a) The initial spark of the youth mobilization facilitated by the social media and covered by the mass media during the first 12 days of January; (b) The Alanganallur peasant-youth polemic commencing from the sixteenth encapsulating strategies of the peasant warfare and (c) The Marina People's movement commencing from the seventeenth focusing on an unprecedented mass Satyagraha. As such, it was a movement that only lasted for nearly 15 days, but it made a tremendous impact on the psyche of the people in making them believe that mere passivity would not suffice and that resistance would alone re-humanize them against being dehumanized.

CONCLUSION

Social media revolution has overtaken the past in a significant way as to cause an unprecedented mobilization of the youth, enable the latter to seize the reins of social vanguardship and the utilization of their creative energies for the conscientization of their fellow citizens. First and foremost, social media has filled in the vacuum created by fossilized formal politics which has only frozen the issues instead of energizing them to get resolved. Second, it has revolutionized social communication with its low-cost facility. Third, it has democratized social participation by facilitating interpersonal communication access transcending all the social barriers which are physical and act as stumbling blocks against social mingling. Fourth, it has made instant social reaction possible where formal organizational action would normally demand time or may even miss it, too. Fifth, social media operates through the popular communication codes intelligible to all thereby offering an alternative to the dominance of the elitist mode. Sixth, it forms the real basis for a thousand flowers to bloom. No formal movement, organization or political party has such operation space for democratic interactions. Seventh, because of this, the youth attain better enlightenment of the social dynamic, which is often hushed up, distorted or obfuscated by the formal movements of all categories. Eighth, the romanticizing effect of social media has a positive dimension. It has the ability to portray the often ignored and scorned as trivia in their real seriousness which, otherwise, confront the formal organizations later in their cumulative form as hurdles or even as catastrophes. Ninth, the youth have acquired the crucial capability to counter the vested interests and enlighten the people and clear their doubts on burning issues, thereby, preventing unnecessary head-on collisions among people. In this aspect, usually, before the formal organizations reach the people, the clash erupts. The pace of the social media reach is incomparably greater. Finally, by opinion moulding through interactions, the youth are able to create an atmosphere of values and they are truth-loving. Since the youth are full-time users of social media, their social status and role have attained unprecedentedly greater heights.

The review of contemporary world movements and their signifi-cance in the world context reveals the pivotal role played by social media in mass mobilization. In every social movement analysed, the upsurge and the ultimate political agenda are unearthed and in the pro-cess, the active role of social media in effecting such mass mobilization was also brought to light. In conclusion, it can be said that in the era of globalization and a boundaryless world, the movement of people in search of opportunities is inevitable, and the world is more inter-dependent now than ever. In such a global context, the influence of social media is imperative and unavoidable. Hence, it becomes crucial for social science researchers, especially media scholars, to continually explore the efficacies of what people do with social media.

REFERENCES

Benford, R. D., & Snow, D. A. (2000). Framing processes and social movements: An overview and assessment. *Annual Review of Sociology, 26*(1), 611–639.
Blumer, H. (1939). Collective behaviour. In Park, R. E., & Reuter, E. B. (Eds.), *An Outline of the Principles of Sociology* (p. 175). New York: Barnes & Noble.

Breuer, A., Landman, T., & Farquhar, D. (2015). Social media and protest mobilization: Evidence from the Tunisian Revolution. *Democratization*, *22*(4), 764–792.

Breuer, A. (2012). The role of social media in mobilizing political protest: Evidence from the Tunisian Revolution. German Development Institute (Discussion Paper), (10), 18600441.

Cammaerts, B. (2015). Social media and activism. *The International Encyclopedia of Digital Communication and Society*, 1–8. https://doi.org/10.1002/9781118767771. wbiedcs083

Chowdhury, M. (2008). The role of the Internet in Burma's Saffron Revolution. Berkman Center research publication, 2008–8.

Clark, E. (2012). Social movement & social media: A qualitative study of Occupy Wall Street. (Dissertation). Retrieved from http://urn.kb.se/resolve?urn=ur n:nbn:se:sh:diva-16787

Coleman, J. S. (1988). Social capital in the creation of human capital. The *American Journal of Sociology*, 94, S95–S120.

Conover, M. D., Ferrara, E., Menczer, F., & Flammini, A. (2013). The digital evolution of Occupy Wall Street. *PLOS one*, *8*(5), e64679.

Diani, M. (1992). The concept of social movement. *The Sociological Review*, *40*(1), 1–25.

Eltantawy, N., & Wiest, J. B. (2011). The Arab Spring| social media in the Egyptian Revolution: Reconsidering resource mobilization theory. *International Journal of Communication*, *5*(18), 1207–1224.

Ferreira, C. J. (2016). The role of social media during the Brazilian protests of 2013. Research project, Summit Institutional Repository, Department of Communication, Art & Technology, School of Communication, Simon Fraser University (pp. 45–47). Retrieved from https://ir.lib.sfu.ca/item/16735

Gainous, J., & Wagner, K. M. (2013). *Tweeting to power: The social media revolution in American politics*. Oxford University Press.

Gerlach, L. P., & Hine, V. H. (1970). People, power, change: Movements of social transformation. *American Journal of Sociology*, *78*(1). https://doi.org/10.1086/225315

Harlow, S. (2012). Social media and social movements: Facebook and an online Guatemalan justice movement that moved offline. *New Media & Society*, *14*(2), 225–243.

Kalaiyarasan, A. (2017). Politics of jallikattu. *Economic & Political Weekly*, *52*(6), 11.

Lopes, A. R. (2014). The impact of social media on social movements: The new opportunity and mobilizing structure. *Journal of Political Science Research*, *4*(1), 1–23.

McCaughey, M., & Ayers, M. D. (Eds.). (2003). *Cyberactivism: Online activism in theory and practice*. Psychology Press.

Oliver, P. E., Cadena-Roa, J., & Strawn, K. D. (2003). Emerging trends in the study of protest and social movements. *Research in Political Sociology*, *12*(1), 213–244.

Padmanabhan, T. (2015). A study of social media and mass mobilization with special reference to Facebook in India. (Unpublished doctoral dissertation). Bharathiar University, Coimbatore, India.

Rane, H., & Salem, S. (2012). Social media, social movements and the diffusion of ideas in the Arab uprisings. *Journal of International Communication, 18*(1), 97–111.

Raja, V. R. R. & Velayutham, C. (2017). The new media and Tamil diaspora identity: A case study of Jallikattu protests. *International Journal of Current Research, 9*(09), 576.

Seebaluck, A. (2014). *How social media affects the dynamics of protest.* [Thesis, Naval Postgraduate School Monterey].

Snow, D. A., and Benford, R. D. (1988). Ideology, frame resonance, and participant mobilization. *International Social Movement Research, 1*(1), 197–217.

Statista. (2021, April 7). Global digital population as of January 2021. Statista.com. Retrieved from https://www.statista.com/statistics/617136/digital-population-worldwide/

Statista. (2021a, January 28). Number of social network users worldwide from 2017 to 2025. Statista.com. Retrieved from https://www.statista.com/statistics/278414/number-of-worldwide-social-network-users/

Stelzner, M. A. (2014). 2014 Social Media Marketing Industry Report, Sixth annual report of the Social Media Examiner, (pp 1–40). Retrieved from https://www.socialmediaexaminer.com/social-media-marketing-industry-report-2014/

Swank, E. (2000). In newspapers we trust? P.G. Coy (Ed.) *Research in Social Movements, Conflicts and Change,* (pp. 27–52). Emerald Group Publishing Limited.

Tarrow, S. (1988). National politics and collective action: Recent theory and research in Western Europe and the United States. *Annual Review of Sociology, 14*(1), 421–440.

Tilly, C. (1984). Social movements and national politics. C. Bright, & S. Harding, (Eds.) *Statemaking and Social Movements,* (pp. 297–317). University of Michigan Press.

Tufekci, Z., & Wilson, C. (2012). Social media and the decision to participate in political protest: Observations from Tahrir Square. *Journal of Communication, 62*(2), 363–379.

Tusa, F. (2013). How social media can shape a protest movement: The cases of Egypt in 2011 and Iran in 2009. *Arab Media and Society, 17,* 1–19.

Valenzuela, S. (2013). Unpacking the use of social media for protest behavior: The roles of information, opinion expression, and activism. *American Behavioral Scientist, 57*(7), 920–942.

Van Laer, J., & Van Aelst, P. (2009). Cyber-protest and civil society: The internet and action repertoires in social movements. In Yvonne J. & Majid Y. (Eds.), *Handbook on Internet Crime,* 230254.

Van Laer, J., & Van Aelst, P. (2010). Internet and social movement action repertoires: Opportunities and limitations. *Information, Communication & Society, 13*(8), 1146–1171.

Westd, D. (2004). New social movements. In Gerald F. G. & Chandran K. (Eds.), *Handbook of Political Theory,* (pp. 265–276). SAGE Publications.

Chapter 8

Use and Misuse of Social Media in Disaster Relief and Rehabilitation

Binish Parveen and Nikhil Kumar Gouda

INTRODUCTION

Social media are 'a group of Internet-based applications that build on the ideological and technological foundations of Web 2.0, and that allow the creation and exchange of user-generated content' (Kaplan & Haenlein, 2010). It is emerging as an important technology for communication during disasters. The Kerala floods damaged the state's traditional communication network lock, stock and barrel. Till the networks were re-established, social media played its role to fill the void to a large extent especially in its disaster management efforts. It became one of the popular media among victims, government agencies, NGOs, rescue teams, activists and many more who used it for disseminating and accessing information required for rescuing people affected by the floods (Mohan, 2018). Social media used during the floods were WhatsApp, Facebook and Twitter. Volunteers and people around the world used various hashtags, for instance, #StandWithKerala, #DoForKerala, #SOSKerala, #SaveChengannurCampaign, #KeralaFloods, #KeralaRains, etc., in their posts to work under the same theme and made their contributions (Sidhardhan, 2018; Trends Desk, 2019) to the cause.

Kerala—*God's own country*— is considered as one of the most successful and developed states of India in terms of various development indicators, such as literacy, life expectancy, infant mortality among others defying its susceptibility to natural hazards such as landslides, drought, floods, lightning, forest fires, coastal erosion and high wind speed. The state has been experiencing devastating floods continuously for the last few years. In 2018, floods hit seven districts of the state including Alappuzha, Ernakulam, Idukki, Kottayam, Pathanamthitta, Thrissur and Wayanad. It had affected 5.4 million people, displaced 1.4 million and 433 people lost their lives. It caused great damage to agriculture and infrastructure. The Post Disaster Needs Assessment estimates the total damage and loss of ₹26,720 crore (UNDP, 2018). The flash floods had destroyed the roads submerging several villages and shut down Kochi airport (HumanityRoad, 2018). Devastating flood repeats again in 2019, affecting the northern districts of the state, that is, Wayanad, Malappuram and Kozhikode in which around 121 people lost their lives, displacing 13,000 people and many were injured. Once again communication and transportation services were affected resulting in the Kochi International Airport being closed and some districts were placed under red alert (Kambli, 2020; Trends Desk, 2019). With the loss of traditional communication channels during the floods in Kerala, social media rose to the occasion and thus helped rescue around 1.5 lakh people in 2018 (Firstpost, 2018).

LITERATURE REVIEW

Social media being a relatively new phenomenon on the horizon of communication is emerging as a powerful tool to cope with disaster management (Babu et al., 2019). People spend time on social media for getting information about weather conditions, safety measures, traffic conditions, location sharing and other disasters (Varghese & Yadukrishnan, 2019). Social media was a supplemental listening platform that helped in each phase when the floods struck in Chennai and Kerala in 2015 and 2018 respectively. Different categories of contents were shared through social media for rescue, relief and healthcare (Rajendiran, 2018). People actively participated and collaborated to disseminate and assess information during emergencies. People used different innovative tools for communicating information during emergencies. Previously, emergency managers used one-way communication but now they are using information that is public generated. Social media was extensively used for various activities such as search and rescue, availability of first aid, victim evacuation, online help, providing information about disaster preparedness, warnings, requests for help, survival response, current situation, donations, well wishes, rehabilitation, social unity among others (Pandey & Natarajan S, 2016; Simon, Goldberg & Adini, 2015).

During the floods, mobile phones and social media were used as tools of citizen journalism. People were helping in rescue efforts by collecting, verifying and sharing information (Paul & Sosale, 2019) particularly WhatsApp and Facebook.

Social media started reverse agenda-setting by flagging off issues that were taken up later by the mainstream media (Bhuvana & Aram, 2019). Similar activities were witnessed during the Uttarakhand flood disaster of 2013, where social media played a vital role in information sharing for relief and rebuilding efforts. Online campaigns were launched which helped in finding out missing people. Online pages and hashtags were made and put to use for the purpose (Kaur, 2018).

The study by Cheong and Cheong in 2013 identified active online communities for crisis communication during the Australian floods in 2010–2011. Twitter was actively used by local authorities, political personalities, social media volunteers, traditional media reporters, people from not-for-profit, humanitarian and community associations. Four categories of social media users were recognized, that is, innovative, reactive, responsive and proactive users (Simon, Goldberg & Adini, 2015). Adding to the literature, Mauroner and Heudorfer in 2016 investigated the social media actions taken by volunteer groups and aid organizations during the floods in Germany and during Typhoon Haiyan in the Philippines in 2013. The findings showed the volunteer groups and aid organizations used social media to a large extent during disasters.

A Twitter analysis of the Chennai floods of 2015 revealed the spatio-temporal distribution of negative emotions before, during and after the floods. Negative emotions, for example, tweets containing anger, disgust, fear and sadness were highest when the disaster hit the city and reduced with the flood. Identification of negative emotions will help to prioritize the rescue and relief operations to deal with the emotional health issues of the affected (Karmegam & Mappillairaju, 2020).

FRAMEWORKS

To analyse social media usage in disaster management, authors have identified and adopted various frameworks. One study (Kaewkitipong, Chen & Ractham, 2012) adopted a social media-based crisis management framework and structuration theory which focuses on three phases of social media usage for managing crisis during Thailand floods that lasted for seven months. First, social media was used before floods for mitigation and preparedness. Second, it was used during floods for response and at last after floods for recovery. People collaborated among themselves for quick and efficient communication. Communication flows from agencies to agencies, agencies to communities and communities to communities. Houston et al. in 2014 wrote about a functional framework that can be used to facilitate the creation of disaster social media tools, implementation process and scientific study of social media effects. In addition to this, social media is used for listening to public debate, situation monitoring, integration of social media into emergency planning and crisis management, crowd-sourcing, creating social cohesion, promoting therapeutic initiatives, enhancing research (Alexander, 2014), monitoring open-source data of situational awareness, encouraging citizens' and organizations' communication, monitoring data on time were strategies for situation awareness (Wukich, 2015). Another study (Simon, Goldberg, & Adini, 2015) discusses the uses of social media in emergencies.

Aim

To review the role of social media in disaster rescue, relief and rehabilitation works of disaster management.

Objectives

1. To review the role social media played during Kerala Floods 2018 and 2019
2. To describe the social media platforms and pages used during Kerala flash floods for rescue, relief and rehabilitation
3. To identify the innovative tools of social media used during Kerala Floods 2018 and 2019

Methodology

Research through literature review lays the foundation for knowledge furtherance, development of new and existing theories along with finding the gaps for future research (Webster & Watson, 2002). The researchers in this study opted for secondary data sources in order to find out the role of social media during the floods in Kerala in 2018 and 2019. The data collected from previous literature, online news articles, websites, reports were used to analyse the role played by social media in disaster management efforts. News articles from the months of August 2018 to September 2018 and August 2019 were used for the study.

POSITIVE ROLE OF SOCIAL MEDIA

A detailed secondary analysis showed that three applications were used extensively during and after the floods—WhatsApp, Facebook and Twitter and to some extent Google Maps.

WhatsApp

Kerala, having one of the most literate populations in the country, used social media skilfully during the phases of floods (Ayyappan, 2018). Volunteers and activists realized early the power of WhatsApp platform as a powerful and effective communication tool for such a scenario. Several volunteers came together through WhatsApp groups for disseminating information for rescue and relief. Helpline numbers were made public in the groups for the ease of stranded people seeking help. Several volunteers served as part of many WhatsApp groups.

They helped the victims by being in touch with the rescue teams through social media. One volunteer, *Johann Binny Kuruvilla* joined five WhatsApp groups and sent his contact number for any emergency mentioning that he could contact police, army and navy personnel. Immediately, he received around 300 calls from people asking for help (Thiagarajan, 2018). Through WhatsApp groups, volunteers came to know the exact nature of requirements at different relief camps on a real-time basis and supplied required materials as most of the victims had left their houses only with their clothes on (Sabu and Joby, 2018). Specific demands as 'mobile battery' for unavailability of electricity at relief camps were met by mobile phone 'power banks' by the authorities (Thiagarajan, 2018). Text, audio and multimedia messages were forwarded throughout the country and outside at the speed of light (Express News Service, 2018). WhatsApp was the last resort to many when all other means failed. An Indian Police Services (IPS) officer, Rema Rajeshwari's family was rescued to safety when the family members sent photos of them being trapped due to heavy rains, to name a few (FirstPost, 2018). Apart from rescue and relief efforts, WhatsApp also served as a platform to motivate people during the crises with many motivational messages to keep the spirit up. One of the viral posts was, 'Hollywood has Spiderman, Batman, Ironman, but we Keralites have all under one name – fishermen' to celebrate the exemplary courage and skills and selflessness shown by the fishermen to save the people from drowning or bringing them to safer places (Kurien, 2018). Next year saw similar efforts from volunteers using this freeware, cross-platform Facebook-owned Messenger to highlight the requirement of stranded people (Nair, 2019) and supply relief materials in time by creating groups and flashing the contact numbers of volunteers (Athira, 2019).

Facebook

Facebook—a popular social networking service—was used in a similar manner for rescue and relief operations extensively. Requests were floated on Facebook groups for help from people stranded in various places to reach state and Central government authorities and other rescue teams (Sabu & Joby, 2018). Facebook served as an effective go-between. With its unique features such as appealing posts and live videos, it allowed users to reach online communities with much more vividness within no time (IANS, 2018). Facebook groups were created like 'Trivandrum Indian', 'Where in Trivandrum' and 'Eat-At Trivandrum' for availing relief materials (ExpressNewsService, 2018; IANS, 2018). All groups were active during the floods to help the victims (Mohan, 2018) like the control rooms. 'Anbodu Kochi', one of the Facebook groups, worked for relief and rehabilitation by supplying materials to various camps. Around 300 volunteers were involved in helping the affected ones (Dey, 2018). Facebook was also used to disseminate awareness materials on rehabilitation work post floods. Tailor-made awareness materials on how to cope with various problems like burying animals to prevent the spread of diseases, removing moisture content from car lights, getting rid of plastic garbage collection in the form of infographics were circulated in Facebook for a wider audience (Thiagarajan, 2018). The 2019 floods saw similar efforts from a similar set of people and groups in the rescue, relief and rehabilitation work. Volunteers posted in Facebook group posts about the various requirements of victims whose houses were drowned in floods (Nair, 2019). The needs of the people were posted in groups like 'Trivandrum, Let's make our city the best' for all possible help (Nair, 2019). One Facebook group consisting of fans of the actress and video jockey Pearle Maaney, distributed cattle feed to the flood victims in a village of Wayanad (Daksham, 2019). A campaign 'I Am For Alleppey' was launched by an IAS officer on Facebook for rehabilitation purposes. The campaign, starting with a simple post on a Facebook page, could manage to help 40,000 people for the rehabilitation of women, fishermen, children, the specially abled, senior citizens and infrastructure (Nath, 2019).

Twitter

The microblogging site stood apart in its use for continuous and quick updating of the flood situation. Some of the government agencies that used Twitter were National Disaster Response Force (@NDRFHQ), the Indian Navy (@indiannavy), the office of Chief Minister of Kerala (@CMOKerala), Indian Coast Guard (@IndiaCoastGuard), Press Information Bureau of India (@PIBIndia) (IANS, 2018). People tweeted for all sorts of assistance including that of baby food, sanitary napkins, medical care and other services (Mandhani, 2018; Thiagarajan, 2018). Sandhya Menon, a freelance journalist raised ₹10.9 lakhs and distributed trucks of relief material including food and cleaning material using Twitter (Jose et al., 2018). A US-based relief organization, 'Khalsa Aid' arranged *langar* (where food is served for free) for flood victims, furthermore, requested people on Twitter to donate. Trusts were continuously updating the money they were receiving on Twitter (Kumar, 2018). Volunteers and relief camp coordinators who were on the rescue operations were posting live videos on Twitter to engage more volunteers, relief materials and donations (Ayyappan, 2018). Phone numbers were published of those people who were on boats for rescue operations. People tweeted not to send expired materials, requested to send volunteers with laptops, asked people if they knew a company that can give them perishable materials at a discounted price. Celebrities and politicians contributed to relief funds and despite having busy schedules updated people on Twitter about their next steps for the victims (Mukherjee, 2018; Sabu & Joby, 2018). Some Bollywood actors tweeted advising people to donate funds for the Kerala floods (Mandhani, 2018). Noted industrialist of the country, Anand Mahindra, the chairman of Mahindra & Mahindra, was very active on Twitter during Kerala Floods (Business Today, 2018). Some people tweeted that their homes are open for those people who were stuck in other cities of the state (Mandhani, 2018). People updated rehabilitation information like restoration of electricity transformers and cleaning of houses (Moneycontrol, 2018). In 2019, people from their Twitter account shared informational messages, videos and pictures of their respective places about flood status and updated people about the relief camps (Trends Desk, 2019).

Important Organizations and Personalities Using Social Media for Flood Rescue, Relief and Rehabilitation

Sometimes, the importance of a medium is known by the credibility, popularity and frequency of its users. Many important organizations and personalities from different walks of life fell back upon social media and other online tools for communication during crises.

National Disaster Management Authority (Thiagarajan, 2018) and State Disaster Management Authority used Google Maps to find the victims when people uploaded their locations on social media (FirstPost, 2018). They also reached out to various volunteers through social media platforms who contributed to their efforts in rescue and relief operations (Sabu & Joby, 2018). Indian Army, Indian Air Force and Indian Navy used social media platforms for rescue and relief operations. They used location and tracking features of the medium (FirstPost, 2018) for the purposes. Other government organizations that used social media during Kerala Floods were the Indian Red Cross Society, Corporate Disaster Resource Network (CDRN India), Ministry of Health and Family Welfare, Indian Coast Guard, India Meteorological Department and National Disaster Response Force (NDRF) (HumanityRoad, 2018). Kerala's state government collaborated with software engineers of the world on a communication platform called 'Slack' and created a website www.keralarescue.in to help the victims as soon as possible (Sabu & Joby, 2018; Thiagarajan, 2018). Many organizations such as *Bhoomika Trust* involved in flood relief sent their helpline numbers through social media for wider spread (Thiagarajan, 2018).

Important public figures including the Chief Minister of Kerala resorted to Twitter requesting people to donate money for the flood relief (Mukherjee, 2018). Several journalists including freelancers used social media in their personal capacity for providing information to the victims. They had also designed a platform on Google Maps that helped the people in searching for their specific needs. Google's Person Finder coupled with various social media came to be very handy in getting information about people (FirstPost, 2018). In the 2019 floods, many eminent and prominent public figures including Rahul Gandhi, the central leader of the Congress party used Twitter about the situation in Wayanad—his constituency—asking for assistance from the Central government (The Economic Times, 2019). Forest officers with the help of volunteers worked together for the rescue of victims by using social media (Nair, 2019).

The modus operandi of the rescue, relief and rehabilitation work was crowdsourcing (Sabu & Joby, 2018). Volunteers and other people made public helpline numbers on social media for any emergency.

The affected people with the help of social media shared messages and videos informing their locations and other descriptions to their friends and family members. Some even volunteered for the victims. They acted as a link between victims and rescue teams. The rescue teams responded and updated their operations on social media. The volunteers, trust organizations, rescue team and politicians coordinated the work on social media during the operations. The process did not end there. They coordinated the work till the relief and rehabilitation of the affected people was complete.

Important Hashtags used in Social Media and their Purposes

There were some popular hashtags used during the Kerala flood, that is, #keralaflood, #kerala, #standwithkerala, #keralam ('Top 10 Kerala flood hashtags', 2021), #KeralaFloods and #KeralaFloodRelief, #UAEStandsWithKerala (Social Samosa, 2019), keralafloodsrelief, keralaflood2019 ('Top 10 hashtags used with #keralaflood', 2021), etc. Some of the hashtags that were used during the crises are mentioned in Table 8.1.

Table 8.1 Important Hashtags Used in Social Media and their Purposes

S. No.	Hashtags	Purpose
1	#doforKerala	Material supplies to victims (non-monetary)
2	#KeralaFloods	Updates, rescue and relief operations
3	#OpMadad	Rescue operations
4	#KeralaRelief	Relief
5	#KeralaFloodRelief	Rescue, donations for flood survivors
6	#KeralaFloods2018	Relief operation
7	#ThankyouUAE	Appreciation for donation
8	#StandWithKerala	Donation
9	#Kerala SOS	Rescue and relief operations

(Table 8.1 Continued)

(Table 8.1 Continued)

S. No.	Hashtags	Purpose
10	#SaveChengannur	Campaign for authorities to take actions for stranded people in Alappuzha town
11	#KeralaDonationChallenge	Donation
12	#RebuildKerala	Donation for rehabilitation
13	#IndiaForKerala	Relief and donation

#DoForKerala

The hashtag was started by Anbodu Kochi with an aim to provide non-monetary help to Kerala flood victims. The hashtag was promoted by the district administration of Kochi and various volunteers. People were asked to help victims with food, clothes and other essentials by writing a board of #OpenHouse outside their homes signalling they can accommodate flood victims. Essential supplies for relief camps were requested using hashtags on social media (Sidhardhan, 2018) and delivering them to the needy. It was not limited to rescue and relief operations but to the rehabilitation phase where people were provided material that are required to rebuild their lives (Dey, 2018).

#KeralaFloods

Celebrities, cricketers and others came together on social media to request donations and spread awareness about the Kerala floods by sharing important information like safe locations, helpline numbers and other essentials (FirstPost, 2018). The Chief Minister of Kerala, Pinarayi Vijayan used the hashtag for honouring the fishermen community for their help in rescue missions by the government (Gulf News, 2018).

#OpMadad

The hashtag was initiated to help victims with rescue and aid. Victims were asking for help using the #OpMadad hashtag (Social Samosa, 2019).

#KeralaRelief

It was used to inform people about the devastating floods and to donate money for the same (FirstPost, 2018).

#KeralaFloodRelief

This hashtag was started to raise funds for survivors of the Kerala flood (Social Samosa, 2019).

#KeralaFloods2018

The hashtag was used to share information about relief centres and other information regarding relief operations (Social Samosa, 2019).

#ThankyouUAE

UAE was one of the first countries to offer help to the Kerala victims in facilitating food, water, funds, etc. Many people came on social media with the hashtag #ThankyouUAE for thanking UAE for the help during the floods (FirstPost, 2018; Gulf News, 2018).

#StandWithKerala

Some celebrities came forward to spread awareness about the floods in Kerala among people by using this hashtag. People were encouraged and motivated to contribute to the Chief Minister's Distress Relief Fund (CMDRF) by updating their profile pictures with the same hashtags (Sidhardhan, 2018).

#Kerala SOS

The tag #Kerala SOS was used to inform the people about relief campaigns (Natrajkumar, 2018).

#SaveChengannur

Due to massive rainfall, many people were stranded in the Alappuzha district of Kerala as the water level was increased. The champaign

#SaveChengannur was initiated for the government authorities to take actions to save the stranded (Sidhardhan, 2018).

#KeralaDonationChallenge

One of the Chennai floods victims in 2015, Siddharth a Tamil actor used #KeralaDonationChallenge and requested people to donate money to the CMDRF and further asked people to persuade others by posting their payment proofs online (FirstPost, 2018; Sidhardhan, 2018).

#RebuildKerala

It is another hashtag used during the Kerala floods for collecting resources for rehabilitation purposes (Jose et al., 2018).

#IndiaForKerala

Politician and Siromani Akali Dal (SAD) leader Manjinder S. Sirsa posted images of volunteers on Twitter and requested the Sikh community to donate funds for Kerala floods relief (Gulf News, 2018).

Innovative Tools of Social Media used during the Floods

Some innovative or relatively new or social media tools used less frequently before were put to use during the crises in Kerala. WhatsApp has a useful feature in 'location sharing'. People who were affected by the floods started sharing their locations with the rescue teams or other authorities, whom they were in contact. Even pet owners were sending their pet's photos, videos and locations to the military people (IANS, 2018).

Trapped Facebook users activated the 'safety check' button to know about their loved ones' safety. They also used this feature to take help for food, clothing, drinking water, medical help, etc. Facebook's 'Map' feature made it possible for the government, rescue teams, NDMA (National Disaster Management Authority), activists to identify the exact location of the trapped people and shift them to safer places.

In Facebook's 'Community Help' and 'Crisis Donate Button', people posted requests from affected areas for help. Around 1200 persons used the 'Community Help' feature for help in food, water among others and nearly 500 persons used 'Crisis Donate Button' for donation during the 2018 floods (IANS, 2018).

Twitter has a data-friendly feature called 'Twitter Lite' that can be used to check updates even in offline mode. It is available in 42 languages (Social Samosa, 2019). People were advised to use 'Twitter lite' to minimize data usage and to easily connect with government agencies, relief organizations, rescue teams, volunteers, etc. (IANS, 2018).

Google Map and Google's Person Finder were also used in conjunction with social media to trace, track and rescue the affected ones. Around 22,000 people were traced using *Google maps* alone (Jose et al., 2018).

NEGATIVE ROLE OF SOCIAL MEDIA

It is not uncommon to find examples that crises and disasters open the floodgates of opportunities for some people to cash in on for various reasons—monetary or otherwise. When the people of Kerala were reeling under record-breaking floods, a huge quantity of misinformation and disinformation floated on social media platforms as well creating panic (Pierpoint, 2018). Though it is a subject of psychological investigations as to how could people resort to such lows even during crises of such magnitude, the types of misuse of social media technology can be broadly categorized into the following five groups based on the secondary data collected.

Discourage Donations

Most of the fake news on social media targeted to dissuade people from donating to the Chief Minister's Distress Relief Fund (CMDRF). One viral video was circulated on WhatsApp where a man was claiming that only rich people were affected by floods who didn't need help and discouraged people from making donations to the Chief Minister's Relief Fund (Times of India, 2018) trying to stoke an age-old emotion of battle between the rich vs the poor. Another post tried to stop donations on religious grounds by saying that more than half of the population of Kerala being Muslims and Christians eat beef and worship the wrong God. The floods were the consequences of their acts (Ayyappan, 2018). As a result, people were asking whether to help beef eaters or not (Nandy, 2018).

Greed

People started giving dubious account numbers to divert donations including that of a fake account number of the Chief Minister's Distress Relief Fund (CMDRF) unearthed by the Kerala police (*The Hindu*, 2018).

Creating Panic

Those who spread fake news probably took a lot of pleasure in creating panic among people. An audio clip of a man was posted in WhatsApp group telling people to leave Ernakulam district of Kerala as the Mullaperiyar dam was leaking and he had been trapped in deep water adding, within three hours the place would sink (Agency France-Presse, 2018; Varma, 2018). Similarly, there was a rumour claiming that Idukki dam and other dams had reached their full capacity. The WhatsApp post of the Peechi dam in Thrissur being opened was proved to be wrong later (Praveen, 2019). Fake news regarding the closure of petrol pumps in Kerala for three days because of trucks getting stuck on the highways owing to heavy rainfall was found to be wrong (Praveen, 2019). Images and videos of destruction to infrastructure and loss of life to both humans and animals during floods in other parts of the country at different points of time were circulated to create panic among people (Pierpoint, 2018).

Cheap Entertainment

Fake information about the amount of donations from celebrities (football star Cristiano Ronaldo of Portugal, Paytm founder Vijay

Shekhar Sharma) and subsequent ridiculing were circulated on social media (DNA, 2018; Mclaughlin, 2018). Old pictures of volunteers on rescue missions in other parts of the country were posted on Facebook (Rampal, 2018) for reasons best known to them.

Sadism

Some didn't even think twice to play with the lives of affected people by posting fake phone numbers of the rescue team of Indian Navy helicopters on WhatsApp and Facebook (Mclaughlin, 2018).

CURB ON MISUSE OF SOCIAL MEDIA

Assessing the negative impact of fake news on social media in the rescue, relief and rehabilitation operations, the cybercrime agency of the state rose to the occasion by catching hold of many fake posts and their creators and taking appropriate actions against them (Varma, 2018). Various departments and constituents of the state government including the Chief Minister warned cyber offenders (Agency France-Presse, 2018; Kundu, 2018) of actions under Section 54 that is, Punishment for False Warning of the Disaster Management Act, 2005 (Praveen, 2019; The News Minute, 2019a). Kerala's Thrissur District collector used Facebook and warned of legal actions for offences. Nineteen cases were registered related to spreading fake information by the cyber wings of the police (The News Minute, 2019b).

Swift clarifications from agencies helped a lot in the damage control exercise created to tackle false information spread. A video clip went viral in which a man dressed up like an Indian Army officer said that the Chief Minister had stopped rescue operations started by the army. Later, the Army tweeted and requested people not to believe such rumours and asked to report any such seemingly unreliable information. A WhatsApp number was shared for that purpose (Pierpoint, 2018; Times of India, 2018). While giving clarifications, the Kerala State Electricity Board posted on its Facebook page to take legal actions against those who had spread the fake news about electricity services shut down for two days (Pierpoint, 2018; Praveen, 2019).

In a press conference, along with a warning to the offenders, the Chief Minister spoke about the negative impact of propaganda on the rescue, relief and rebuilding work and assured the people of Kerala that donations to the Chief Minister's Disaster Relief Fund would be judiciously used for the purpose it had been collected (The News Minute, 2019b).

LESSONS LEARNT

By studying the two successive floods of Kerala and comparing and contrasting them with the secondary data mentioned in the Literature Review, there can be many broader learnings. For the affected community, people need to know the availability and use of various social media networks that can be put into use to share their situations, respond to rescue calls, update their status of safety or seek help in time (Bird et al., 2012). Studies show people are not always well versed to handle social media (Babu et al., 2019).

Realizing the immense power of social media in managing disasters, various authorities should render it as one of the priority tools for information dissemination and collections during disasters (Allaire, 2016; Philip & Kannan, 2019). The government should encourage people to use emerging technologies such as social media along with collaborating with various social media platforms for better disaster management (Ajay, 2019; Bird et al., 2012; Restrepo-Estrada et al., 2018). For this, the reach of social media has to increase to the extent possible (Allaire, 2016). For all this, the prerequisite is 'charged mobile phones'. Therefore, the emergency kits should contain power banks to charge mobile phones or if possible mobile phones should be fixed with solar cells for emergency charging (Ajay, 2019; Kumar, et al., 2018).

Social media is a double-edged sword. If misused it can do more harm than good (Mauroner & Heudorfer, 2016). Strict monitoring of the platforms especially during disasters by the authorities and countering the rumours with facts is a must. Awareness on the part of the public of the possible misuse of social media by people with vested interests would go a long way in handling fake news during disasters.

CONCLUSION

The tragedy in Kerala due to heavy monsoon rainfall for two consecutive years in 2018 and 2019 was unprecedented and unforgettable. It has affected a large number of people in terms of life and wealth. When all other traditional communication networks were down, social media rose to the occasion allowing people to participate from across the world in rescue, relief and rehabilitation work by fundraising, volunteer coordination, aiding the agencies among others. Civil society, local and Central government agencies, volunteers, trust organizations all collaborated smoothly and used social media platforms for collecting, compiling and disseminating information to rescue as many people as they could, distribute relief materials like never before and see to the rehabilitation of the needy in lesser time.

Contrary to Harold Innis's concept of centralization of power by communication technology, social media decentralizes power and gives control of information to almost everybody. At times, this becomes a bane. People with vested interests misuse the medium which was in full display during the Kerala floods management efforts. The spread of misinformation and disinformation were rampant creating panic, confusion, helplessness to an extent of threatening the noble initiatives of rescue, relief and rehabilitation. However, those were curbed in time by the swift actions of the state machinery. Many purpose-specific social media pages, hashtags were created and used brilliantly for tracing and tracking of both men and materials to aid the aim of rescue, relief and rehabilitation of the affected people. The mammoth efforts by the people and agencies saw the use of many relatively new or lesser-known and used social media tools, for example, WhatsApp's 'location sharing', Facebook's 'safety check', Facebook's 'Map', Facebook's 'Help and the Crisis Donate Button', Facebook's 'community help' and 'Twitter lite' in conjunction with other online tools, for example, 'google map', Google's 'person finder' that proved to be very effective during crisis communication.

REFERENCES

Agency France-Presse. (2018, 19 August). Mint. Fake news adds to Kerala flood torment. Retrieved from https://www.livemint.com/Politics/KLgnO07lu36dnKi2GXk78M/Fake-news-adds-to-Kerala-flood-torment.html

Ajay, A. (2019). Role of technology in responding to disasters: Insights from the great deluge in Kerala. *Current Science*, *116*(6), 913–918. https://doi. org/10.18520/cs/v116/i6/913-918

Alexander, D. E. (2014). Social media in disaster risk reduction and crisis management. *Science and Engineering Ethics*, *20*(3), 717–733. https://doi.org/10.1007/ s11948-013-9502-z

Allaire, M. C. (2016). Disaster loss and social media: Can online information increase flood resilience? *Water Resources Research*, *52*(9), 7408–7423. https:// doi.org/10.1111/j.1752-1688.1969.tb04897.x

Athira M. (2019, August 14). How a group of drone operators in Kerala rose to the occasion during floods. *The Hindu*. Retrieved from https://www.thehindu. com/news/national/kerala/how-a-group-of-drone-opertors-rose-to-the-occasion-during-floods-and-landslips-in-kerala/article29091339.ece

Ayyappan R. (2018, August 23). New trinity of Kerala's flood rescue ops: FB, Twitter, WhatsApp. OnManorama. Retrieved from https://www.onmano-rama.com/news/kerala/2018/08/23/social-media-help-flood-rescue-ops.html

Babu, A. S., Babu S. D., & Harikrishnan, D. (2019). Impact of social media in dissemination of information during a disaster: A case study on Kerala floods 2018. *International Journal of Innovative Technology and Exploring Engineering*, *8*(7), 283–286. https://www.ijitee.org/wp-content/uploads/papers/v8i7s2/ G10490587S219.pdf

Bhuvana, N., & Aram, I. A. (2019). Facebook and Whatsapp as disaster management tools during the Chennai (India) floods of 2015. *International Journal of Disaster Risk Reduction*, *39*, 101135. https://doi.org/10.1016/j. ijdrr.2019.101135

Bird, D., Ling, M., & Haynes, K. (2012). Flooding Facebook? The use of social media during the Queensland and Victorian floods. *Australian Journal of Emergency Management*, *27*(1), 27–33.

Business Today. (2018, August 22). Kerala floods: Anand Mahindra shares heart-warming picture, calls it 'incredible India'. *Business Today*. Retrieved from https://www.businesstoday.in/current/economy-politics/kerala-floods-anand-mahindra-heartwarming-picture-incredible-india/story/281549.html

Daksham. (2019, September 6). Kerala: VJ's FB group distributes cattlefeed to flood victims. *Deccan Chronicle*. Retrieved from https://www.deccanchronicle. com/nation/current-affairs/060919/kerala-vjs-fb-group-distributes-cattlefeed-to-flood-victims.html

Dey, S. (2018, August 25). What Kerala can teach us. *Mint*. Retrieved from https:// www.livemint.com/Leisure/koMFWn56xDpL40aMTjTJCM/What-Kerala-can-teach-us.html

DNA. (2018, August 18). Kerala flood: Twitter brutally trolls Paytm boss Vijay Shekhar Sharma for Rs 10,000 donation. DNA. Retrieved from https://www. dnaindia.com/business/report-kerala-flood-twitter-brutally-trolls-paytm-boss-vijay-shekhar-sharma-for-rs-10000-donation-2651465

ExpressNewsService. (2018, August 21). Kerala floods: Social media on the mission. *The New Indian Express*. Retrieved from https://www.newindianexpress.com/ cities/thiruvananthapuram/2018/aug/21/kerala-floods-social-media-on-the-mission-1860428.html

FirstPost. (2018, August 18). Kerala floods: Stranded people turn to social media to reach out to loved ones, mobilise relief. First Post. Retrieved from https:// www.firstpost.com/india/kerala-floods-stranded-people-turn-to-social-media-to-reach-out-to-loved-ones-mobilise-relief-4988461.html

Gulf News. (2018, August 21). How social media was used during #KeralaFloods; Keralites thank UAE. Gulf News. Retrieved from https://gulfnews.com/ world/asia/india/how-social-media-was-used-during-keralafloods-keralites-thank-uae-1.2268552

Houston, J. B., Hawthorne, J., Perreault, M. F., Park, E. H., Goldstein Hode, M., Halliwell, M. R., Turner McGowen, S. E., Davis, R., Vaid, S., McElderry, J.A., & Griffith, S. A. (2015). Social media and disasters: A functional framework for social media use in disaster planning, response, and research. *Disasters*, *39*(1), 1–22. https://doi.org/10.1111/disa.12092

HumanityRoad. (2018, September 30). *2018 India Kerala Flooding*. Retrieved from https://reliefweb.int/sites/reliefweb.int/files/resources/Humanity Road Sitrep No 2%2C Kerala India Floods%2C 18Aug2018.pdf

IANS. (2018, August 18). Kerala floods: Facebook donates Rs. 1.75 crores for victims. Gadgets 360. Retrieved from https://gadgets.ndtv.com/social-networking/ news/kerala-floods-facebook-donates-rs-1-75-crores-for-victims-1903387

Jose P. J., Narayanan, C., & Vinayak, A. (2018, August 30). *The Hindu BusinessLine*. One tweet and a torrent of aid. Retrieved from https://www.thehindubusinessline.com/news/variety/one-tweet-and-a-torrent-of-aid/article24803584. ece#!

Kaewkitipong, L., Chen, C., & Ractham, P. (2012). Lessons learned from the use of social media in combating a crisis: A case study of 2011 Thailand flooding disaster. *Thirty Third International Conference on Information Systems*.

Kambli, K. (2020, January 8). Top 5: Biggest floods to affect India in 2019. The Weather Channel. Retrieved from https://weather.com/en-IN/india/news/ news/2020-01-08-top-5-biggest-floods-affect-india-2019

Kaplan, A. M., & Haenlein, M. (2010). Users of the world, unite! The challenges and opportunities of Social Media. *Business Horizons*, *53*(1), 59–68. https:// doi.org/10.1016/j.bushor.2009.09.003

Karmegam, D., & Mappillairaju, B. (2020). Spatio-temporal distribution of negative emotions on Twitter during floods in Chennai, India, in 2015: A post hoc analysis. *International Journal of Health Geographics*, 1–13.

Kaur, G. (2018). Role of media and literature during Kedarnath calamity. *Literary Herald*, *4*(3), 124–128.

Kumar, P. (2018, August 18). India for Kerala: Support comes pouring in on Twitter for rain-ravaged state. *India Today*. Retrieved from https://www.indiatoday.in/india/ story/kerala-floods-support-comes-pouring-in-on-twitter-1317436-2018-08-18

Kundu, C. (2018, August 20). Fact check: Now fake news floods Kerala. *India Today*. Retrieved from https://www.indiatoday.in/fact-check/story/kerala-floods-fake-news-fact-check-1319187-2018-08-20

Kurien, J. (2018, August 23). Kerala floods: Residents owe fishermen more than a few words of thanks and social media memes. Scroll.in. Retrieved from https://scroll.in/article/891482/kerala-floods-local-residents-owe-fishermen-more-than-a-few-words-of-thanks-and-social-media-memes

Mandhani, N. (2018, August 20). How Indians are using social media to help flood-hit Kerala. BBC News. Retrieved from https://www.bbc.com/news/world-asia-india-45218556

Mauroner, O., & Heudorfer, A. (2016). Social media in disaster management: How social media impact the work of volunteer groups and aid organisations in disaster preparation and response. *International Journal of Emergency Management*, *12*(2), 196–217. https://doi.org/10.1504/IJEM.2016.076625

Mclaughlin, T. (2018, September 5). WhatsApp disinformation spreads during Kerala floods—*The Atlantic*. Retrieved from https://www.theatlantic.com/international/archive/2018/09/fighting-whatsapp-disinformation-india-kerala-floods/569332/

Mohan, N. (2018, August 30). Kerala flood coverage: Malayalam news channels set an example in the media world. Exchange 4 media. Retrieved from https://www.exchange4media.com/media-tv-news/kerala-flood-coveragemalayalam-news-channels-set-an-example-in-the-media-world-91804.html

Moneycontrol. (2018, August 25). Kerala floods Live: 31% flood-hit houses cleaned; 23 lakh electricity connections restored. Moneycontrol. Retrieved from https://www.moneycontrol.com/news/india/kerala-floods-live-gates-foundation-to-send-600000-aid-for-relief-ops-in-kerala-2845711.html

Mukherjee, R. (2018, August 13). How actors are getting their fans to contribute to the Kerala CM's flood relief fund. News18. Retrieved from https://www.news18.com/news/buzz/how-actors-are-getting-their-fans-to-contribute-to-the-kerala-cms-flood-relief-fund-1842263.html

Nair, A. (2019, August 20). Kerala floods: Benefactors come together on social media, dish out relief in quick time. *The Hindu*. Retrieved from https://www.thehindu.com/news/national/kerala/benefactors-come-together-on-social-media-dish-out-relief-in-quick-time/article29128515.ece

Nandy, A. (2018, August, 20). Blaming women & beef for Kerala floods?! You must be kidding. The Quint. Retrieved from https://www.thequint.com/videos/kerala-floods-women-in-sabarimala-beef-muslims-christians

Nath, S. (2019, January, 18). Kerala: IAS officer's Facebook campaign is rebuilding flood-ravaged Alleppey. Efforts for good. Retrieved from https://effortsfor-good.org/get-inspired/i-am-for-alleppey/

Natrajkumar, N. (2018, August 17). #Kerala SOS trends as social media users help with rescue operations. *Business Times*. Retrieved from International https://www.ibtimes.co.in/kerala-sos-trends-social-media-users-help-rescue-operations-778054

Newsclick. (2019, August 8). Kerala floods 2019: 121 dead, 1,789 houses collapsed. News Click. Retrieved from https://www.newsclick.in/kerala-floods-2019-121-dead-1789-houses-collapsed

Pandey, N., & Natarajan S. (2016). How social media can contribute during disaster events? *2016 International Conference on Advances in Computing, Communications and Informatics (ICACCI)*, 1352–1356.

Paul, S., & Sosale, S. (2019). Witnessing a disaster: Public use of digital technologies in the 2015 south Indian floods. *Digital Journalism*, 1–17. https://doi.org/10.1080/21670811.2019.1636693

Philip, L., & Kannan, S. (2019). An exploratory study on the use of social media as a disaster management tool in India. *International Journal of Scientific Research and Review*, 7(3), 1409–1418. https://doi.org/10.9723/jksiis.2012.17.7.149

Pierpoint, G. (2018, August 20). Kerala floods: Fake news 'creating unnecessary panic'. BBC News. Retrieved from https://www.bbc.com/news/world-asia-india-45245999

Praveen, S. R. (2019, August 9). In Kerala, fake news floods social media adds to panic. *The Hindu*. Retrieved from https://www.thehindu.com/news/national/kerala/in-kerala-fake-news-floods-social-media-adds-to-panic/article28965647.ece

PTI. (2019, August 11). Kerala flood water recedes, death toll rises to 104. Press Trust of India. Retrieved from https://www.indiatoday.in/india/story/kerala-flood-water-recedes-death-toll-rises-to-104-1581202-2019-08-15

Rajendiran, K. (2018). Social media listening during disasters: 2018 Kerala floods in focus. *Latent View*. Retrieved from https://www.latentview.com/social-media-listening-during-floods/

Rampal, N. (2018, August 13). Photos of RSS workers helping out Kerala flood victims are from Gujarat last year. *The Print*. Retrieved from https://theprint.in/hoaxposed/photos-of-rss-workers-helping-out-kerala-flood-victims-are-from-gujarat/97637/

Restrepo-Estrada, C., de Andrade, S. C., Abe, N., Fava, M. C., Mendiondo, E. M., & de Albuquerque, J. P. (2018). Geo-social media as a proxy for hydrometeorological data for streamflow estimation and to improve flood monitoring. *Computers and Geosciences*, *111*, 148–158. https://doi.org/10.1016/j.cageo.2017.10.010

Sabu, S., & Joby, N. E. (2018, September 21). Kerala floods—Rescue and rehabilitation using information technology and social media. AGU website. Retrieved from https://blogs.agu.org/thefield/2018/09/21/kerala-floods-rescue-and-rehabilitation-using-information-technology-and-social-media/

Shaji, K. A. (2019, August 28). As floods repeat this year in Kerala, experts point to climate change. Mongabay. Retrieved from https://india.mongabay.com/2019/08/as-floods-repeat-this-year-in-kerala-experts-point-to-climate-change/

Sidhardhan, S. (2018, August 20). #KeralaFloods: Surging on social media. *Times of India*. Retrieved from https://timesofindia.indiatimes.com/city/kochi/keralafloods-surging-on-social-media/articleshow/65450526.cms

Simon, T., Goldberg, A., & Adini, B. (2015). Socializing in emergencies–A review of the use of social media in emergency situations. *International Journal of Information Management, 35*(5), 609–619. https://doi.org/10.1016/j.ijinfomgt.2015.07.001

Social Samosa. (2019, August 13). 5 tips for using Twitter during Kerala Floods. Social Samosa. Retrieved from https://www.socialsamosa.com/2018/08/twitter-tips-for-crisis-kerala-floods/

Suresh Babu, A., Babu S. D., & Harikrishnan, D. (2019). Impact of social media in dissemination of information during a disaster—A case study on Kerala floods 2018. *International Journal of Innovative Technology and Exploring Engineering, 8*(7), 283–286.

The Economic Times. (2019, August 9). Kerala floods live updates: Kerala toll nears 30, schools shut, 24 landslides reported. *The Economic Times.* Retrieved from https://economictimes.indiatimes.com/news/politics-and-nation/kerala-floods-live-news-updates/liveblog/70601254.cms

The Hindu. (2018, August 18). TN man urges people to donate for Kerala relief, but posts his account details. *The Hindu.* Retrieved from https://www.the-hindu.com/news/national/kerala/tn-man-urges-people-to-donate-for-kerala-relief-but-posts-his-account-details/article24725797.ece

The News Minute. (2019a August 9). Kerala floods: Govt warns of strict action against those spreading fake news, old videos. The News Minute. Retrieved from https://www.thenewsminute.com/article/kerala-floods-govt-warns-strict-action-against-those-spreading-fake-news-old-videos-106929

The News Minute. (2019b, August 13). Kerala police register 19 cases for fake campaigns on social media over flood relief. The News Minute. Retrieved from https://www.thenewsminute.com/article/kerala-police-register-19-cases-fake-campaigns-social-media-over-flood-relief-107130

Thiagarajan, K. (2018, August 22). How social media came to the rescue after Kerala's floods. npr. Retrieved from https://www.npr.org/sections/goatsandsoda/2018/08/22/640879582/how-social-media-came-to-the-rescue-after-keralas-flood

Times of India. (2018, August 20). Kerala battles flood on the ground and disinformation on social media–India News. *Times of India.* Retrieved from https://timesofindia.indiatimes.com/india/kerala-battles-flood-on-the-ground-and-disinformation-on-social-media/articleshow/65468380.cms

Top 10 hashtags used with #keralaflood. (2021). HashtagsforLikes. Retrieved from https://www.hashtagsforlikes.co/hashtag/keralaflood

Top 10 Kerala flood hashtags. (2021, July 21). best-hashtags.com. Retrieved from http://best-hashtags.com/hashtag/keralaflood/

Trends Desk. (2019, August 10). #KeralaFloods, #KeralaRains trend as residents use social media to provide information. The Indian Express. Retrieved from https://indianexpress.com/article/trending/trending-in-india/keralal-floods-kerala-rains-2019-maharashtra-rains-maharashtra-floods-5891020/

UNDP. (2018, December 12). Post-disaster needs assessment—Kerala. United nations Development Programme. Retrieved from https://www.undp.org/publications/post-disaster-needs-assessment-kerala

Varghese, R. R., & Yadukrishnan, T. A. (2019). Role of social media during Kerala floods 2018. *Library Philosophy and Practice (e-Journal).* 2754.

Varma, V. (2018, August 18). Across Kerala's WhatsApp groups, some fake news, but thousands of helping hands. *The Indian Express.* Retrieved from https://indianexpress.com/article/india/kerala-floods-kerala-rains-across-keralas-whatsapp-groups-some-fake-news-helping-hands-5313155/

Webster, J. & Watson, R. (2002). Analyzing the past to prepare for the future: Writing a literature review. *MIS Quarterly,* 26. 10.2307/4132319.

Wukich, C. (2015). Social media use in emergency management. *Journal of Emergency Management, 13*(4), 281–294. https://doi.org/10.5055/jem.2015.0242

PART III

Balancing Autonomy and Regulation

Chapter 9

Fake News
Scenario, Initiatives, Perceptions and Challenges

I. Arul Aram and Parama Gupta

INTRODUCTION

What was yellow journalism in the era of print journalism has taken
the form of fake news in the era of the internet with its fangs becoming
more virulent with passing time. The overload of information and the
labyrinthine nature of the internet make it impossible for users to trace
the source and thus determine the authenticity of what is presented to
them as genuine information. The *English Cambridge Dictionary* defines
fake news as 'false stories that appear to be news, spread on the internet or using other media, usually created to influence political views
or as a joke'. The *Oxford Learner's Dictionary* defines it as 'false reports
of events, written and read on a website'. Yet another comprehensive
definition, as given by the Ethical Journalism Network, is 'information that is likely to be perceived as news, which has been deliberately
fabricated and is disseminated with the intention to deceive others into
believing falsehoods or doubting verifiable facts'. Thus, fake news is a
misnomer, for news, as understood by its most fundamental principle
of truth, cannot be fake if it is to be classified as news. While fake
news is widely used by propagandists in the political and social arena
to fuel their vested interests, it is a matter of concern that fake news

has pervaded the domains of health, an area in which the principles of truth and verification are of paramount importance, more than any other beat, and where misinformation can be detrimental to the lives of people. This has come to the forefront in the times of fighting against COVID-19.

As India, along with the rest of the world, fights COVID-19, disinformation and misinformation have surpassed all previous levels. Propagation of unverified cures and preventions, unproven facts surrounding the disease, ill-informed opinions and dangerously targeted propaganda against specific religious communities have been in the spotlight since the outbreak of the pandemic. COVID-19 had brought to the public eye several fake news, starting with interviews by mediocre doctors in which a range of opinions had been voiced that could be open for contestation. For example, a view that the virus will not affect people in a hot country like India was refuted by the World Health Organization based on scientific data. A Siddha medical practitioner in Tamil Nadu put out a vociferous YouTube video saying that he would inject blood on himself from a corona patient and cure himself with this potion. He later ended up in jail for spreading false information through newspaper interviews and social media posts (Koushik, 2020). Drinking the urine of a black, virgin cow, boiled with turmeric powder and some herbal leaves is thought to cure any type of cancer, at any stage (Krishnan, 2020). But then, one such man who appeared on a YouTube video promoting drinking of virgin cow urine had died of cancer though the popular video is still on the web. Even in this COVID-19 scenario, cow urine has been wrongly advocated as a cure from the virus. A 50-year-old milk trader from Hooghly, West Bengal, was arrested by the police for selling cow urine at ₹500 per litre as a cure for COVID-19 (Awasthi, 2020). In another instance, a self-styled godman released a video of him bathing in cow urine and dung, which led his followers to organize a cow urine party. Police have also arrested people indulging in such superstitious practices which are likely to cause varied infections (Mishra, 2020). And now, as administration of the vaccines for the disease is under way globally, the rampant spread of fake news regarding the effects of vaccines poses a major cause of concern.

Fake news on the subject has ranged from bizarre accounts of the vaccine's capability to turn people into zombies to drug firms declaring the vaccines useless. A WhatsApp hoax message circulated in May 2021 created enough reason for panic as it reported French Nobel laureate Luc Montagnier claiming that administration of COVID-19 vaccines is a mistake and that people who have taken any form of Corona vaccine are likely to die in the next two years. The news has been packaged in a way that it appears to be genuine, with several quotes attributed to the virologist. It was later found that while Montagnier did say in an interview that the vaccines are responsible for creating the variants of the virus, he did not say that people who have taken the vaccines will die in two years. The false claims were busted but not before it had generated enough perplexity among those who had received the news. Besides spreading panic among people, such false information does not augur well for the collective well-being of society, both in terms of people's physical and mental health. The COVID-19 situation in India has not only led to an increase in concerns over health-related fake news but has also triggered several incidents of attacks of communal nature propelled by malicious online content. Media Scanner, a fact-checking organization, identified 69 doctored videos targeted at spreading hatred against Muslims after the Tablighi Jamaat gathering came to a spotlight as a contributor to India's COVID-19 chain (Jain, 2020). The poison did not stay restricted in the online space but spilled over to the real world with 28 attacks spurred by online hatred.

TYPES OF FAKE NEWS

The term 'fake news' is often casually used to refer to a wide variety of content, so much so that it becomes important to distinguish at the outset as to what does not fall within its purview. Satirical content, which includes intentional distortion of facts with the aim to mock or criticize, does not fall under the categorization of fake news. Fake news also does not refer to false information that is a result of inadvertent mistake to obtain or verify accurate information by a reporter or an editor belonging to an organization that is otherwise committed to truthful journalism (Watson, 2018). Contrary to these, fake news is the intentional fabrication or manipulation of facts with ulterior motives at play.

There are several categorizations of fake news. The most common ones include disinformation and misinformation. As active consumers of the media, it is important to understand what each of these implies to be able to detect them and guard against being misled by them. Disinformation is the deliberate propagation of false and manipulated information. Misinformation, on the other hand, can be understood as false or baseless information which arises out of lack of verification or negligence and is spread widely. While misinformation lacks harmful intent on the part of the propagator, disinformation is driven entirely by the malicious intent to malign or cause harm to individuals, organizations or particular societies.

WHY DOES FAKE NEWS SPREAD?

With the emergence of the internet and the development of phenomena such as citizen journalism and user-generated content, the power to disseminate information is now no longer restricted to the hands of professional journalists who are trained in the trade and committed to the cardinal principles of journalism. The web provides all its users immense freedom to generate content. In such a scenario, the traditional gatekeepers, who are the perceived custodians of accurate and authentic journalism, are missing. This can be seen as a strong reason for the mushrooming of fake news websites and content.

Publication is no longer the privilege of a select few. Today, anyone with access to a computer or mobile phone has the means to write, edit and publish material online, throwing the traditional methods of news gathering, gatekeeping and disseminating for a toss. This privilege has turned into a double-edged sword. On the one hand, it has created the opportunity for voices to be heard, and on the other it has opened the doors for propagandists and mischief mongers to manipulate content. Moreover, lack of adequate media literacy and the knowledge of ways to detect authenticity results in inadvertent widespread sharing of such content by users as it appeals to them at an emotional level triggering a need to share with friends and acquaintances. Allcott and Gentzkow

(2017) identify two main motives behind the creation and propagation of fake news. The first is of a pecuniary nature, driven by the prospect of gaining monetary benefits by attracting a huge traffic to one's site through sensational content propagated on social media, which can then bring in huge advertising revenue online. The second motive is to fuel an ideological warfare, by either spreading self-promotional content or propaganda directed at maligning adversaries.

INITIATIVES TO CURB THE MENACE

Several initiatives in recent times have been taken by non-profit organizations as well as social media sites to curb the menace. The following is a brief round-up of such initiatives which will help media professionals as well as users to enhance their ability to check the veracity of information received online. The internet while posing a challenge also makes it possible to detect the authenticity of news by placing certain tools and mechanisms at our disposal.

The efforts of various organizations and groups are a testimony to the fact that the strength of technology can very well be harnessed to minimize the extent of reach of the false content that fake news propagates. In April 2020, Google, the world's leading search engine, announced a package of US$6.5 million to combat fake news to strengthen the efforts of fact checkers and organizations involved in the efforts to stem the flow of fake news. Besides offering funding to fake news busters and collaborating with various organizations from across the world such as DataLead, First Draft and Meedan to provide training to journalists in authentic news gathering, verification and production, Google has rolled out a fact check feature in Google Search and News. For the first time, when one conducts a search on Google that returns an authoritative result containing fact checks for one or more public claims, one will see that information clearly on the search results page—information on the claim, who made the claim and the fact check of that particular claim.

In 2017, Facebook outlined its strategy against fake news propagation on its platform, stating their focus on three key areas which are to disrupt the monetary gain sought by fake news propagators, building new features and empowering users to identify and filter out fake news. While acknowledging the limitations arising from their scale and the platform's focused role as a social networking site and not the arbiters of truth, Facebook has tied up with third-party fact checkers to curb the flow of fake news in their space. In 2019, Facebook unveiled on a trial basis the news tab for users in the United States to access news stories from credible sources. This is yet to be rolled out at a large scale and if done can be expected to minimize considerably the impact of fake news, provided users are made sufficiently sensitized towards the menace.

WhatsApp has consistently been in the eye of the storm throughout this chaotic scenario. The platform has been taking several initiatives in the last few years. In India, during the 2019 Lok Sabha elections, WhatsApp in collaboration with a start-up PROTO introduced a tip line feature to keep a tab on circulating rumours. This feature made it possible to check and classify information as false, true, misleading, disputed or out of scope based on users reporting to a WhatsApp number. This service was made available for posts in various Indian languages. In January 2020, WhatsApp took further steps to demarcate messages shared more than five times to indicate their potentiality of going viral and thus in a way serving as a caution for anyone sharing it to stop and ponder about its authenticity and the consequences of sharing. WhatsApp also experimented with the 'suspicious link detection', a feature made available only on Android phones. This feature seeks to identify fraudulent links through the characters used in the links. With the infodemic ushered in by COVID-19, WhatsApp took more stringent steps to limit the forwarding of messages after it was shared a certain number of times.

Moreover, it has tied up with several organizations to ensure the dissemination of authentic information through its platform. According to the India head of public policy for WhatsApp, Shivnath Thukral (2020),

WhatsApp takes the safety of its users very seriously. People across the country rely on WhatsApp to talk to their loved ones, doctors, teachers and businesses during this challenging time of COVID-19. Our priority is to empower people to directly connect with health officials and government agencies to rely on these credible sources to receive verified updates during the pandemic. This campaign helps convey our collective responsibility and the need to always verify before sharing information.

Apart from social media platforms, mainstream news outlets have also taken up the cause of fighting fake news. The British Broadcast Corporation (BBC) has emerged as one of the frontline warriors in this battle, undertaking and publishing extensive research studies to map trends in fake news creation and propagation. The organization has also made available on its website a huge repository of resources to help media users learn how to spot and derail fake news from its track. Major Indian news organizations such as the *Indian Express*, *The Hindu Business Line*, CNN-IBN and NDTV have dedicated sections for reports and discussions on fake news.

In February 2021, researchers hailing from Germany and Slovenia developed a new approach based on the power of machine learning to identify fake news (Sheth, 2021). The model developed by these researchers uses an advanced mechanism of classification where fake news is detected through the identification of specific words or styles of writing. Such a model, as the researchers acknowledge, has already been existent though has been rendered ineffective or is at least not adequately effective in curbing fake news as propagators of such news have learnt to modify content to avoid detection. Thus, detection rates of fake news have continued to be low. The latest approach seeks to plug the hole and make detection possible even when fake news spreaders change styles of content. While it can be hoped that advanced algorithms can bring the rate of detection up to some extent, a large onus to fight fake news would still lie on well-informed consumption of media content by the general user. Ireton and Posetti (2018) aver that journalists have a greater onus to adhere to the standards of ethical journalism in these times of rampant disinformation. They have a duty to bring to the public information about the existence of fact-checking organizations and their efforts in debunking fake news. They stress on strengthening the mechanism of internal fact-checking at the pre-publication stage, which is in line with the journalistic principle of verification. A proactive approach towards keeping a tab on new ways in which false information is spread can go a long way in safeguarding against publication of unauthentic information.

REVIEW OF LITERATURE

A review of literature of recent academic research on fake news reveals significant insights on the extent of its reach, the identified motives of the propagators, factors leading to its rise and the role that is being played by various stakeholders.

In a 2018 research by Stanford University (Allcott et al., 2019), new and significant findings were presented on the volume of unauthentic content that was circulated on social media in the period between January 2015 and July 2018 by identifying 570 websites that were pinned down as sources of misinformation, drawn from previous studies undertaken on the subject as well as online resources. The researchers then measured the level of engagement with content from the identified sites on popular social media platforms such as Facebook and Twitter.

This is then compared with the level of engagement with content from sites which are established as authentic such as big news outlets and smaller news media sites that are known to adhere to the principles of journalism. It was found that with Facebook introducing new features to curb the flow of fake news, the level of engagement with fake news had come down towards the end of the period of study.

Allcott and Gentzkow (2017) did an extensive online survey of over 1,200 respondents in addition to a study of 156 fake news stories surrounding the 2016 U.S. presidential campaign. A noteworthy finding of the study was the reportedly low levels of trust on social media as a source of important election news, with only 14 per cent of the respondents choosing social media over traditional media as a credible source of information. Further, the study presents evidence of how there were greater number of fake stories that projected Donald Trump in a favourable light, identifying 115 such pro-Trump stories as against 41 stories that were pro-Hillary Clinton. The study also shows the high rate of sharing of the pro-Trump fake stories with 30 million shares recorded on social media as against around seven million shares for the pro-Clinton stories. The study reveals the massive extent of the reach of fabricated content by placing on record evidence of over 159 million visits to fake news websites.

In yet another study of fake news conducted during the 2016 U.S. presidential elections, fake news was understood to have two dimensions, one that of fake news genre and the other of fake news label (Egelhofer & Lecheler, 2019).

While the former implies the deliberate manipulation of information under the garb of authentic journalistic techniques, the latter refers to the use of the term fake news by political actors to undermine the credibility of news media. Both forms are equally detrimental to the overall perception of news media and political knowledge of the public.

Research has also thrown the spotlight on the propagators of fake news and their various motives. Schulman and Siman-Tov (2020) list out the players involved in this murky scenario where institutions as high as states are found to have masterminded efforts to propagate false and manipulated information with the aim of destabilizing other states. Examples of China spreading rumours about Taiwan hiding COVID-19 figures and websites with links to Russia, as claimed by the U.S., circulating information that the virus was a creation of the U.S. and was unleashed on China as a biological weapon to hit a blow to their economy are cited to support this point. Anti-establishment groups have been identified as another category that produces fake news to deflate establishments. The media themselves, traditionally the custodians of truth, have been found to be lacking in their commitment to meet the highest standards of the profession and thus contributing to the chaos.

Delving into the motives of fake news propagators, Watson (2018) indicates that fake news, which is most often a product of the minds of 'opportunists who seek financial gain or hyper-partisans who want to influence political beliefs', often finds oxygen through widespread dissemination enabled by the structures of social media and 'humans responding to inflamed emotions'. The content of fake news is manipulated in such a way so as to instigate dormant outrage or to strengthen existing biases.

In another study, Brun and Roitman (2019) discuss the four factors that have contributed to the proliferation of fake news. These factors include the challenges of distinguishing facts from fabrications, the dilemma over the need to clarify reality, the lack of universal concern over what can be believed to be a credible source of information and the use of organized power by interest groups to undermine and suppress the efforts of institutions committed to the cause of truth. They argue that the scientific method of fact finding grounded largely on empirical worth has taken the back seat in these times of unrestrained propagation of unauthentic information. The free marketplace of ideas, which was once regarded highly by Western democracies and media theorists, has indeed been desecrated by the current onslaught of manipulated content.

In a survey conducted among faculty members from across various disciplines at the California State University, Northridge (CSUN) in Los Angeles, California, Weiss et al. (2020) found that there exists a divide in the levels of awareness, perceptions and attitudes of faculty members from different disciplines, which they opine can hold long-term implications on how students belonging to different disciplines are likely to regard the issue of fake news.

Recent research also underlines the worrisome trend of hatred spread through malicious content against specific communities with the aim to gain political capital. Cerase and Santoro (2018) draw attention to how racially discriminatory material have become a major fuel for hoaxes that are vehemently driven towards creating and reinforcing negative stereotypes of certain communities which promote a culture of exclusion of groups resulting in polarization of votes during elections. In their words, 'racial hoaxes have relevant political and social implications: spread across multiple channels, they can foster exclusionary discourse on immigration, migrants, refugees, and other minorities, with concrete consequences on people and policies'. Banerjee and Haque (2018) draw attention to the polarizing motives of vested political interests behind the rampancy of fake news in India. They note that fake news can have devastating effects given the population dynamics of the country and raise concerns over the inability of social media platforms to prevent its spread.

Further, a survey conducted by Raj and Goswami (2020) points towards popular public opinion in favour of setting up concrete national policies and statutory bodies specially to tackle fake news. Self-regulation was regarded as an ineffective method in the survey whereas the call for increasing social media literacy was voiced by a majority of respondents.

Studying COVID-19 related online fake news in India, Al-Zaman (2021) notes that most of the fake news studied are international rather than national. The study identifies Twitter, Facebook, WhatsApp and YouTube as the main platforms where such news is shared, with Twitter taking the dubious lead with its potential as a quick platform for sharing information turning into a double-edged sword. In an earlier study, Farooq (2018) comments on the emergence of WhatsApp as a tool of political propaganda, which may be attributed to the usage patterns on the application. This includes the prevalence of first-time social media users who have negligible exposure to other social media platforms and are therefore unaware of the concept and trends of fake news. Moreover, the platform also makes it possible for users to participate in ideologically driven groups which are the fertile grounds of propagandist content.

Delving into the reasons why people tend to share fake news on social media, Pennycook and Rand (2021) pinpoint the lack of attentive consideration on the part of users while sharing information they receive. This presents an alternative to the common belief that political biases are at work when people spread misinformation online. The study also highlights the intervention social media can play in veering people into a mode of active thinking and fact-checking and thus improving the rate of curbing fake news. Guadagno and Guttieri (2019) point towards a complex interaction between three key influencing factors—*social, contextual and individual*—leading to the proliferation of fake news. These factors include existing cultural values, the type of content or message carried by fake news as well as personal opinions and preferences of individuals. Nielsen and Graves (2017) present crucial findings in relation to audience perceptions of fake news. They find that while people are aware of the term fake news, they are largely unable to clearly distinguish fake news in the real sense of the term from instances of poor journalism. Their study suggests a general discontent among people regarding the credibility of information sources rather than a clear understanding of what fake news is.

A growing body of research is now also focussing on the challenges involved in debunking fake news. Brashier et al. (2021) observe that corrective messages issued after the spread of fake news fail to undo the damage caused by the spread entirely, especially when there is a considerable time lapse between fake news and its counter message. Lewandowsky and van der Linden (2021) reiterate the seriousness of this challenge with evidence from an experimental study, which suggests a 'continued influence effect of misinformation'. Wiping away the original impact of fake news from people's memory is not easy as memories of false information persist.

Shu et al. (2018) present a research-based data analysis of a comprehensive fake news data repository called FakeNewsNet that understands fake news in terms of their information content, social context and the time and space in which they are created and shared. The researchers argue in favour of the efficacy of a huge repository such as FakeNewsNet in collating and analysing the dynamics of fake news, which is a crucial process in its detection and debunking. In the war against unmitigated proliferation of fake news, all stakeholders including governments, non-governmental organizations, educational institutions and technological start-ups are key players. Haciyakupoglu et al. (2018) enumerate measures that are crucial in enhancing media literacy among users and creating a culture of critical thinking, which are effective weapons in the fight against fake news.

Fact-checking websites are one among these efforts. The authors also report that in countries such as Canada, Italy and Taiwan, school curriculums have incorporated lessons on differentiating between authentic and inauthentic information, thus paving the way for early training in false news detection. The role of opinion leaders and social media influences has also been identified as being of paramount importance by many countries. Government-funded research on developing technology in the form of artificial intelligence and machine learning to combat fake news is yet another measure that is being adopted. Claimbuster, a project funded by the U.S. National Science Foundation, which spots factual claims made in textual content, is cited as a successful example of such efforts.

CASE STUDIES

Fake News Case 1: WhatsApp Hoax of Nano-GPS-fitted ₹2000 Currency Notes

In 2016, during the demonetization drive, a WhatsApp hoax was being widely circulated claiming that the new 2000-rupee notes released by the RBI carried nano GPS chips to help the government track the notes with the aim to prevent the hoarding of black money. The message, which carried images of the newly introduced 2000-rupee notes, made several claims regarding the high level of technology the chip was fitted with. The images even marked the areas that were said to contain the nano chips. It said that the chips contained signal reflectors and would alert the government about the exact location coordinates of the currency and that it could be tracked from 120 metres below the ground level. The message also claimed that the authorities would be alerted if too many 2000-rupee notes were kept together as a means to discourage corruption by amassing wealth through bribes. Later, newspaper reports busted the hoax saying that the Reserve Bank of India has mentioned no such chip while releasing information about the new currency notes.

Fake News Case 2: Rumours of Shortage in Salt Supply

In November 2018, rumours of shortage of salt supply went viral through WhatsApp forwards to cause widespread panic buying in different parts of India. More recently, such rumours of salt shortage resurfaced in the state of Assam in April 2020 prompting the Assam

Police to issue a fake news alert notice. The source of the news, the police said, was a fake unofficial mobile app on the Google play store in the name of the *Assam Tribune*, a leading daily in the state. The notice issued by the Assam police sought to clearly state that there was no salt shortage and that there was mischief underway in spreading the rumour about shortage of salt. The notice further asked citizens not to pay any heed to such baseless information and also assured that there was enough stock of all essentials including salt. In 2016, word of a salt shortage in North India spread widely. The fake news unleashed panic, and in Hyderabad, among other places, salt prices increased by a factor of four. It even extracted a victim, a woman who died in Bakarganj Bazaar, Kanpur, when she slipped and fell into a drain in a panic buying melee (Bansal, 2017). It was reported that certain salt merchants benefitted by raising the price of salt taking advantage of the situation. It came at a time when the demonetization drive had left several in need of cash. All these facts point towards a motive that is pecuniary in nature. However, the exact propagators were neither identified nor brought to book.

Fake News Case 3: Fake Audio of Dr Devi Shetty issuing Advisory on Corona Testing

In March 2020, an audio clip was circulated on social media with an image of the eminent cardiologist Dr Devi Shetty at the backdrop, a voice claiming to be issuing an advisory for patients suspecting themselves to be infected with COVID-19 to not get tested. The post appeared on the Facebook page of the Karnataka Medical Association on which a comment by the official page of Narayana Health clarified that the audio was being wrongly attributed to Dr Shetty. Besides Facebook, it was shared on other social networks such as Twitter and WhatsApp. On Twitter, it was re-tweeted over 2,000 times before it was found to be fake.

A report by Boom Live revealed that the voice in the audio clip was that of a Chennai-based orthopaedic Dr Santhosh Jacob, who is reported to have said that he had sent the audio to a personal friend. The doctor himself expressed surprise at how an audio recording by him had gone viral. The audio bore the logo of 'Daijiworld Television', a news portal based in Karnataka, which later brought out news stories on the rise of fake news and a report about Dr Santhosh Jacob's advisory. In the story about rising cases of fake news, Daijiworld mentioned the instance of the fake audio clip attributed to Dr Devi Shetty but neither took responsibility nor made any comments on the appearance of the portal's logo on the clip. There are no reports on the further probe as to how the fake audio had managed to be released and circulated.

Fake News Case 4: Fake Video of Corona Patients Being Beaten by Doctors

A widely circulated video in April 2021 claimed that Corona patients were being beaten to death in hospitals for monetary gains. The footage showed a man in a hospital bed being 'attacked', which was later revealed to be from an unrelated incident reported to have taken place in Bangladesh. The clipping also showed a patient being thrashed by a hospital staff, which was found to be footage of a depressed patient being treated in a hospital in Patiala. But the entire video was packaged in a way to give the impression that Corona patients were being killed so that the hospital rumoured to be in Karnataka could gain money. The Karnataka police pinned the source to an Instagram account and said that the intent was to spread fear and panic among people. Later, according to news reports, the police also put up an image that showed images of apology by the Instagram account holder. However, there has been no information of action taken against the perpetrators of the mischief.

Fake News Case 5: Fake Video of a Corona Patient Being Administered Vaccine from an Empty Syringe

In yet another instance of manipulation of facts taken from a different context, in April 2021, a video shared on social media showed a man being administered vaccine from an 'empty syringe' by a healthcare worker that sought to cast aspersions on healthcare officials in India and their trustworthiness in administering vaccines to patients. The rumour the video stoked was that hospital authorities were administering fake vaccines and were selling real vaccines in the black market. The source of the video was later revealed to be a Mexican vaccination camp where, as part of the Phase III trial, a placebo was being injected into a patient's body. A placebo, which is a harmless and inactive substitute for an actual vaccine, is a viable method of vaccination trial.

From these cases, it can be seen that while fake news is debunked, very little is done to reach its roots and the propagators are seldom tracked or brought to book. By the time action is taken to counteract the effect of fake news, enough damage is done through the spread of false information. The intent for spreading false information varies from the lure of making easy lucre to mere mischief-mongering. In certain instances, fake news baffles not only the general public but also mainstream media outlets that are committed to providing verified information. The potential for damage carried by the fake news far exceeds the counteractive measures as is seen by the case studies. In the case of health-related fake news, the absence of prior knowledge of medical phenomena on the part of the general public makes the fang of fake news all the more poisonous. In such circumstances, increasing awareness about the prevalence of misinformation is the only option available to minimize its impact.

SURVEY RESULTS

In a survey conducted among 100 respondents, certain significant insights came forth with reference to their consumption and reception of fake news and perceptions about fabricated content. The respondents included people from the 21–50 age group. As much as 34 per cent of the respondents were college students, constituting the largest chunk, data specialists accounted for 15 per cent, quality analysts 16 per cent, software engineers 14 per cent, unemployed 14 per cent and other engineers 12 per cent.

When asked as to what prompts them to share messages on social media when they are received without checking for authenticity (Figure 9.1), 47 per cent respondents admitted to having shared unverified information out of habit, which reflects an inherent need to

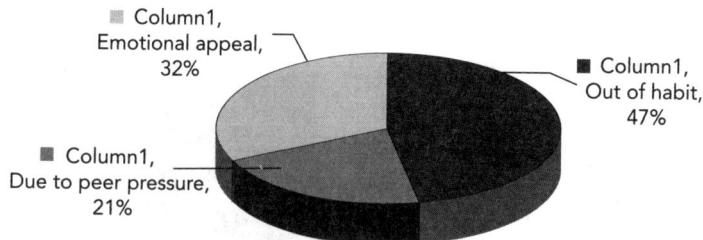

Figure 9.1 *Reasons Why People Share Forwards on Social Media*

share information simply for the sake of sharing something and being perceived as active on social media. As much as 21 per cent of the respondents said they shared 'received' messages due to some prevailing peer pressure, hinting at the need to win approval from friends by sharing 'interesting stuff' in common groups or because someone they know asked them to share it. As much as 32 per cent said they shared such information because it appealed to them emotionally.

As much as 89 per cent of the respondents said they received such forwarded information with content whose authenticity was debatable (Figure 9.2) through WhatsApp groups and 11 per cent said they received such messages in private chats. This again points to the need to either gain some recognition in groups or at least to stay relevant and active. At the same time, this also brings to the forefront concerns regarding the widespread reach of such messages through groups on social networking platforms. A single forward can gain several viewers when shared in groups. As much as 71 per cent of respondents said they carefully read

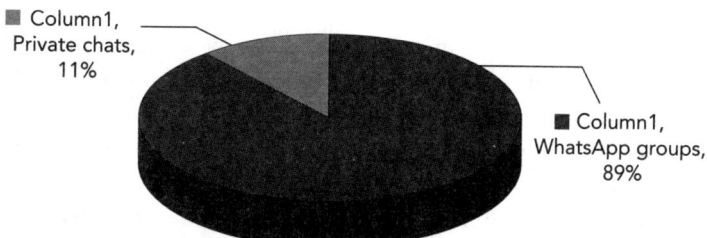

Figure 9.2 *Source of Receiving Forwarded Messages with Debatable Content*

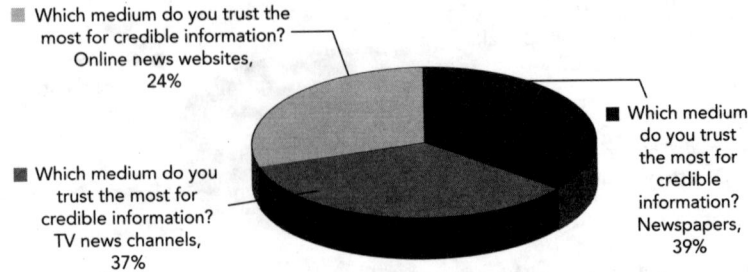

Figure 9.3 *Sources Most Trusted by Users for Credible Information*

messages before forwarding them, whereas 29 per cent said they did not. This is indicative of the tendency to pay attention to messages.

To know the mechanisms that users are likely to use to guard against misinformation, respondents were also asked about how they would seek to verify the information they received through social media (Figure 9.3). As many as 39 per cent of users, which constituted the majority, said they would cross-check with reports published in newspapers in order to ascertain the authenticity of the information received through social media.

This indicates that many still consider newspapers as the most credible source of information. Moreover, 37 per cent of respondents said they would turn to television news for authentic information, placing the medium a close second to print media as a trusted source of information. As much as 24 per cent said they would check the online medium to verify the source of information they received on social media.

Further to a survey, in-depth interviews were conducted with 10 persons to gain qualitative insights and viewpoints surrounding fake news. The respondents included a professor, a research scholar, a journalist, an advertising professional, a public relations official, a human resources management professional and four students. While five respondents were from the media background, five were from non-media backgrounds in terms of profession and educational qualifications. When asked about general understanding and awareness of fake news, all the interviewees said they were aware of what fake news is. Four of the 10 interviewees promptly recalled at least 5–7 recent fake news stories, showing a well-informed awareness of the issues. Of these, three were from the media background and one from a non-media background. All the respondents pointed out that the singular element which marks fake news is the intentional manipulation of facts driven by ulterior motives. Health-related fake news and communally motivated fake news were believed by most interviewees to be the most dangerous in terms of the reach and magnitude of the negative impact they could have.

While fake news did not have any direct personal impact on the interviewees, most related instances of when someone known, either a relative or a friend, was fooled into believing false information to be true. One interviewee related how a relative informed her of a war declared by China on India believing it to be true, which was just an exaggerated narration of existing tension between the two countries. Conspiracy videos have been a common concern, according to some. Two interviewees said they encountered the use of celebrity images to spread false news on a regular basis. Sometimes, posts shared by celebrity profiles on Twitter or official pages on Facebook are taken seriously by a huge number of fans.

One interviewee cited the example of popular Hollywood actor Leonardo de Caprio whose post about the Amazon fire was later revealed to have used images that were not actually of the fire. When celebrities can be misled easily and share posts without checking the veracity of information, their followers on social media are also likely to tread the same path. All interviewees stressed the importance of increasing one's awareness about the issues surrounding fake news and the ways to verify the information. Only two interviewees could name organizations that debunk fake news and said that they referred to sites like Alt News to clarify information for authenticity. Another interviewee said that while she was aware of the existence of fake news and took every post circulated on social media with a pinch of salt, older members in her family who had lesser exposure to social media tended to take everything posted through WhatsApp and other social networking platforms at face value. These inputs underscore the need for increasing levels of awareness about defences available against fake news.

CHALLENGES

Tracking the source of any fake news is the biggest challenge in stopping it in its tracks. So far, fake news busters have been involved in discovering if news is fake or not, but they can seldom trace the creators of such content. According to an article published in *The Hindu* (Gupta, 2019), measures to track the source would require social media platforms to 'de-anonymise all social media accounts ... is fraught with serious issues concerning the invasion of privacy and free speech ...'. The issue of protection of privacy thus comes as a hindrance to bringing to book the creators of fake news, who go scot-free and no punitive actions can be taken against them even if the content is proven to be false or manipulated.

Even when social media platforms such as WhatsApp and Facebook have enabled fact-checking in different Indian languages, not all the 23 official languages of the country are covered under this provision. Major languages such as Kannada and Odiya are not included in the list of languages for which fact-checking is enabled.

A large number of users remain uninformed about the concept of fake news or even if they do know about it, they lack the adequate level of media literacy to track the sources and hence determine the authenticity of news. The inherent human need to share posts that appeal to them instantly to get approval in the form of likes, re-tweets, comments or shares may be yet another deterrent to rational thinking and the push to check facts before sharing. According to an article published in the *Economic Times* (Rai, 2019), India lacks an adequate taskforce to debunk fake news. The amount and rate at which fake news spreads far exceed the speed with which it can be tracked and exposed.

CONCLUSION

The growing importance of social media has led to changes in public communication, shifting the power-centre. The provisions of developing user-generated content and sharing it multiple times have opened up a new dimension. The level of awareness about fake news and the defences against it among users of social media as well as the efforts being made to curb the proliferation of fake news are inadequate. While information overload and busy lifestyles pose challenges for social media users to filter fake news actively from social networking platforms, more focused efforts to increase awareness about the extent of spread and virulence of fake news can minimize, if not fully eliminate, the propagation and impact of fake news. The efforts of social networking sites to introduce new features, though still at a nascent stage, will hold the key to solving this problem. This has to be backed by fast-paced efforts at making people aware of the wide reach and negative impacts of fake news. Thus, increasing media literacy among the general public with a specific focus on developing strong resistance towards manipulative information is the foremost requirement to fight fake news. Also, existing fact-checking organizations, which are currently fighting a valiant battle, need to be strengthened by roping in trained professionals to handle the task of verifying mammoth amounts of information circulating online for authenticity. This can be seen as an opportunity for aspiring media professionals who want to make a career in social media to have a professional approach to the news even in the absence of gatekeeping. In India, statutory policies and regulatory bodies need to be set up in addition to enhancing media literacy among the masses.

REFERENCES

Al-Zaman, M. S. (2021). Covid-19-related social media fake news in India. *Journalism and Media, 2*(1), 100–14.

Allcott, H., & Gentzkow, M. (2017). Social media and fake news in the 2016 election. *The Journal of Economic Perspectives, 31*(2), 211–235. Retrieved from www.jstor.org/stable/44235006

Allcott, H., Gentzkow, M., & Yu, C. (2019). Trends in the diffusion of misinformation on social media. *Research & Politics, 6*, 1–8. Retrieved from https://doi.org/10.1177/2053168019848554

Awasthi, P. (2020, March). One held for selling cow urine and dung as cure for coronavirus. *The Hindu Business Line.* Retrieved from https://www.thehindubusinessline.com/news/national/one-held-for-selling-cow-urine-and-dung-as-cure-for-coronavirus/article31097518.ece

Banerjee, A. N., & Haque, M. N. (2018). Is fake news real in India?. *Journal of Content, Community & Communication, 8*(4), 46–49. doi:www.doi.org/10.31620/JCCC.12.18/09

Bansal, S. (2017, May 19). Faking it on WhatsApp: How India's favourite messaging app is turning into a rumour mill. *Hindustan Times*. Retrieved from https://www.hindustantimes.com/india-news/faking-it-on-whatsapp-how-india-s-favourite-messaging-app-turned-into-a-rumour-mill/story-QAkM-4RnF3NeeulOXlFDyUK.html

Brashier, N.M., Pennycook, G., Berinskye, A. J. & Rand, D.G. (2021). 'Timing Matters when Correcting Fake News'. *Proc. Natl. Acad. Sci. USA*. 118.

Brun, I., & Roitman, M. (2019). 'National Security in the Era of Post Truth and Fake News'. *Institute for National Security Studies*. https://bit.ly/30XXb92

Cerase, A., & Santoro, C. (2018). From racial hoaxes to media hypes: Fake news' real consequences. In P. Vasterman (Ed.), *From media hype to Twitter storm* (pp. 333–354). *Amsterdam University Press*. doi:10.2307/j.ctt21215m0.20

Egelhofer, J. L., & Lecheler, S. (2019). Fake news as a two-dimensional phenomenon: A framework and research agenda. *Annals of the International Communication Association*, *43*, 97–116.

Farooq, G. (2018). Politics of fake news: How WhatsApp became a potent propaganda tool in India. *Media Watch*, *9*(1), 106–117.

Guadagno, R. E., & Guttieri, K. (2019). Fake news and information warfare: An examination of the political and psychological processes from the digital sphere to the real world. In Innocent E. Chiluwa and Sergei A. Samoilenko (Eds.), *Handbook of research on deception, fake news, and misinformation online* (pp. 167–191). IGI Global.

Gupta, R. (2019, September 19). Shaking the foundation of fake news. *The Hindu*. Retrieved from http://www.thehindu.com/

Haciyakupoglu, G., Yang Hui, J., Suguna, V., Leong, D., & Rahman, M. (2018). Countering fake news: A survey of recent global initiatives (pp. 5–13, Rep.). *S. Rajaratnam School of International Studies*. Retrieved from www.jstor.org/stable/resrep17646.5

Ireton, Ch. & Posetti, J. (2018). *Journalism, fake news and disinformation: Handbook for journalism education and training*. UNESCO Publications.

Jain, R. (2020, April 21). Covid-19: How fake news and Modi government messaging fuelled India's latest spiral of Islamophobia. *Scroll.in*. Retrieved from http://www.https://scroll.in/

Koushik, J. (2020, May 7). Tamil Nadu police arrest man who claimed to have found 'herbal' cure for Covid-19. *The Indian Express*. Retrieved from https://indianexpress.com/article/cities/chennai/tamil-nadu-police-arrest-man-who-claimed-to-have-found-herbal-cure-for-covid-19-6398039/

Krishnan, J. (2020, January 31). No, magic potion of cow urine and turmeric cannot cure cancer. *Health Analytics Asia*. Retrieved from https://www.ha-asia.com/no-magic-potion-of-cow-urine-turmeric-cannot-cure-cancer/

Lewandowsky, S. & Sander van der Linden, S. (2021). Countering misinformation and fake news through inoculation and prebunking. *European Review of Social Psychology*. doi:10.1080/10463283.2021.1876983

Mishra, I. (2020, April 6). Bathing in cow dung: Superstitions abound on how to tackle Covid-19. *The Times of India*. Retrieved from http://timesofindia.indiatimes.com/articleshow/74998817.cms?utm_source=contentofinterest&utm_medium=text&utm_campaign=cppst

Nielsen, R. K., & Graves, L. (2017). News you don't believe: Audience perspectives on fake news. https:// reutersinstitute.politics.ox.ac.uk/sites/default/files/2017-10/Nielsen%26Graves_factsheet_1710v3_FINAL_download. pdf

Pennycook, G. & Rand, D.G. (2021). The psychology of fake news. *Trends in Cognitive Sciences*, 25(5), 388–402. https://doi.org/10.1016/j.tics.2021.02.007.

Rai, S. (2019, May 21). Alarming lessons from Facebook's push to stop fake news in India. *The Economic Times*. Retrieved from http://www.https:https://economictimes.indiatimes.com/

Raj, A., & Goswami, M. P. (2020). Is fake news spreading more rapidly than Covid-19 in India?. *Journal of Content, Community and Communication*, 11, 208–220.

Schulman, R., & Siman-Tov, D. (2020, March 18). From biological weapons to miracle drugs: Fake news about the coronavirus pandemic. INSS Insight No. 1275.

Sheth, H. (2021, February 2). Researchers develop new approach to help detect fake news: Report. *Business Line*. Retrieved from https://www.thehindubusinessline.com/news/researchers-develop-new-approach-to-help-detect-fake-news-report/article33729127.ece

Shu, K., Mahudeswaran, D., Wang, S., Lee, D., & Liu, H. (2018). FakeNewsNet: A data repository with news content, social context and dynamic information for studying fake news on social media. arXiv preprint arXiv:1809.01286 (2018).

Thukral, S. (2020, May 15). WhatsApp Launches 'Check It Before You Share It' Campaign to Stem Misinformation. *Economic Times*. Retrieved from https://economictimes.indiatimes.com/news/politics-and-nation/whatsapp-launches-check-it-before-you-share-it-campaign-to-stem-misinformation/articleshow/75762404.cms?utm_source=contentofinterest&utm_medium=text&utm_campaign=cppst

Watson, C. A. (2018). Information literacy in a fake/false news world: An overview of the characteristics of fake news and its historical development. *International Journal of Legal Information*, 46(2), 93–96. doi: http://dx.doi.org/10.1017/jli.2018.25

Weiss, A. P., Alwan, A., Garcia, E. P., & Garcia, J. (2020). Surveying fake news: Assessing university faculty's fragmented definition of fake news and its impact on teaching critical thinking. *International Journal for Educational Integrity, 16*(1). https://doi.org/10.1007/s40979-019-0049-x

Chapter 10

Social Media Regulation
A Review of Legal Frameworks

Balashanmugam S. K.

INTRODUCTION

In India, social media consumption has experienced a 75 per cent increase as compared to that of the preceding week of the first lockdown due to COVID-19 in 2020 (Keerely, 2021). Fifty per cent of the world's population avail the services of online social media (Hootsuite, 2021). Further, social media has made tremendous changes replacing the traditional media in the sphere of information and communication, post-liberalization (Mellor, 2014). Despite its development, the users' privacy concerns of social media have spiked in recent decades.

Over the years, online social media has attracted a lot of criticism for fake news, hate speech, misogynistic and anti-minority content and most importantly, its manipulative impact on electoral democracy (Aichholzer, 2020; Gil de Zúñiga & Hsuan-Ting, 2019). The Cambridge Analytica Scandal is found as the best instance that throws light on how companies steal the data of users and share it with the third-party websites (Kawaljeet, 2018). Therefore, the deteriorated concern of the public trust and their control over their data has been at a recent stake (Turner, 2018).

Further, there is no specific legislation to regulate online social media platforms and intermediaries in India (Basu & Jones, 2005). Therefore, this chapter attempts to review the significance of laws and the institutional framework that were developed worldwide to ensure data privacy and data protection. Further, the chapter will bring out the significance of the development of legislation and the institutional framework governing online social platforms and especially data protection and data privacy with reference to India.

SOCIAL MEDIA THREATS

The following types of social media threats have been continuously creating privacy threats since 2000 and particularly, the concern is huge since 2020 and 2021:

- Data mining
- Malware sharing
- Over the top
- Phishing attacks

Data Mining

Data mining refers to the phenomenon of automated analytical techniques to explore data for trends, patterns and other important information (Flavian et al., 2015). Online social media has been functional in allowing users over the internet to disseminate particular information and exchanging opinions will further open up to expose their identity to communicate with users of similar interests at the other end (Ahmad et al. 2014). The recent online social networking sites are internet-based, and the contents are stored on cloud storage through a centralized access management system (Ud Din et al., 2018). While creating a social media account, users present their personal information which includes name, date of birth, geographical location and personal interests (Irshad & Soomro, 2018). Further, users share information about their daily routine, friends, colleagues, photos and videos. Additionally, the respective site owners collect information about the user's behaviour. The contents of such may be accessed by end users from anywhere using an internet connection (Kim, 2002). Inadvertently, site owners disseminate such information about users to third-party networks without the knowledge or consent of the users. The accessibility of such sensitive information may lead to the disclosure of privacy of users. Further, the users' privacy has been at risk because of the traceability of publicly available data (Senthil Kumar et al., 2016).

Malware Sharing

Malware has become the first choice of weapon to perform hateful incidents on the cyber platform (Bakdash et al., 2018). It refers to a class of attack without the knowledge of the host/legitimate owner to benefit the adversary. For instance, viruses, worms, Trojan horses, spyware are some of the exemplary classes of malware.

It shall be used to filch sensitive information, extract money once malware has been infiltrated into the users' computer (Eze & Chiaghana, 2018). Ransomware is a category of malware that employs encryption which spreads like a worm and prevents the users from accessing their system either by system lock or file lock until after ransom is paid (Khalida et al., 2019). At present, social media becomes an ideal delivery system for distributing malware (Arunlal, 2019). Often, malware is used to target public or corporate websites to collect essential information and then to disrupt their operations (Jang-Jaccard & Nepal, 2014). Cybercriminals further distribute malware to friends' accounts/contacts of the users' by compromising users' account (Rokkathapa & Kanrar, 2019).

Phishing Attacks

Phishing is a category of social network attack often used to steal users' data, login information and numbers of the credit and debit cards of the users. It occurs when an attacker, concealed as a trusted organization, make the victim open an email and by sending an instant message or text message. It is one of the most prominent routes that criminals adopt to get access to insightful individual information. There has been a steady rise in phishing attacks from 76 per cent in 2017 to 83 per cent in 2018 and the number of phishing attacks is remarkably higher than the number recorded in the first half of 2019 (Proofpoint, 2020). Phishing attacks employ a combination of social networking and technology spoofing methods to influence the users to communicate essential information that the invader exercise to make a financial gain (Banu & Banu 2013). Phishing attacks occur in various forms. Email Spoofing and Web Spoofing are considered to be the most pressing cybersecurity threat for all internet users (Alkhalil et al., 2021). It has impacted many stakeholders, including victims from the corporate sector to government agencies. For instance, a massive phishing campaign in the year 2019 targeted the users of Instagram by using a two-factor authentication system, prompting the users to log in to a false Instagram page.

Over the Top (OTT)

In times of the COVID pandemic, the 'Over the top' (OTT) video consumption has rapidly evolved given advancements in digital infrastructure and compelling consumers to avail such services (Saini, 2020). It is estimated that India will become the second-largest OTT market after the United States in 2023 (Fitzgerald, 2019). The OTT service providers viz. Netflix, YouTube, Amazon Prime Videos and Spotify have seen excessive growth in a developing country like India and have the potential to capitalize as a strong communication channel on digital media (Kumari, 2020; Gupta & Singharia, 2021).

The OTT services possess a hybrid character as it combines the consumer choice of the web and the passive consumption of television (Chaithra, 2020). The censorship justification and the significance of films have produced a lot of attention during the growth of live streaming sites in times of the COVID pandemic. The issue that arose in respect of digital content regulation is state censorship and self-regulation.

INTERNATIONAL FRAMEWORK

Social networks across the globe consider revolving with the adaptation to the needs and responses of subjects of various nations (Clark et al., 2018; Muller, E., & Peres, 2019; Schlagwein, 2014). In spite of various international regulations at the place, users' freedom of expression has been given much attention through the international instruments and particularly through agreements under the aegis of the United Nations (Howie, 2018). Therefore, the analysis of the international legal framework for online social media is necessary to bring out the determination of the most important covenants that represent a source of media law and its implementation strategies.

Highlighting the importance of speech and expression over the use of the internet and social media, the relevance of agreements negotiated under the ambience of the United Nations needs a peculiar analysis. The United Nations plays a significant role in the protection and promotion of human rights across the world (Wehbe, 2018). The Universal Declaration of Human Rights (UDHR) draws its attention to addressing the needs and developments of human rights. According to Article 19 of the UDHR,

> Everyone has the right to freedom of opinion and expression; this right includes freedom to hold opinions without interference and to seek, receive and impart information and ideas through any media and regardless of frontiers.

The United Nations General Assembly adopts the UDHR as a set of regulations or principles that every member nation agreed to implement into their national regulations. Thus, the freedom of formulating opinions and expression is considered to be an international human right protected by the United Nations. Freedom of expression is not an absolute right, and it presumes to be an individual responsibility. It sounds fundamental to democracy and the media acts as a guardian. According to Article 19(2) of the International Covenant on Civil and Political Rights (ICCPR), 1966,

> 1. Everyone shall have the right to hold opinions without interference.

> 2. Everyone shall have the right to freedom of expression; this right shall include freedom to seek, receive and impart information and ideas of all kinds, regardless of frontiers, either orally, in writing or in print, in the form of art, or through any other media of his choice.

The important feature of this covenant is that it contains binding legal obligations for state actors and the member nations (Carpenter, 2000). Further, the article intends to recognize the global expression of the right to formulate and express an opinion (Haxhiraj, 2013; O'Flaherty, 2012). Thus, the freedom to formulate opinion, speech and expression is considered as fundamental under the international instruments.

DOMESTIC JURISDICTION AND ITS REGULATORY FRAMEWORK

Several countries around the globe paid their attention in regulating online social media as this is of serious concern not only for individual countries but also of transnational (Muller & Peres, 2019; Schlagwein, 2014). The countries such as Germany, European Union, Australia, China and the U. S. have been undertaken for analysis (see Table 10.1).

Table 10.1 *Comparison of Online Social Media Regulations in Domestic Jurisdictions*

Country	Existing Legislation	New Legislation	Nature of Legislation
Germany	NIL	Network Enforcement Act, 2018	Stringent liability regime & self-regulation
European Union	NIL	General Data Protection Regulation, 2018	Self-regulation
Australia	NIL	Enhancing Online Safety Act, 2015	Stringent liability regime & self-regulation
United States	NIL	Sector-specific legislations	Stringent liability regime & self-regulation
China	NIL	Data Security Law, 2020 (in draft stage)	Self-regulation
India	Information Technology Act, 2000	NIL	Self-regulation

Germany

In Germany, the existing Network Enforcement Act (NetzDG), 2018, enforces an important obligation for the social media platforms to remove hate speech within a set deadline or otherwise the offender will face a case with a fine of up to 50 million pounds and the penalty is higher for non-compliance (Zipursky, 2019). The significance of this legislation is to strengthen the rights of the users and to ensure transparency, simplifying the notifications of the users and the objection procedures against the abusive content made easier (Tworek & Leerssen, 2019). Another important feature of the legislation is the introduction of an intermediary liability regime that incentivizes severe administrative penalties.

Further, it forces the social networking sites to report about violence, murder or rape threats, terrorist attacks and sexual abuse of children if any to the Office of the Federal Criminal Police (Wagner et al., 2020). Though the legislation strengthens the transparency and accountability of large social network platforms, it also raises serious concerns regarding the formulation of opinion and the freedom of expression.

European Union

The issues concerning data privacy are well addressed in the European Convention on Human Rights and Fundamental Freedoms and particularly with respect to Article 8 of the Convention. The bare provision reads as follows:

> 1. Everyone has the right to respect for his private and family life, his home and his correspondence.
>
> 2. There shall be no interference by a public authority with the exercise of this right except such as is in accordance with the law and is necessary in a democratic society in the interests of national security, public safety or the economic wellbeing of the country, for the prevention of disorder or crime, for the protection of health or morals, or for the protection of the rights and freedoms of others.

It enunciates the right for every human individual to respect one's private and family life, one's home and correspondence without any unlawful hindrances by the public authority. Further, the General Data Protection Regulation (GDPR) has been enforced in 2018 with an aim to harmonize the privacy and data protection laws making consumer-friendly legislation (al, C. J., 2019). Through the new set of regulations, the EU attempted to introduce rules to maintain and manage the users' data and other information (Chassang, 2017; Dove, 2018). Though the user interactions with GDPR-sparked initiatives are on the rise, the attitude of the citizen and hope of data governance are not keeping enough paces (Aichholzer, 2019).

Consumer awareness against the protection of data and data privacy has increased in the EU, which is considered a welcome step in the development of regulations (Daigle & Khan, 2020). In view of this, the member countries of the EU are directed to implement the community directive into their domestic legislations within 2021. But the implementation of the GDPR requires financial and human resources as well as capacity building of employees. This seems to be a difficult task for the companies to comply with it (Christina et al., 2018).

Australia

In 2015, legislators enacted the Enhancing Online Safety Act. The important objective of the act is to prohibit the posting or threatening to post an intimate image, relevant electronic service without consent on a social networking site. It further encourages complaints and objection system with proper channelling through the establishment of the Office of the e-safety Commissioner. Therefore, after the introduction of such legislation, complaints concerning harassing, posting obscene contents on social media sites have been considerably reduced (Mason & Czapski, 2017). Additional with a jail sentence the penalty has also been imposed for any kind of violations on online social media networks. The Office of the e-Safety Commissioner's has been entrusted to impose takedown notices and penalties for posting obscene contents over online social media.

China

In addition to the Cyber Security Law, 2016, the Data Security Law of the People's Republic of China has been presented by the Standing Committee of China's National People's Congress to put forth the implementing regulations, standards and guidance (Parasol, 2018). It contains an expressive provision for the right of privacy and personal information protection (Qi et al., 2018). The act further aimed at establishing a comprehensive state-directed data security system that comprises the hierarchical data classification management that would reduce the harm to the national economy, national security and public interest (Lasiello, 2017). Another feature of this act is the introduction of a centralized data security risk assessment, monitoring mechanism, reporting strategies, sharing of information and early warning system. The new administrative structures have been connected with the existing cybersecurity administrative structures for their better implementation.

United States

The exploitation of secret information of over 50 million users of Facebook by the consulting agency Cambridge Analytica has been a turning point that sought the attention of the legislators towards the development of legislation (Balke, 2018). There is no single legislation to cover the data security threats in the United States (Boyne, 2018). There have been laws enacted at federal and state levels to protect the personal data, safeguarding data, disposing data and privacy issues of citizens of the United States (Bernadette & Vince, 2019). In addition to that, sector-specific legislations have been enacted and made applicable to financial sectors, personal health, telemarketing, telecommunication sectors, credit report information and information pertaining to children (Ducato, 2020).

LEGISLATIVE AND INSTITUTIONAL FRAMEWORK IN INDIA

There is no specific legislation to ensure data privacy and data protection laws in India. In such a scenario, the primary source of data privacy and data protection is protected under the existing Information

Technology Act (IT Act), 2000. The primary intent of this legislation is to provide legal recognition for all transactions performed through electronic path for exchanging data, e-commerce to reform the earlier way of paper-based communication. The legislation has been enacted in conformity with the obligations made in the United Nations Commission on International Trade Law (UNCITRAL). The UNCITRAL instituted the UNCITRAL Model law on E-Commerce in the year 1996. The intended law is to facilitate the use of online social media with a focus on the storage and communication of information.

Out of which, Section 43A of IT Act, 2000 reads as follows:

Penalty and compensation for damage to computer, computer system, etc. – If any person without permission of the owner or any other person who is in charge of a computer, computer system or computer network,–

(a) accesses or secures access to such computer, computer system or computer network [or computer resource];

Section 43A creates a corporate liability towards data handling, storage and disseminates information for an unfair loss or unlawful gain to any person by way of paying compensation to the affected users (Rajvanshi & Singhal, 2016). Further, Section 43 A enunciates the framing of the Information Technology (Reasonable Security Practices and Procedures and Sensitive Personal Data or Information) Rules, 2011. This rule has been framed to protect the personal data collected by an individual who has been indulged in commercial or specialized activities (Singh, 2011). While Section 43A provides compensation for private organizations, Section 72 imposes a penalty to the officials including government officials for disclosing the electronic records, books, register, information, etc., related to any person without obtaining his prior consent. Section 72 of the IT Act, 2000, reads as follows:

Penalty for Breach of confidentiality and privacy.– Save as otherwise provided in this Act or any other law for the time being in force, if any person who, in pursuance of any of the powers conferred under this Act, rules or regulations made there under, has secured access to any electronic record, book, register, correspondence, information, document or other material without the consent of the person concerned discloses such electronic record, book, register, correspondence, information, document or other material to any other person shall be punished with imprisonment for a term which may extend to two years, or with fine which may extend to one lakh rupees, or with both.

Section 66A of the IT Act, 2000, prohibits the sending of offensive messages through online networking sites. This could be well understood through the analysis of the landmark case, *Shreya Singhal vs Union of India*. The insertion of S.66A to the IT Act, 2000 extends the scope of the legislation to deal with offences like cyberstalking, threatening mails, phishing mails and spam (Fatima, 2007). This process involves various intermediaries in delivering such information to the end users through online medium (Bahl et al., 2020). For instance, a user interested in launching a website will initially open an account with a host. Then he uploads necessary information on his web pages available with the host network and is directly accessible through the operations on the internet (Flavian et al. 2009).

When such information is added to the server, the uploaded information becomes immediately available to all other internet users (Batra & Batra, 2020). Therefore, Internet Service Providers (ISPs) play a significant role in disseminating the content of third-party content (Azmi et al., 2017). The wording of Section 66A has ambiguity in it. The basic issue with the section, particularly with respect to clauses (b) and (c), and usage of words such as 'inconvenience', 'obstruction', 'annoyance' which are neither defined in the primary legislation nor introduced by way of amendment to the legislation. This leads to absurdity in interpretation which further develops the likelihood of misuse of the provision. So, there are many undefined words that needed a definition because of which it is ineffective to deal with such issues.

Further, Section 69 of the IT Act, 2000 empowers the Central government to hold control over online data and to arrest the offender.

69A. Power to issue directions for blocking for public access of any information through any computer resource.–(1) Where the Central Government or any of its officers specially authorised by it in this behalf is satisfied that it is necessary or expedient so to do, in the interest of sovereignty and integrity of India, defence of India, security of the State, friendly relations with foreign States or public order or for preventing incitement to the commission of any cognizable, offence relating to above, it may subject to the provisions of sub-section (2), for reasons to be recorded in writing, by order, direct any agency of the Government or intermediary to block for access by the public or cause to be blocked for access by the public any information generated, transmitted, received, stored or hosted in any computer resource.

While observing the powers under Section 69A of the Information Technology Act read with the Information Technology (Procedure and Safeguards for Blocking of Access of Information by Public) Rules 2009, the Ministry of Electronics and Information Technology (MEITY), Government of India has blocked 118 mobile applications considering the emerging nature of threats in late 2020.

So, the need for imposing greater liability for the ISPs is of utmost concern in the recent scenario. Section 79 of the IT Act grants restricted protection to intermediaries from liability for any third-party incidents. Section 79(1) of the IT Act provides conditional immunity to the intermediaries regarding any information, data or communication link of a third party hosted by them. Further, Section 79(2) basically covers the cases where the activity undertaken by the intermediary is of a technical nature. Thus, the intermediaries must possess adequate knowledge and control over the information which is intended to get transmitted or communicated.

Furthermore, Section 79(3)(b) envisages a 'notice and take down' rule, wherein the intermediary is obligatory to remove unlawful content upon receiving actual awareness of its existence. In the case of *Avnish Bajaj vs State*, the managing director of the company Bazee.com was charged with criminal provisions for the circulation of content on its e-commerce platform by a third party. The judgement on this case led to the observation of widening the scope of the intermediary protection. Through an amendment to the IT Act, the Government of India enacted intermediary guidelines 'The Information Technology (Intermediaries Guidelines) Rules, 2011' making it mandatory for all intermediaries to follow due diligence requirements.

As a given effect, in the case of *Kamlesh Vaswani vs Union of India*, the intermediaries were directed to disable the content relating to child pornography. The vicarious liability plays a very important role in the fixation of liability for the intermediaries. Based on this rule, the ISP is strictly bound to be liable for any unlawful or illegal activity that is transmitted on its platform. Moreover, it is not an easy task to regulate the flow of data as it deemed to be a larger size by the ISP. Finally, the ISP was often unsuccessful in protecting its users from economic, religious and sociopolitical offences which might misuse freedom of formulation of opinions, speech and data protection (Mathew, 2016).

Therefore, through the analysis, it is clear that the IT Act, 2000 has its very limited application on data privacy and the development of standards. Privacy also has an implication for the formulation of opinion and expression. The rise in the number of litigations is clear evidence for this. As envisaged in various international instruments, privacy considered an important fundamental human right forms the basis of a democratic country (La Rue, 2013). Though Article 21 of the Indian Constitution expands the scope of right to life to include privacy, there is no comprehensive law in India to ensure privacy.

The nine-judge bench of the Supreme Court of India expanded the scope of 'right to life' as envisaged under Article 21 of the Constitution of India to include 'right to privacy' through the landmark decision of *Justice K. S. Puttaswamy vs Union of India*. This landmark judgement streamlined and influenced the Government of India to develop legislation towards data privacy and protection across its territory. Subsequently, a petition has been filed before the Supreme Court of India to regulate Twitter and other social media networks by framing regulations/guidelines including criminal prosecutions for wrongdoings. In the month of March 2021, Twitter withheld around 250 accounts upon request by MEITY under Section 69A of the IT Act, 2000. It was informed that the reason to withheld was to ensure law and order at the time of farmers' protest.

In line with further developments, MEITY constituted a committee under the chairmanship of Hon'ble Retd. Justice B. N. Srikrishna of the Supreme Court of India to draft a Bill on data protection. The Personal Data Protection Bill, 2019 aimed to propose a stringent legislative framework to safeguard the individual privacy of their personal data, storage, use and communication, creating a trust between individual users and the corporate in processing data. One of the significant features of this Bill is that it is proposed to establish a mechanism for implementing organizational and technical measures towards processing data and formulating norms for the transborder regulation of personal data. The successful adoption of this Bill ensures accountability of sites processing individual data and lays down remedies for unauthorized and harmful processing. It further handed over the responsibility of regulating by the creation of Data Protection Authority to oversee and administer the processing activities. At present, the Bill is being examined by a 30-member team of the Joint Parliamentary Committee (JPC), which is obligated to present its report.

So far, in India, the exclusive legislation that has its control on data privacy and data protection falls under the Information Technology Act, 2000 through the framing of rules thereunder and the penal provisions concerned under the Indian Penal Code (IPC). Very recently, India has notified stringent guidelines, that is, 'The Information Technology (Guidelines for Intermediaries and Digital Media Ethics Code) Rules, 2021' wherein the 'originator' of any unlawful message has to be identified and punished (Muller & Peres, 2019; Rajkhowa, 2015). In view of compliance to this, MEITY has enacted its draft Information Technology (Intermediary Guidelines and Digital Media Ethics Code) Rules, 2021 which require the online social networking sites to communicate the details of the 'originator' of whenever an offensive message is in circulation.

The recent initiative of the government sounds with a self-regulatory mechanism for the OTT Platforms and the online portals as well (Banday & Mazood, 2013; Mathew, 2016). In order to adjudicate the grievances and issues surrounding online platforms, a three-tier grievance redressal system has been planned to introduce in consequence of the acceptance of the Data Protection Bill (Menon, 2020). The important aspect of the Bill is that it self-regulates publishers. Further, it requires the appointment of an India-based officer to take charge of the complaints and grievances and to adjudicate the same with a duration of around 15 days. Additionally, the Ministry of Information and Broadcasting has been entrusted to formulate an oversight mechanism and to develop a charter for self-regulating bodies which include Codes of Practices and to constitute an inter-departmental committee for hearing such grievances.

Realizing the need to create a censor screen for the OTT platforms, the government came up with recommendations for the OTT players to classify their films on the basis of age appropriateness, for instance, 13+, 16+ and adults, etc. Though the government stepped up with an enormous measure to regulate the online platforms, there should be an appropriate parental lock mechanism as Netflix has an option at the front.

CONCLUSION

The progress of technology cannot be on hold under any circumstances. Despite its growth, it has led to various cyber threats in India and across the globe. The challenge here is for the regulators to develop measures to handle and manage the users' data. Further, the freedom of forming opinions and expression, though it is considered to be an important fundamental right recognized by the United Nations covenants and also Indian legislation, it is still violated in various forms. In addition to this, the Indian laws on data protection are still in the nascent stage of their development though it seems to be pending with the Parliamentary Committee for its evaluation. It is to conclude that the cybersecurity and data protection faces a significant threat because of the absence of such appropriate legislative and institutional framework. Though self-regulation seems to reduce the constraints to a certain level, the development of community-wise legislation is also equally important as this issue of data protection is of transnational concern.

REFERENCES

Ahmad. A. Afnan S., Hanan, B. & Maha, S. (2014). Social networks' benefits, privacy, and identity theft: KSA case study. *International Journal of Advanced Computer Science and Applications,* 5(12), 129–143.

Alkhalil, Z., Hewage, C. Nawaf, L., Khan, I. (2021). Phishing attacks: A recent comprehensive study and a new anatomy. *Frontiers in Computer Science,* 3. 2624–9898.

Aichholzer, R. L. (2020). E-Democracy: Conceptual foundations and recent trends. In Hennen, L., Van Keulen, I., Korthagen, I., Aichholzer, G., Lindner, R., Nielsen, R.Ø. (Eds.) *European E-Democracy in Practice*, (pp.11–45).

Arunlal, V. (2019). Impact of malware in modern society. *Journal of Scientific Research and Development, 2*(3), 593–600.

Azmi, I., Ismail, S., & Daud, M. (2017). Internet service providers liability for third party content: Freedom to operate? *5th International Conference on Cyber and IT Service Management*, 1–5.

Bahl, V. S., Rahman, F., & Bailey, R. (2020). Internet intermediaries and online harms: Regulatory responses in India. *Data Governance Network*. Working Paper 06.

Bakdash, J. Z., Hutchinson, S., Zaroukian, E. G., Marusich, L. R., & Thirumuruganathan, S., Sample, C., Hoffman, B. & Das, G. (2018). Malware in the future? Forecasting of analyst detection of cyber events. *Journal of Cyber Security, 1*(10). https://doi.org/10.1093/cybsec/tyy007

Balke, L. (2018). China's new cybersecurity law and U. S.–China cybersecurity issues. *Santa Clara Law Review, 58*(1), 137–162.

Banday, M. T. & Mazood, M. (2013). Social media in e-governance: A study with special reference to India. *Social Networking, 2*(2), 47–56.

Banu, M. N. & Banu, S. M., (2013). A comprehensive study of phishing attacks. *International Journal of Computer Science and Information Technologies, 4*(6), 783–786.

Basu, S. & Jones, R. (2005). Indian Information and Technology Act 2000: Review of the regulatory powers under the act. *International Review of Law, Computers & Technology, 19*(2), 209–230.

Batra, Nayyar, V., & Batra, R. (2020). 'Does Online Media Self-Regulate Consumption Behavior of Indian Youth?' *International Review on Public and Nonprofit Marketing, 17*, 277–288.

Bernadette K. & Vince, M. (2019). Your data is my data: A framework for addressing interdependent privacy infringements. *Journal of Public Policy & Marketing, 38*(4), 433–450.

Boyne, S. M. (2018). Data protection in the United States. *The American Journal of Comparative Law, 66*, 299–343.

Carpenter, K. D. A. (2000). The international covenant on civil and political rights: A toothless tiger. *North Carolina Journal of International Law and Commerce Regulation, 26*(1). https://scholarship.law.unc.edu/ncilj/vol26/iss1/1

Chaithra, R. (2020). Proliferation of OTT apps in India: An empirical study of OTT apps and its impact on college students. *International Journal of Research and Analytical Reviews, 7*(1), 427–435.

Chassang, G. (2017). The impact of the EU general data protection regulation on scientific research. *E-Cancer Medical Science, 11*, 709.

Chen, F., Deng, P., Wan, J., & Zhang, D. (2015). Data mining for the internet of things: Literature review and challenges. *International Journal of Distributed Sensor Networks, 9*, 1–14.

Christina, T. P., Anna, R. & Markkula, J. (2018). EU general data protection regulation: Changes and implications for personal data collecting companies. *Computer Law & Security Review, 34*(1), 134–153.

Clark, J. L., Algoe, S. B., & Green, M. C. (2018). Social network sites and well-being: The role of social connection. *Current Directions in Psychological Science, 27*(1).

Daigle, B., & Khan, M. (2020). The EU general data protection regulation: An analysis of enforcement trends by EU data protection authorities. *Journal of International Commerce and Economics, 12*(1), 1–38.

Dove, E. S. (2018). The EU general data protection regulation: Implications for international scientific research in the digital era. *The Journal of Law, Medicine & Ethics, 46*(4), 1013–1030.

Ducato, R. (2020). Data protection, scientific research, and the role of information. *Computer Law & Security Review, 37*. 105412

Eze, A. O. & Chiaghana, C. E. (2018). Malware analysis and mitigation in information preservation. *IOSR Journal of Computer Engineering, 20*(4) 53–62.

Fatima, T. (2007). Liability of online intermediaries: Emerging trends. *Journal of the Indian Law Institute, 49*(2), 155–178.

Fitzgerald, S. (2019). Over-the-top video services in India: Media imperialism after globalisation. *Media Industries, 6*(2). doi:10.3998/mij.15031809.0006.206

Flavian, C. R. Gurrea, R., Orús, C. (2009). Web design: A key factor for the website success. *Journal of Systems and Information Technology, 11*(2), 17.

Gil de Zúñiga, H. & Hsuan-Ting, C. (2019). Digital media and politics: Effects of the great information and communication divides. *Journal of Broadcasting & Electronic Media, 63*(3), 365–373.

Gupta, G., & Singharia, K. (2021). Consumption of OTT Media Streaming in COVID-19 Lockdown: Insights from PLS Analysis. *Vision, 25*(1), 36–46.

Haxhiraj, A. (2013). The covenant on civil and political rights. *Juridical Tribune, 3*(2)., 308–315.

Hootsuite. (2021). The global state of digital 2021. Retrieved from https://www.hootsuite.com/resources/digital-trends

Howie, E. (2018). Protecting the human right to freedom of expression in international law. *International Journal of Speech-Language Pathology, 20*(1), 12–15.

Hoofnagle, C. J., van der Sloot, B., & Borgesius, F. Z. (2019). The European Union general data protection regulation: What it is and what it means. *Information & Communications Technology Law, 28*(1), 65–98.

Irshad, S., & Soomro, T. R. (2018). Identity theft and social media. *International Journal of Computer Science and Network Security, 18*(1), 43–55.

Jang-Jaccard, J. & Nepal, S. (2014). A survey of emerging trends in cybersecurity. *Journal of Computer and System Sciences, 80*(5), 973–993.

Kawaljeet K. K., (2018). Advances in social media research: Past, present and future. *Informatiion Systems Frontiers, 20*(3), 531–558.

Keerely, S. (2021, August 2). Social Media Usage in India—Statistics & Facts. statista.com. Retrieved from https://www.statista.com/topics/5113/social-media-usage-in-india/#dossierSummary

Khalida, M. A., D. Z. M., Nadhim, M. H., & Abdellah, R. H. (2019). A study of ransomware attacks: Evolution and prevention. *Journal of Social Transformation and Regional Development, 1*(1), 18–25.

Kim, D. L. (2002). 2-Data Mining. *Database and Data Communication Network Systems, 1,* 41–76.

Kumari, T. (2020). A study on growth of over the top (OTT) video services in India. *International Journal of Latest Research in Humanities and Social Sciences, 3*(9), 68–73.

Lasiello, E. (2017). China's cyber initiatives counter international pressure. *Journal of Strategic Security, 10*(1), 1–16.

Mason, G., & Czapski, N. (2017). Regulating Cyber Racism. *Melbourne University Law Review, 41*(1), 1–53.

Mathew, M. (2016). Media Self-Regulation in India: A Critical Analysis. *Indian Law Institute Law Review,* 25–37.

Mellor, N. (2014). The two faces of media liberalization. *Mediterranean Politics, 19*(2), 265–271.

Menon, D. P. (2020). 'The Personal Data Protection Bill, 2018: India's Regulatory Journey towards a Comprehensive Data Protection Law'. *International Journal of Law & Information Technology, 28*(1), 1–19.

Muller, E., & Peres, R. (2019). The effect of social networks structure on innovation performance: A review and directions for research. *International Journal of Research in Marketing, 36*(1), 3–19.

O'Flaherty, M. (2012). Freedom of expression: Article 19 of the international covenant on civil and political rights and the human rights committee's general comment No 34. *Human Rights Law Review, 12*(4), 627–654.

Parasol, M. (2018). The impact of China's 2016 cyber security law on foreign technology firms, and on China's big data and smart city dreams. *Computer Law & Security Review, 34*(1), 67–98.

Proofpoint. (2020). 2020 State of the Phish: An in-depth look at user awareness, vulnerability and resilience. Annual Report of Proofpoint Inc. Retrieved from https://cdw prod.adobecqms.net/content/dam/cdw/on-domain-cdw/brands/proofpoint/gtd-pfpt-us-tr-state-of-the-phish-2020.pdf

Qi, A., Guosong, S., & Wentong, Z. (2018). Assessing China's cybersecurity law. *Computer Law & Security Review, 34*(6), 1342–1354.

Rajkhowa, A. (2015). The spectre of censorship: Media regulation, political anxiety and public contestations in India (2011–2013). *Media, Culture & Society, 37*(6), 867–886.

Rajvanshi, G., & Singhal, M. (2016). Data privacy law and growth of e-commerce: An Indian perspective. *Bharati Law Review, 4*(4), 1–36.

Rokkathapa, E., & Kanrar, S. (2019). A novel approach for predicting the malware attacks. *International Journal of Computer Applications, 181*(45), 30–32.

Rue, F. L. (2013). Report of the special rapporteur on the promotion and protection of the right to freedom of opinion and expression. *United Nations General Assembly Documents* A/HRC/23/40.

Saini, N. (2020). Usage of OTT platforms during COVID-19 lockdown: Trends, rationale and implications. *PalArch's Journal of Archaelogy of Egypt/Eqyptology*, *17*(6), 4212–4222.

Schlagwein, D. (2014). Social media around the globe. *Journal of Organizational Computing and Electronic Commerce*, *24* (2), 122–137.

Senthil Kumar, N., Saravanakumar, K., & Deepa, K. (2016). Privacy and security in social media—Comprehensive study. *Procedia Computer Science*, *78*, 114–119.

Singh, S. S. (2011). Privacy and data protection in India: A critical assessment. *Journal of the Indian Law Institute*, *53*(4), 663–677.

Turner, G. (2018). The media and democracy in the digital era: Is this what we had in mind? *Media International Australia*, *168*(1), 3–14.

Tworek, H. & Leerssen, P. (2019). *An analysis of Germany's NetzDG Law*. Transatlantic Working Group.

Ud Din, I., Islam, N., Rodrigues, J., & Guizani, M. (2018). Privacy and security issues in online social networks. *Future Internet*, *10*(114).

Wagner, B. Sekwenz, M. T., Cobbe, J., & Singh, J. (2020, January). Regulating transparency? Facebook, Twitter and the German Network Enforcement Act. Proceedings of the 2020 Conference on Fairness, Accountability, and Transparency, 261–271. doi.org/10.1145/3351095.3372856

Wehbe, A. (2018). Increasing international legal protections for freedom of expression. *Notre Dame Journal of International & Comparative Law*, *8*(2), 45–61.

Zipursky, R. (2019). Nuts about NETZ: The network enforcement act and freedom of expression. *Fordham International Law Journal*, *42*(4), 1325–1373.

Chapter 11

Balancing Social Media Autonomy, Privacy and Regulation

Francis P. Barclay, Boobalakrishnan N.
and Anushiya K.

INTRODUCTION

Social media may just be yet another medium through which a part of social interaction is channelled—exchanges such as hate speech, ridicule, blasphemy, gossip and rumour happen on multiple mediums just as they are delivered offline—but on these connected social media applications, such communications get amplified, sometimes, with desolating effects.

Social media may have become a necessary political tool in India, with politicians, media persons and partymen to the *aam aadmi* claiming their rightful online space for political activism and discourses. In politics and propaganda, online platforms are known and accepted to play crucial roles, determining successes and failures, and the earliest and well-known examples were the success of Barack Obama's 2008 presidential campaign and Howard Dean's failed 2004 presidential bid and the first-ever Tea Party rally, respectively (Ratkiewicz et al., 2011). Online social media may have played major roles in the last two Indian Lok Sabha elections (Barclay et al., 2014, 2015, 2016). Since 2014, political parties have been investing heavily in digital campaigns and are using social media aggressively to propagate their ideologies and discredit oppositions, as campaign successes are now dependent on innovative deployment of social media (Mahapatra & Plagemann, 2019). Social media is also at the forefront, providing a wealth of political data and opinion that can be used to gain wide-and-varied insights about the users and their attitudes and behaviours (Barclay, 2017; Nair & Barclay, 2017).

Social media reaching a wider section of the electorate increases political possibilities (Ceron et al., 2014). As the digital communication space gets denser with increased flow of user-generated information, netizens are able to garner wider and deeper access to valuable and timely information, participate in public discussions, exchange opinion and coordinate mass social movements (Shirky, 2011). Though the social media space encourages free and mass flow of opinions and ideas, aided by accessible and affordable internet, it could mean increased communicative capabilities and social development; yet little is 'understood about how online opinions emerge, diffuse and gain momentum' (Sobkowicz et al., 2012).

Facebook fosters the flow of user-generated information and supports the seamless sharing of information between networks, whereas 'politeness is lower in the more anonymous and deindividuated YouTube' (Halpern & Gibbs, 2013).

More recently, microblogging services such as Twitter and social network sites such as Facebook which are also open to public deliberation through posting, sharing and commenting are believed to have the ability to increase public participation in politics. Not just people are able to air out their political opinions freely on platforms such as Twitter and WhatsApp, even political parties and leaders have adopted these applications to establish direct contact and for two-way communication with the electorate, increasing political participation and discussion of political issues (Stieglitz & Dang-Xuan, 2013).

SOCIAL MEDIA MISUSE

Though social media platforms have wide and varied political applications, from propaganda and political opinion mining to poll prediction, on the other side of the spectrum, such social media platforms also pose several sociopolitical challenges (Cogburn & Espinoza-Vasquez, 2011). Social media has also raised several ethical and privacy issues, with fake messages used in unethical ways for propaganda and controversial regulatory mechanisms drawing flak.

In several instances, social media platforms have been squarely blamed for spreading rumours and misleading information, triggering tensions, leading to lynching, provoking anti-national and anti-social sentiments, defaming politicians and personalities, deepening discriminations, triggering religious intolerance and leading to clashes.

In 2012, one of the earliest cases of social media misuse called for government attention, when morphed pictures and videos of earthquake victims went viral. Miscreants used morphed images of quake victims to show them as minority victims of civil riots in Assam and Burma. This was intended to provoke further riots and it did bring about a reaction (Debu, 2015).

There have also been instances of arrests for posting indecent jokes about political leaders and for insulting the national flag (Express News Service, 2017; *Hindustan Times*, 2015).

Social media websites are banned to calm tensions in disputed regions as such applications are misused (Associated Press, 2017). Online social media was said to have a role in one of the recent Bhima-Koregaon protests that took place in Mumbai in the Indian state of Maharashtra. Wrong and misleading information was posted about the riots as tweets and Facebook posts (Sharon 2018). In yet another incident, two people were arrested for posting child-kidnapping rumours on WhatsApp and fake news on social media that caused lynching of seven innocent people (TNN, 2017). There have also been instances of social media users being jailed for unmindful posts and comments (TNN, 2017a).

Mass sharing of messages on social media platforms such as WhatsApp without concerns about credibility, fake messages and article links being shared through such applications and posting of inaccurate messages on social media platforms such as Facebook creating unrest and for political propaganda have been a major political issue of late, demanding critical examination. Social media have been conceived and viewed as an alternative medium of communication, offering a space for the sidelined to air out their opinions. But experience and research have shown social media to reflect dominant thoughts propagated through mainstream media, further thwarting alternative ideas and opinion (Barclay, 2017).

With social media platforms, one can reach out to the world with relative ease and broadcast his or her opinion to a wider section of audience. It is indeed crucial to have a free space for information–opinion exchange and sociopolitical deliberations without fear of repercussions—and the online social media platforms serve that purpose. Such liberty, however, comes with a cost, which has to be weighed in for the democratic tenets to hold ground.

While the idea of free expression is encouraging, social media poses challenges such as privacy and security threats (Venkat et al., 2014), problems of data security and management, inequalities in accessibility, lack of social inclusion, challenges in governance and creating a robust information policy. Although the fundamental guiding principles behind many regulations are still relevant, advancements and rapid adoption of social media applications have made the regulatory framework related to management of these online social networks seem outdated (Bertot et al., 2012). Even while it is the right to freedom of expression to post personal opinions online, it becomes tricky when those comments border on blasphemy, and their credibility and validity are questionable and they unduly affect another person, group or organization. Accusations have also pointed to misuse of user data (VID Community, 2020) and privacy invasion by social media companies for commercial reasons and to exacerbate social media usage, apart from data exploitations from outside sources (Leetaru, 2018). A section of social media users, even while aware that their privacy is at stake, are still unable to stay away from the popular social media platforms. Social media, even though an understandably necessary tool, wields a lot of communicative power that can be harnessed and misused.

While there is little difference of opinion when it comes to economic crimes perpetrated through online social media, there may be contentions when it comes to several other cyber offences, including porn consumption and political criticism. Even in the recent past, there have been numerous instances in India of voyeuristic, scandalous, gangrape and child porn videos going viral and state crackdowns leading to arrests (ABP News Bureau, 2021; HTC, 2020; Karindalam, 2020; OIS, 2021; Thaver, 2020; Unnithan, 2020; Veerappan, 2021).

India seems to have a serious fake news issue (Patil, 2019) and Indians are stated to be the most likely to encounter fake news and internet hoaxes (FPJ Bureau 2021; MNCI, 2019).

Reports say India is 'facing information wars of an unprecedented nature and scale' and a significant part of 'misinformation campaigns are developed and run by political parties with nationwide cyber armies' (Poonam & Bansal, 2019).

Users—equipped and exhilarated with their new-found ability to broadcast and reach the masses in no time—knowingly or unknowingly play a part in the spread of misinformation and disinformation. A lack of clarity and ordained documentation about where autonomy and privacy ends and regulation should begin adds to the mayhem. Hence, it becomes necessary to study various aspects of online social media related to regulation and invent ways to streamline communication on those networks for their sustainability and good use. There is also a difference of opinion with regard to ethical concerns, autonomy, liberty and regulations and this chapter intends to address these by examining the status quo and user perceptions.

SOCIAL MEDIA REGULATION IN INDIA AND ALLIED ISSUES

Information Technology Act, 2000, is the primary law in India that deals with electronic commerce and related offences, though several sections and offences in the Indian Penal Code and Code of Criminal Procedure may still either be relevant in or related to these matters. Of the cybercrimes defined and which penalties are prescribed for in the original Act are hacking, publishing obscene content, refusal to decrypt data and breach of confidentiality and privacy.

After the rise of the online social media and in a major amendment made to the IT Act in 2008, provisions were introduced to address password theft, cheating, publishing private images and sexual acts, pornography, child porn, predating children online and cyber terrorism. Controversial sections introduced through this amendment included Section 66A which penalized 'grossly offensive' and 'false' messages and Section 69 that gave the authorities the power to intercept, monitor and decrypt online information when deemed necessary.

After Section 66A was infamously applied in instances against political criticism, accusation and insult, in 2015, the apex court declared it as unconstitutional and struck it down, commenting that, 'Section 66A arbitrarily, excessively and disproportionately invades the right of free speech and upsets the balance between such right and the reasonable restrictions that may be imposed on such right' (Sriram, 2017). No new law was framed to replace this repealed section, though the repeal could 'encourage social media miscreants' (PTI, 2015).

Both the mainstream media and public opinion have mostly been critical of government or police action based on social media posts, especially political, resulting in acquittals without convictions and complicating social media regulation (BBC News, 2017b; Behl, 2021; Chaudhuri, 2017; Kaul, 2017; Masih & Das, 2015; Shantha, 2021). Social media regulatory actions have also been garnering widespread media attention (Agrawal, 2020; BBC News, 2017; HT Correspondent, 2017; Pahwa, 2020; Scroll Staff, 2019; Trends Desk, 2020).

Amid this untidiness, untrammelled issues such as social media misuse, fake news, obscenity, user privacy and security, child pornography, rape and gangrape imageries led to a government resolve to strengthen the legal frameworks and make social media applications more accountable, preparation of the draft Information Technology (Intermediary Guidelines) Rules in 2018 and the roll-out of the Information Technology (Intermediary Guidelines and Digital Media Ethics Code) Rules in 2021 as a secondary or subordinate legislation to the IT Act and suppressing the Intermediary Guidelines Rules introduced in 2011.

In February 2021, India notified the new rules imposing significant due diligence on significant social media intermediaries (such as

Facebook and Twitter) that have more than five million registered users in the country. As per the new rules, such intermediaries have to prominently publish rules and regulations, privacy policy and user agreement and inform users about prohibited content. These apart, the renewed code laid down a host of new rules for active and proactive timely censorship of prohibited content. Such intermediaries have also been asked to enable the identification of the first originator of prohibited information 'as may be required by a judicial order passed by a competent court or authority'.

This latest act and development in social media regulation in India have led to a face-off between the Government of India and social media intermediaries (Agarwal, 2021; Deka, 2021) and drawn commentaries from experts (Aravind, 2021). In contemporary times, even while the importance of free speech in perhaps the world's largest democracy is valued and social media is recognized as a medium of empowerment, experts welcome a robust regulatory mechanism to weed out misinformation and other objectionable content from the platforms (Deka, 2021).

It is also propounded that vocal and creative freedom should be guided by a sense of ethics and responsibility. However, experts are critical about making the government the final arbiter with the superpowers of censorship and fear that the traceability clause may be prone to misuse. Clear and transparent mechanisms are sought to prevent misuse of social media to spread misinformation and for defaming people (Deka, 2021).

While the government maintains that the new rules will benefit only the social media users, tackle misuse and put in place a robust and timely grievance redressal mechanism, social media firms have raised concerns over the clause relating to employees being jailed under the new rules and abatement of user privacy (Bhargava, 2021).

While Google and Facebook have reportedly agreed to comply with the new rules, WhatsApp has sent across a different message (Mint, 2021). On 25 May 2021, the last day for the intermediaries to comply with the new rules, WhatsApp sued the government, terming the identification of the first originator of information as a violation of privacy rights (Menn, 2021; Reuters, 2021). Petitions have also been filed by a flurry of news websites and editors challenging the new rules (Latest laws, 2021) and digital rights outfits have sought a rollback (Alawadhi, 2021).

Twitter is also reported to be at loggerheads with the Indian government (ITWD, 2021; Shrivastava, 2021). On the other side of the argument, the Indian government reasoned that the new rules were framed to protect the rights of the Indian social media users because the intermediaries have failed to do so (Sidhartha & Doval, 2021). The Indian government also assured that the new rules are not aimed at thwarting freedom of expression or political criticism but to check rampant misuse and uphold the rights of users (Ramachandran, 2021).

In this backdrop, with the new social media rules at the eye of the storm in the battle between the Indian regulators and tech firms, this chapter seeks to consolidate mass opinions and considerations about social media regulation and related issues.

RESEARCH PROBLEM

Political applications of social media may vary depending upon the motivations, purposes and ideology of the users, which could also determine how they view the medium. In this chapter, hence, user perceptions about autonomy, privacy and regulation are measured and political ideology, extent of usage of social media and online political participation are studied as related concepts. The following are the primary objectives of the present study:

- To analyse political ideology, participation and extent of usage of social media
- To analyse user perceptions about privacy, autonomy and regulation of social media
- To check if political ideology, participation and extent of usage of social media are associated with user perceptions about privacy, autonomy and regulation of social media
- To find ways to balance the triad of privacy, autonomy and regulation and recommend strategies for regulation of social media and frame policies

PAST STUDIES AND OBSERVATIONS

Gamson et al. (1992) concluded that the media generally operate in ways that 'promote apathy, cynicism, and quiescence, rather than active citizenship and participation'. Gil de Zúñiga et al. (2012) observed that even traditional media have started making use of online and social media resources to gauge social capital and civic and political participatory behaviours, online and offline. Dahlgren (2005) also weighed in on the importance of online political deliberations.

In her submission, Trepte (2020) differentiates privacy in general (selective control of information sharing, where control is key) and on online social media, where an individual user's information isn't necessarily under his or her control. Her model is based on

> four propositions: Privacy in social media is interdependently perceived and valued. Thus, it cannot always be achieved through control. As an alternative, interpersonal communication is the primary mechanism to ensure social media privacy. Finally, trust and norms function as mechanisms that represent crystallised privacy communication.

A social networks theory of privacy proposed by Strahilevitz (2004) bases its arguments on binaries: 'What facts are public and what facts are private? It is the fundamental, first-principles question in privacy law, and a necessary element in the two most important privacy torts, public disclosure of private facts and intrusion upon seclusion.' While privacy is mostly related to invasion of personal privacy and control of information, political criticisms have become a serious social media issue of late, with the rise in popularity of these online platforms, raising questions about what kinds of criticism and comments are acceptable or unacceptable. Another interesting concept of algorithmic 'folk theories' could also offer a theoretical foundation for the current study. Peterson–Salahuddin and Diakopoulos (2020) studied negotiated autonomy and the role of perceptions about social media algorithms in editorial decision making. They interviewed journalists to understand how they make sense of social media algorithms and to what extent this influences editorial decision making. In the current study, too, user understanding about social media algorithms and perceptions about how these platforms work and can be regulated is analysed as it could influence their usage.

In all, it makes sense to study user perceptions about the concepts of autonomy, privacy and regulation and relate them with political ideology and SM usage.

Napoli (2019), in his book on media regulation in the disinformation age, presents a 'timely and persuasive case for understanding and governing social media as news media, with a fundamental obligation to serve the public interest'. There again, it becomes limited in its scope as it examines social media as a news outlet.

After the likes of Twitter, Facebook, WhatsApp and Instagram brought widespread popularity to the online social media platforms—aided by the availability of affordable smartphones—a dominant part of scholarly research in this area focussed on the positive potentials of these platforms, viewing them as alternative media and decisive enablers booming the communicative capabilities of the humankind for their good. But now, online social media is evolving as a dominant source of information (Niklewicz, 2017) and mainstream medium of mass communication, with advertorials and paid actions, and there is a need to subject them as well to the same regulations and ethical codes as conventional media organizations. Indian law regarding censorship in traditional media is fairly developed. With social media becoming an entwined part of our lives, thanks to its independent and undisciplined nature, it is prone to misuse and proving to be disturbing and deleterious at times, calling for regulation.

Hence, it becomes perceptive to revisit and review the values of freedom of expression, privacy and regulation and on how to balance these for the better use of online social media platforms. Though the legal framework comprises several provisions that can be used to censor online content and check misuse, timely remedies for the common users still remain a far cry, when they are exploited, or their privacy is invaded, and the social platforms are misused to harm them. In this age of disinformation, conventional thoughts about social media need to be rethought to develop newer social attitudes towards social media user privacy and control the extent to which information is disseminated.

Niklewicz (2017) also favoured viewing online social media as a traditional news outlet or media firm that could be regulated with morphed press laws. Niklewicz prescribed a 'notice and correct' strategy to check the spread of misinformation and save the victims. Napoli (2019) also justified social media regulation presenting a view that user-generated data may be considered as a public resource. Citing instances of social media misuse, Napoli puts forth arguments favouring monitoring and regulation of social media by government entities to keep up the interest of the public on the lines of traditional media.

It is not without opposition though: scholars such as Thierer (2012) have highlighted the side effects of viewing social media platforms and resources as public utilities.

Obar and Wildman (2015) suggested 'regulatory innovation' to match advancements in the digital spaces and the emergence of social media. Wu (2015) suggested international communities for the regulation of social media to increase coordination among the states and establish an effective monitoring regime. Mueller (2015) views government regulation of errant behaviour (with punishment of users with malafide intentions) as more beneficial to control of generic technological capabilities (platforms). Riedl et al. (2021) observed that understanding user perceptions about social media content moderation and platform regulation was crucial.

Reviewing the past studies, it can be inferred that the popularity of social media has raised several research problems related to privacy, security, autonomy and regulation, and social media needs a robust framework within the law to streamline these mostly unregulated communication systems, for which public opinion about these is paramount.

RESEARCH METHOD

In the quantitative survey, a sample of 2,500 social media users were selected from across the Indian state of Tamil Nadu, using a multistage cluster sampling procedure during January 2020–January 2021. The survey questionnaire used to measure political ideology, political participation, extent of usage of social media, user perceptions about privacy, autonomy and regulation of social media was part of a larger instrument that was created for a state-wide project funded by the Indian Council of Social Science Research (ICSSR) under the IMPRESS scheme. In this project, a range of variables are measured through a mixed methods research and the relationship that they share among them are examined to propose recommendations for the formation of policies to regulate the sprawling social media space.

First, the Indian state of Tamil Nadu was divided into five strata or zones: north, south, east, west and central. For each of these five zones, two or three districts were chosen as prime points for data collection, and respondents were chosen from each of these zones leading to a grand total of 2,015 respondents. Data was collected from as many as 50 respondents using a survey instrument that had 135 items, under 16 sections. Based on respondent feedback, the instrument was revised to finally have 98 items under 16 sections.

In the final instrument, there were 44 questions operationalizing the six variables—political ideology, political participation, extent of usage of social media, user perceptions about privacy, autonomy and regulation of social media—apart from demographic variables—age, education, gender, occupation and family monthly income.

As many as 20 focus group discussions (FGDs)—with 10–12 participants in each of the discussions—were also conducted during the same window of examination.

For the qualitative analysis using FGD data, the grounded theory approach (Corbin & Strauss, 1990) was employed, where data were collected, coded and analysed simultaneously, through constant comparison. Thus, data collection and analysis became an interrelated process in our study. At the start of the study, we made only tentative decisions about the initial collection of data instead of planning the entire procedure. Choices regarding data collection were not entirely prearranged because the analysis was conducted simultaneously, and the analysis of data will reveal the need for more data. Theoretical sampling is performed until the point of saturation. Using the data and analysis, several categories and concepts were developed, related and mapped to build a unified theory.

DATA ANALYSIS

Quantitative Analysis

A quantitative survey was used to measure political ideology, political participation, extent of usage of social media, user perceptions about privacy, autonomy and regulation of social media and their descriptive statistics are presented in Tables 11.1 and 11.2.

Of the total 2,500 respondents who participated in the study, 379 (15.2%) respondents were low on power distance (favouring equality and opposing hierarchy), while 1,054 (42.2%) respondents moderately supported the power structure and the remaining 1,067 (42.7%) respondents exhibited high levels of power distance, support-ing hierarchy. Similarly, 1,281 (51.2%) respondents favoured curb-ing of social freedom, while 1,082 (43.3%) respondents moderately favoured social freedom and the remaining 137 (5.5%) respondents were in support of social freedom. Of the total 2,500 respondents who participated in the study, 1,825 (73%) respondents were against economic freedom, while 598 (23.9%) respondents moderately sup-ported economic freedom and only a meagre 77 (3.1%) respondents were in favour of economic freedom.

Table 11.1 Descriptive Statistics: Political Ideology

Frequencies					
Power structure	Against	379	Economic Freedom	Against	1,825
	Neutral	1,054		Neutral	598
	For	1,067		For	77
Social freedom	Against	1,281	Social Justice	Against	111
	Neutral	1,082		Neutral	668
	For	137		For	1,721
Political participation	Low	210	Usage	Low	1,249
	Moderate	1,601		Moderate	1,067
	High	689		High	184

Table 11.2 *Descriptive Statistics: Privacy, Autonomy, Regulation*

Frequencies		
	Against	560
Privacy	Neutral	1,553
	For	387
	Against	2,069
Autonomy	Neutral	426
	For	5
	Against	503
Regulation	Neutral	1,417
	For	580

As many as 111 (4.4%) respondents were not in favour of social justice and equality, while 668 (26.7%) respondents moderately favoured social injustice and the remaining 1,721 (68.8%) respondents were in support of social justice.

Of the total 2,500 respondents who participated in the study, 210 (8.4%) respondents had low levels of political participation, while 1,601 (64%) respondents had moderate levels of political participation and the remaining 689 (27.6%) respondents exhibited high levels of political participation.

Similarly, 1,249 (50%) respondents had low levels of social media usage, while 1,067 (42.7%) respondents had moderate levels of social media usage and the remaining 184 (7.4%) respondents had high levels of social media usage.

Of the 2,500 respondents who participated in the study, 560 (22.4%) respondents were not in favour of privacy on social media, while 1,553 (62.1%) respondents had moderate opinion about privacy on social media, and the remaining 387 (15.5%) were in strong support of social media privacy. As many as 2,069 (82.8%) respondents favoured social media autonomy the least, while 426 (17%) respondents held moderate opinions on the subject and only a meagre five (0.2%) were

Table 11.3 *Correlations: Political Ideology, Privacy, Autonomy and Regulation*

		Privacy	Autonomy	Regulation
Power structure	Correlation	0.059**	0.069**	0.322**
	Sig.	0.003	0.001	0
Social freedom	Correlation	−1.78**	−0.130**	−0.254**
	Sig.	0	0	0
Economic freedom	Correlation	−0.330**	−0.18**	−0.246**
	Sig.	0	0	0
Social justice	Correlation	0.369**	0.087**	0.239**
	Sig.	0	0	0

in strong support of autonomy on social media. As many as 503 (13.1%) respondents were not in favour of regulation of online social media platforms, while 1,417 (56.7%) respondents held moderate opinions and the remaining 580 (23.2%) were in strong favour of social media regulation.

To test the relationships between political ideology, privacy, autonomy and regulation, Pearson's product–moment correlation was run, and the test results are presented in Table 11.3. Power structure was positively correlated with privacy ($r = 0.059$; $p = 0.003$), autonomy ($r = 0.069$; $p = 0.001$) and regulation ($r = 0.322$; $p < 0.0005$).

Social justice was also positively correlated with privacy ($r = 0.369$; $p < 0.0005$), autonomy ($r = 0.087$; $p < 0.0005$) and regulation ($r = 0.239$; $p < 0.0005$). Social freedom was negatively associated with privacy ($r = −1.78$; $p < 0.0005$), autonomy ($r = −0.130$; $p < 0.0005$) and regulation ($r = −0.254$; $p < 0.0005$). Economic freedom was also negatively associated with privacy ($r = −0.330$; $p < 0.0005$), autonomy ($r = −0.18$; $p < 0.0005$) and regulation ($r = −0.246$; $p < 0.0005$).

To test the relationships between political participation, privacy, autonomy and regulation, Pearson's product–moment correlation was run, and the test results are presented in Table 11.4. Political participation was positively associated with privacy ($r = 0.118$; $p < 0.0005$)

Table 11.4 *Correlations: Political Participation, Privacy, Autonomy and Regulation*

		Privacy	Autonomy	Regulation
Political participation	Correlation	0.118**	−0.076**	0.020**
	Sig.	0	0	0
Privacy	Correlation		−0.019	0.186
	Sig.		0.331	0
Autonomy	Correlation			0.114
	Sig.			0

Table 11.5 *Correlations: Usage, Privacy, Autonomy and Regulation*

		Privacy	Autonomy	Regulation
Usage	Correlation	−0.198**	−1.165**	−0.201**
	Sig.	0	0	0

and regulation and negatively associated with autonomy ($r = -0.076$; $p < 0.0005$). Positive correlations were observed between regulation and privacy ($r = 0.186$; $p < 0.0005$) and autonomy ($r = 0.114$; $p < 0.0005$). Negative correlations were found between privacy and autonomy ($r = -0.019$; $p = 0.331$).

To test the relationships between usage, privacy, autonomy and regulation, Pearson's product–moment correlation was run, and the test results are presented in Table 11.5. Social media usage was negatively associated with privacy ($r = -0.198$; $p < 0.0005$), autonomy ($r = -1.165$; $p < 0.0005$) and regulation ($r = -.201$; $p < 0.0005$).

Qualitative Analysis

Focus group discussions were conducted to gauge stakeholder opinion on social media privacy, autonomy and regulation and how to balance them and the results are presented in Table 11.6.

Table 11.6 *FGD Results*

Categories	Themes	Overarching Concepts
Data misuse, data sale, targeted advertising, cookies, usage tracking, AI prompting	Privacy invasion by tech firms	Privacy threat
Hacking, identity theft, information threat, phishing, spamming, pornography, cyber stalking	Privacy invasion by those with malicious intent	
Illiteracy unavailability of terms and conditions in local languages ignoring terms and conditions	Lack of awareness	Privacy challenges
Unwarranted censorship	Regulatory misuse	Autonomy threat
Misinformation, disinformation, creating division (polarization), instigating violence, attacking communities, hurting or outraging sentiments, feelings and beliefs, data theft, economic crime political crime, sexual and allied crime	Misuse	Regulatory need
Fake accounts	Anonymity	Regulatory challenges
Awareness (about issues and ethical usage), media-information literacy, stricter and elaborate laws, registration, account verification, regular updation of media laws, simplified forms of terms and conditions, privacy management (personal) through privacy settings, privacy management (tech firm) through maximum privacy, increasing accountability (user), increasing accountability (tech firm), restriction in data use	Proactive regulation	(Multifaceted) Regulation

(Table 11.6 Continued)

(Table 11.6 Continued)

Categories	Themes	Overarching Concepts
Platform-based restriction, self-regulation (information control, avoiding unmindful posting and sharing), information verification mechanism	Simultaneous regulation	
Legal action, censorship, blocking, timely action (quick complaining system and redressal of grievance)	Retroactive regulation	
Government (establishment), users, independent regulators, tech firms	Stakeholders	

TRIANGULATION AND DISCUSSION

A majority of online social media users either moderately favoured (42.2%) or strongly advocated (42.7) hierarchy or a well–defined power structure, while being against social freedom (51.2%) and economic freedom (73%). When it comes to social justice or reduction of social inequality, a major section of social media users (68.8%) were in favour of this facet of political ideology. A majority of the social media users moderately participated in politics (64%) and about 27 per cent reported to actively participate in politics online and offline. Given the plethora and proliferation of social media platforms, usage was reported to be majorly low (50%) or moderate (42.7%) on social media.

Public opinion was mostly neutral or mixed about social media privacy (62%) and regulation (56.7%), while it was strongly against autonomy (82.8%).

Exploring the reasons for such an outcome, it can be cautiously assumed that the recent issues related to social media privacy and controversial regulations could be crucial factors. While regulation is crucial for a section of social media users, recent political social media regulatory attempts have widely been criticized by the mainstream media and censured by the judiciary as well. Privacy concerns arose over technological companies selling user data for commercial purposes.

Interestingly, the dominant public opinion was squarely against unrestrained freedom of expression online. While the imperative opinion emerging here is that social media users should not have the freedom to post or share unmindful messages online, there is mixed opinion about regulation as it is not seen as the primary way to streamline the online social space. FGDs also revealed that regulation of the sprawling social media space in real time would pose a challenge. Social media information literacy and awareness generation are seen as possible ways to impede the misuse of social media.

Power structure and social justice had positive associations with privacy, autonomy and regulation, while social freedom and economic freedom were negatively associated with those variables. That is, those who favoured social hierarchy and social equality were in favour of social media regulation and preservation of user privacy. Those who wanted social and economic freedom, however, were against regulation of online social media and wanted them to be open-public networks for online deliberations and opinion exchange.

Conceptual qualitative analyses identified several invasion threats to social media user privacy from the tech firms themselves that run the websites and the others with malicious intent, including data sale and misuse, cookies and usage tracking, AI prompting and targeted advertising, hacking, identity theft, information threat, phishing, spamming, pornography and cyber stalking. Lack of awareness about social media issues and ethical use complicate this situation, thanks to illiteracy, unavailability of terms and conditions in local languages, ignorance and lethargy. Misuse of social media for spreading misinformation, creating division (polarization), instigating violence, attacking communities, hurting or outraging sentiments, feelings and beliefs, data theft, economic crimes, political crimes, and sexual and allied crimes called for a robust regulatory framework. A multifaceted regulatory framework—involving all stakeholders such as the government, users, tech firms and independent regulators with shared responsibilities—is prescribed at three stages: proactive, simultaneous and retroactive.

Proactive regulation is about awareness generation (about issues and ethical usage), increasing media information literacy at the primary school level, bringing in stricter and elaborate laws that are regularly updated to match the pace at which the tech world evolves, registration and account verification to increase user accountability, simplified forms of terms and conditions in local languages, privacy management (personal) through privacy settings, privacy management (tech firm) by prescribing maximum privacy as default settings, increasing accountability of the tech firms and restricting data use by them.

Simultaneous regulation of online social media would entail platform-based restrictions that could thwart misuse, self-regulation following ethical usage and avoiding unmindful sharing of misinformation, malignant messages and personal information and promoting quick information verification mechanisms. Lastly, retroactive regulation could be executed with prompt legal action serving social media victimized users through punishment, censorship of content, blocking of accounts and timely action through quick complaint-lodging systems and redressal of grievances. As statistics show (Statista, 2021; Statista, 2021a; United Nations, 2021) the rise of social media, the study findings also indicate that a major section of the people value these platforms considerably and consider them important for development, in line with the observations of scholars such as Ceron et al. (2014); Dahlgren (2005); Gil de Zúñiga et al. (2012); Ratkiewicz et al. (2011); Shirky (2011); Sobkowicz (2012); Stieglitz & Dang-Xuan (2013). Notwithstanding, the view opposing unrestrained freedom and predisposed privacy is overbearing and this concern has also been raised by several scholars reviewed (Bertot et al., 2012; Cogburn & Espinoza-Vasquez, 2011). People seek a robust regulatory framework with regular revisions, on the lines of traditional media, as advocated by scholars such as Mueller (2015); Napoli (2019); Niklewicz (2017); Obar and Wildman (2015), and but feel that the social media policy and guiding principles need to accord equal paramountcy to promote freedom of expression and the safety and progress of the users.

STUDY FINDINGS AND POLICY IMPLICATIONS

The study findings and policy implications are discussed as follows:

- **Prone to misuse:** Social media platforms are highly prone to misuse, threatening the safety and well-being of users, courtesy the resourcefulness of the internet, acumen of those with malignant or misguided intent and the prelusion of anonymity that online applications offer, apart from general apathy and insensitivity to the concerns of the third person.

- **Opinion about social media regulation is changing:** A while ago, the idea of regulating social media, if proposed, would have met with strife: terming it either impossible or treacherous. But now, thanks to the social media blemishes, public opinion about social media regulation is changing, with a wider section wanting a robust regulatory framework.

- **Social media as alternative media?** Social media seems to reflect dominant thoughts espoused by the mainstream media, further thwarting alternative opinion.

- **Embracing the known devil:** Social media users, even while aware that their privacy is at stake and social media can harm them, are still unable to stay away from the popular platforms. As social media has become an integral part of human lives, it is time for measures to make these platforms safer for users.

- **Negativity thriving on social media:** A dominant opinion that emerged was that political content shared on social media was highly unreliable and mostly hostile and fault-finding.

- **Dangers are outweighing benefits:** It is indeed crucial to have a free space for information-opinion exchange and sociopolitical deliberations without fear of repercussions—and the online social media platforms serve that purpose. Such liberty, however, comes with a cost. Social media dangers are now outweighing their benefits.

- **Timely remedy still remains elusive:** When the common social media user is victimized, timely remedy still remains elusive.

- **Traceability clause:** It may be judiciously applied to threatening social media content that are posted in open public networks.

- **More social than political:** Social media regulation needs to be viewed more as a social than a political problem, even while possible misuse of regulatory frameworks needs to be checked.

- **Opinion about privacy and regulation is mixed:** Exploring the reasons for such an outcome, it can be cautiously assumed that the recent issues raised related to social media privacy and controversial regulations could be crucial factors. While regulation is crucial for a section of social media users, recent political social media regulatory attempts have widely been criticized by the mainstream media and censured by the judiciary as well. Privacy concerns arose over technological companies selling user data for commercial purposes. Interestingly, the dominant public opinion was squarely against unrestrained freedom of expression online. While the imperative opinion emerging here is that social media users should not have the freedom to post or share unmindful messages online, there is mixed opinion about regulation as it is not seen as the primary way to streamline the online social space.

- **Mainstream media rules may be relevant:** A reflection of the changing attitudes about social media is that social media need to be treated as mainstream media. After the likes of Twitter, Facebook, WhatsApp and Instagram brought widespread popularity to the online social media platforms—aided by the availability of affordable smartphones—a dominant part of scholarly research in this area focussed on the positive potentials of these platforms, viewing them as decisive enablers booming the communicative capabilities of the humankind for their good. But now, online social media is evolving as a dominant source of information and mainstream medium of mass communication, with advertorials and paid actions, and there is a need to subject them as well to the same regulations and ethical codes as conventional media organizations.

- **Privacy invasion threats:** Conceptual qualitative analyses identified several invasion threats to social media user privacy from the tech firms themselves that run the websites and the others with malicious intent, including data sale and misuse, cookies and usage tracking, AI prompting and targeted advertising, hacking, identity theft, information threat, phishing, spamming, pornography and cyber stalking.

- **Awareness still low:** Users—equipped and exhilarated with their new-found ability to broadcast and reach the masses in no time—knowingly or unknowingly, play a part in the spread of misinformation and disinformation. They do not think twice before believing in a social media message or even sharing it. Social media information literacy and awareness generation are seen as possible ways to impede the misuse of social media.

- **Open to multiple interpretations and misuse:** The problem of vagueness also haunts information technology laws and social media rules. An increase in clarity and specificity instead of generalized abstractness and (problematic) offences that heavily rely on subjective interpretation can make regulation and conviction easier.

- **Free speech or hate speech?** While the overarching opinion was against social media autonomy (unchecked freedom of expression), public opinion about privacy and regulation was squarely mixed. Social media users want to be more accountable, but they do not view one-sided regulation—proclaiming it as the responsibility of the government—as the only way to streamline this sprawling social digital space.

- **Social media regulation needs to be multifaceted:** A multifaceted regulatory framework—involving all stakeholders such as the government, users, tech firms and independent regulators with shared responsibilities—is prescribed at three stages: proactive, simultaneous and retroactive.

- **Proactive regulation:** It is about more rigorous awareness generation (about issues and ethical usage), increasing media information literacy at the primary school level, bringing in stricter and elaborate laws that are regularly updated to match the pace at which the tech world evolves. While proactive regulation is about measures to avoid future occurrence of undesired social media actions, simultaneous regulatory mechanisms could be put in place by the social media intermediaries to stop unethical or undesired social media practices and actions during execution (for instance, consider increasing the capability of a social media website to instantly review and refuse upload of pornographic material and warn the user) and retroactive regulation could be through timely grievance redressal and punishment for offences.

- **Promote usage of verified social media accounts:** Minimizing social media anonymity and encouraging people to trust and use verified accounts can increase accountability.

- **Reduce opacity:** Simplified forms of terms and conditions in local languages may be encouraged. Transparency should be encouraged among tech firms with regard to the extent of usage of user data, how they are used and for what purposes. Information about data usage needs to be shared to users in simplified forms.

- **Privacy settings:** People need to be educated on privacy management (personal) through privacy settings. Platforms may have maximum privacy as default settings, increasing accountability of the tech firms and restricting data use by them.
- **Balance:** Social media policy and the guiding principles of such policies need to a have a balanced design aimed at promoting free online speech and at the same time ensuring safety of users and checking misuse of the medium and data, understanding that any shift to either side of the balance could lead to issues threatening the sustainability of this essential medium. Radical, populist and extremist regulatory measures may be called for dire-demanding times, while a pragmatic and balanced regulatory framework with a long-term purview needs to be the standard and established schema.

CONCLUSION

Dominant political ideologies emerging among online social media users in India are in favour of political hierarchy and social justice (reducing social inequality), even at the cost of social and economic freedom. Social media usage, political participation and political ideologies of the users were observed to affect people's opinion about social media privacy, autonomy and regulation. Those who favoured social hierarchy and social equality were in favour of social media regulation and preservation of user privacy. Those who wanted social and economic freedom, however, were against regulation of online social media and wanted them to be open-public networks for online deliberations and opinion exchange. Political participation favoured social media regulation and privacy and was against autonomy. Social media is seen as a challenge for the politically seasoned, given its unregulated nature and potentials of its prone misuse. A dominant opinion that emerged was that political content shared on social media was highly unreliable and mostly hostile and fault-finding.

While the overarching opinion was against social media autonomy, public opinion about privacy and regulation was squarely mixed. Social media users want to be more accountable, but they do not view one-sided regulation—proclaiming it as the responsibility of the government—as the only way to streamline this sprawling social digital space.

As a whole, social media users want tougher laws, stricter implementation and a robust regulatory framework with regular updation even at the cost of losing a little of their autonomy and unregulated freedom of expression.

A multifaceted regulatory framework—involving all stakeholders such as the government, users, tech firms and independent regulators with shared responsibilities—is prescribed at three stages: proactive, simultaneous and retroactive. Public opinion seems to also be in line with the current social media policy, as informed by the Indian government (Bhargava, 2021), shifting from the lopsided insistence on free speech towards a balanced check of misuse, ready to give up some of the unrestrained freedom of expression online in favour of regulation for the common good and making all stakeholders more accountable.

REFERENCES

ABP News Bureau. (2021, February 17). Watching porn on your smartphone? Uttar Pradesh govt is monitoring you. Retrieved from https://News.Abplive.com/. https://news.abplive.com/news/india/watching-porn-on-your-smartphone-uttar-pradesh-govt-is-monitoring-you-1444680

Agarwal, S. (2021, June 3). India IT Rules 2021: Industry groups seek end to govt-social media standoff. *The Economic Times.* Retrieved from https://economictimes.indiatimes.com/tech/tech-bytes/india-it-rules-2021-industry-groups-seek-end-to-govt-social-media-standoff/articleshow/83189318.cms

Agrawal, S. (2020, March 1). Assam lecturer posts remarks against RSS-BJP, Modi on Facebook, lands in jail after protest. *The Print.* Retrieved from https://theprint.in/india/assam-lecturer-posts-remarks-against-rss-bjp-modi-on-facebook-lands-in-jail-after-abvp-protest/373526/

Alawadhi, N. (2021, June 11). Digital rights outfits call upon Indian govt to roll back IT Rules. www.Business-Standard.com. Retrieved from https://www.business-standard.com/article/economy-policy/digital-rights-outfits-call-upon-indian-govt-to-roll-back-it-rules-121061101277_1.html

Aravind, V. (2021, May 29). From social to antisocial: How the new IT rules will accelerate India's democratic decline. Newslaundry. Retrieved from https://www.newslaundry.com/2021/05/29/from-social-to-antisocial-how-the-new-it-rules-will-accelerate-indias-democratic-decline

Associated Press (2017, April 27). India bans social media in Kashmir for one month, Retrieved from https://www.telegraph.co.uk/technology/2017/04/27/india-bans-social-media-kashmir-one-month/

Barclay, F. P. (2017). Media effect on media: Progression of political news and tweets during India 2014. *Journal of Media and Communication*, *1*(1), 1–28.

Barclay, F. P., Chinnasamy, P., & Pichandy, P. (2014). Political opinion expressed in social media and election outcomes—US presidential elections 2012. *GSTF International Journal on Media & Communications (JMC)*, *1*(2), 15–22.

Barclay, F. P., Pichandy, C., Venkat, A., & Sudhakaran, S. (2015). India 2014: Facebook 'like' as a predictor of election outcomes. *Asian Journal of Political Science*, *23*(2), 134–160.

Barclay, F. P., Pichandy, C., Venkat, A., & Sudhakaran, S. (2016). Twitter sentiments: Pattern recognition and poll prediction. In *Communication and Information Technologies Annual*. Emerald Group Publishing Limited.

BBC News. (2017, April 26). India bans social media in Kashmir amid violent unrest. Retrieved from https://www.bbc.com/news/world-asia-india-39719795

BBC News. (2017b, June 16). India internet shutdowns 'violate human rights'. Retrieved from https://www.bbc.com/news/world-asia-india-40298722

Behl, T. N. S. (2021, May 31). This is what's happening in the name of national security. *The Times of India*. Retrieved from https://timesofindia.indiatimes.com/india/this-is-whats-happening-in-the-name-of-national-security/articleshow/83108970.cms

Bertot, J. C., Jaeger, P. T., & Hansen, D. (2012). The impact of polices on government social media usage: Issues, challenges, and recommendations. *Government Information Quarterly*, *29*(1), 30–40.

Bhargava, Y. (2021, June 6). New IT rules only to tackle misuse of social media, give users redressal mechanism, says Ravi Shankar Prasad. *The Hindu*. Retrieved from https://www.thehindu.com/news/national/union-minister-ravi-shankar-prasad-interview-with-the-hindu/article34743824.ece

Ceron, A., Curini, L., Iacus, S. M., & Porro, G. (2014). Every tweet counts? How sentiment analysis of social media can improve our knowledge of citizens' political preferences with an application to Italy and France. *New Media & Society*, *16*(2), 340–358.

Chaudhuri, P. (2017, November 6). Cartoonist in Tamil Nadu arrested for exercising free speech on social media. *The Logical Indian*. Retrieved from https://thelogicalindian.com/news/bala-cartoonist-arrested-tamil-nadu-cartoon-edappadi/

Cogburn, D. L., & Espinoza-Vasquez, F. K. (2011). From networked nominee to networked nation: Examining the impact of Web 2.0 and social media on political participation and civic engagement in the 2008 Obama campaign. *Journal of Political Marketing*, *10*(1–2), 189–213.

Corbin, J. M., & Strauss, A. (1990). Grounded theory research: Procedures, canons, and evaluative criteria. *Qualitative Sociology*, *13*(1), 3–21.

Dahlgren, P. (2005). The Internet, public spheres, and political communication: Dispersion and deliberation. Political Communication, *22*(2), 147–162.

Debu (2015, September 28). Undue use and misuse of social media, MyIndia. Retrieved from https://www.mapsofindia.com/my-india/society/undue-use-and-misuse-of-social-media

Deka, K. (2021, June 11). The battle for online privacy. *India Today*. Retrieved from https://www.indiatoday.in/magazine/special-report/story/20210621-the-battle-for-online-privacy-1813369-2021-06-11

Express News Service (2017, November 2). Section 66A: Seven instances of alleged abuse on social media. *Express News Service*. Retrieved from https://indianexpress.com/article/india/india-others/section-66-a-instances-of-alleged-abuse-on-social-media-2324927/

FPJ Bureau. (2021, May 27). Sending any negative post or video against PM Modi can lead to arrest? Govt is recording WhatsApp calls? Here's the truth behind viral message. *Free Press Journal*. Retrieved from https://www.freepressjournal.in/india/sending-any-negative-post-or-video-against-pm-modi-can-lead-to-arrest-govt-is-recording-whatsapp-calls-heres-the-truth-behind-viral-message

Gamson, W. A., Croteau, D., Hoynes, W., & Sasson, T. (1992). Media images and the social construction of reality. *Annual Review of Sociology, 18*(1), 373–393.

Gil de Zúñiga, H., Jung, N., & Valenzuela, S. (2012). Social media use for news and individuals' social capital, civic engagement and political participation. *Journal of Computer-Mediated Communication, 17*(3), 319–336.

Halpern, D., & Gibbs, J. (2013). Social media as a catalyst for online deliberation? Exploring the affordances of Facebook and YouTube for political expression. *Computers in Human Behavior, 29*(3), 1159–1168.

Hindustan Times. (2015). Facebook trouble: 10 cases of arrests under Sec 66A of IT Act, published March 24, 2015, retrieved November 20, 2018 from https://www.hindustantimes.com/india/facebook-trouble-10-cases-of-arrests-under-sec-66a-of-it-act/story-4xKp9EJjR6YoyrC2rUUMDN.html

HT Correspondent. (2017, March 24). Arrest over a Facebook status: 7 times people landed in jail for posts against politicians. *Hindustan Times*. Retrieved from https://www.hindustantimes.com/india-news/arrested-over-a-facebook-status-7-times-people-landed-in-jail-for-posts-against-politicians/story-ON1jukoStfV6T8aYcJEVGJ.html

HTC. (2020, December 28). In Kerala, 41 held for promoting child pornography. *Hindustan Times*. Retrieved from https://www.hindustantimes.com/india-news/in-kerala-41-held-for-promoting-child-pornography/story-DnTZydkkR5GtAcWHerzKkM.html

ITWD. (2021, May 29). Do business in India by all means but follow the laws: RS Prasad on social media rules: Exclusive. *India Today*. Retrieved from https://www.indiatoday.in/india/story/ravi-shankar-prasad-social-media-rules-exclusive-1808268-2021-05-29

Karindalam, V. (2020, October 7). Operation 'P Hunt' by Kerala Police to monitor viewing and sharing of child pornography. *Times Now*. Retrieved from https://www.timesnownews.com/mirror-now/in-focus/article/operation-p-hunt-by-kerala-police-to-monitor-viewing-and-sharing-of-child-pornography/663866

Kaul, M. (2017, March 27). Social media becomes the scapegoat in India. Index on Censorship. Retrieved from https://www.indexoncensorship.org/2013/10/india-social-media/

Latest laws. (2021, March 21). In another challenge to the new IT Rules 2021, Kannada News portal 'Pratidhvani' files petition. Latestlaws.com. Retrieved from https://www.latestlaws.com/latest-news/in-another-challenge-to-the-new-it-rules-2021-kannada-news-portal-pratidhvani-files-petition/

Leetaru, K. (2018, December 5). Social media platforms are still powerless to stop data misuse. *Forbes*. Retrieved from https://www.forbes.com/sites/kalev-leetaru/2018/12/05/social-media-platforms-are-still-powerless-to-stop-data-misuse/?sh=7e42555c742b

Liu, C., & Ma, J. (2018). Development and validation of the Chinese social media addiction scale. *Personality and Individual Differences, 134*, 55–59.

Masih, N., & Das, M. (2015, March 18). Class 11 student in jail over Facebook post attributed to UP minister Azam Khan. NDTV.com. Retrieved from https://www.ndtv.com/india-news/class-11-student-arrested-for-reportedly-putting-up-a-facebook-post-in-up-minister-azam-khans-name-747520

Menn, J. (2021, May 26). WhatsApp sues Indian government over new privacy rules—sources. *Reuters*. Retrieved from https://www.reuters.com/world/india/exclusive-whatsapp-sues-india-govt-says-new-media-rules-mean-end-privacy-sources-2021-05-26/

Mint (2021, May 27). Google to comply with India's new IT rules: Sundar Pichai. *Mint*. Retrieved from https://www.livemint.com/companies/news/google-to-comply-with-india-s-new-it-rules-sundar-pichai-11622093673533.html

MNCI. (2019, February 5). Microsoft releases digital civility index on Safer Internet Day. Microsoft. Retrieved from https://perma.cc/545B-7YVN

Mueller, M. L. (2015). Hyper-transparency and social control: Social media as magnets for regulation. *Telecommunications Policy, 39*(9), 804–810.

Nair, P. S. and Barclay, F. P. (2017). Twitter usage patterns as a predictor of user gender. *Journal of Media and Communication, 1*(2), 1–23.

Napoli, P. M. (2019). *Social media and the public interest: Media regulation in the disinformation age*. Columbia University Press.

Napoli, P. M. (2019). User data as public resource: Implications for social media regulation. *Policy & Internet, 11*(4), 439–459.

Niklewicz, K. (2017). Weeding out fake news: an approach to social media regulation. *European View, 16*(2), 335–335.

Obar, J. A., & Wildman, S. S. (2015). Social media definition and the governance challenge: An introduction to the special issue. *Telecommunications Policy, 39*(9), 745–750.

OIS. (2021, May 27). Viral video showing brutal gang rape is not related to the Jodhpur suicide case. Details. OpIndia. Retrieved from https://www.opindia.com/2021/05/woman-gang-rape-viral-video-not-related-to-nagaland-girl-suicide-case-police-clarify/

Pahwa, N. (2020, August 7). What Indians lost when their government banned TikTok. *Slate Magazine*. Retrieved from https://slate.com/technology/2020/08/tiktok-india-ban-china.html

Patil, S. (2019, May 1). Opinion—India has a public health crisis. It's called fake news. *The New York Times*. Retrieved from https://www.nytimes.com/2019/04/29/opinion/india-elections-disinformation.html

Peterson-Salahuddin, C., & Diakopoulos, N. (2020). Negotiated autonomy: The role of social media algorithms in editorial decision making. *Media and Communication, 8*(3), 27–38.

Poonam, S., & Bansal, S. (2019, April 1). Misinformation is endangering India's election. *The Atlantic*. Retrieved from https://perma.cc/Y39M-KGWU

PTI. (2015, April 2). Centre working on new law similar to Section 66A: Devendra Fadnavis. *The Times of India*. Retrieved from https://timesofindia.indiatimes.com/social/centre-working-on-new-law-similar-to-section-66a-devendra-fadnavis/articleshow/46780443.cms?pcode=461

Ramachandran, S. K. (2021, June 6). 'India won't compromise its digital sovereignty': Ravi Shankar Prasad. *Hindustan Times*. Retrieved from https://www.hindustantimes.com/india-news/india-won-t-compromise-its-digital-sovereignty-ravi-shankar-prasad-101622919207459.html

Ratkiewicz, J., Conover, M., Meiss, M., Gonçalves, B., Flammini, A., & Menczer, F. (2021). In Proceedings of the International AAAI Conference on Web and Social Media. *Detecting and tracking political abuse in social media. 5*(1), 297–304. Retrieved from https://ojs.aaai.org/index.php/ICWSM/article/view/14127

Reuters. (2021, May 26). WhatsApp sues India govt, says new rules mean end to privacy: Report. *Mint*. Retrieved from https://www.livemint.com/companies/news/whatsapp-sues-india-govt-says-new-rules-mean-end-to-privacy-report-11621998397369.html

Riedl, M. J., Whipple, K. N., & Wallace, R. (2021). Antecedents of support for social media content moderation and platform regulation: The role of presumed effects on self and others. *Information, Communication & Society*, 1–18. Routledge. doi: 10.1080/1369118X.2021.1874040

Scroll Staff. (2019, June 14). Eight people have been arrested in four states over social media posts in India this week. *Scroll.in*. Retrieved from https://scroll.in/latest/927004/in-india-this-week-at-least-eight-people-have-been-arrested-in-four-states-over-social-media-posts

Shantha, S. (2021, January 12). Mumbai Police 'arrests' activist for sharing a Facebook post, releases her in few hours. *The Wire*. Retrieved from https://thewire.in/rights/mumbai-police-arrest-harshali-potdar

Sharon (2018, January 24). Advantages and misuse of social media during disasters and crisis. Retrieved from http://www.webtraffic.agency/2018/01/advantages-and-misuse-social-media-disasters-crisis/

Shirky, C. (2011). The political power of social media: Technology, the public sphere, and political change. *Foreign Affairs, 90*(1) 28–41.

Shrivastava, R. (2021, May 27). Govt vs Twitter: Gloves come off as Centre says Twitter cannot dictate policy in India. *India Today*. Retrieved from https://www.indiatoday.in/india/story/govt-vs-twitter-centre-says-twitter-cannot-dictate-policy-india-1807816-2021-05-28

Sidhartha, & Doval, P. (2021, June 1). Rules protect rights of users, were framed because social media giants failed to do so: IT and law minister Ravi Shankar Prasad. *The Times of India.* Retrieved from https://timesofindia.indiatimes. com/india/rules-protect-rights-of-users-were-framed-because-social-media-giants-failed-to-do-so-it-and-law-minister-ravi-shankar-prasad/article-show/83128246.cms

Sobkowicz, P., Kaschesky, M., & Bouchard, G. (2012). Opinion mining in social media: Modeling, simulating, and forecasting political opinions in the web. *Government Information Quarterly, 29*(4), 470–479.

Sriram, J. (2017, September 23). SC strikes down 'draconian' Section 66A. *The Hindu.* Retrieved from https://www.thehindu.com/news/national/supreme-court-strikes-down-section-66-a-of-the-it-act-finds-it-unconstitutional/article10740659.ece

Statista. (2021). Number of internet users in India from 2015 to 2020 with a forecast until 2025. Statista.com. Retrieved on January 6 from https://www.statista. com/statistics/255146/number-of-internet-users-in-india/

Statista. (2021a, April 27). Number of social network users in India from 2015 to 2018 with a forecast until 2023. Statista.com. Retrieved from https://www. statista.com/statistics/278407/number-of-social-network-users-in-india/

Stieglitz, S., & Dang-Xuan, L. (2013). Social media and political communication: A social media analytics framework. *Social Network Analysis and Mining, 3*(4), 1277–1291.

Strahilevitz, L. (2004). A social networks theory of privacy. *University of Chicago Law & Economics,* Olin Working Paper No. 230; University of Chicago, Public Law Working Paper No. 79. doi:10.2139/ssrn.629283

Thaver, M. (2020, December 15). Explained: How Maharashtra Police will use software to crack down on child porn. *The Indian Express.* Retrieved from https://indianexpress.com/article/explained/maharashtra-police-interpol-child-porn-software-7096513/

Thierer, A. (2012). The perils of classifying social media platforms as public utilities. *CommLaw Conspectus – Journal of Communications Law and Policy, 21*(2). http://dx.doi.org/10.2139/ssrn.2025674

TNN (2017, May 31). Fake WhatsApp messages led to Jharkhand lynching: Urgent call to verify messages received. Times Now. Retrieved from https://www.timesnownews.com/india/article/fake-news-whatsapp-social-media-jharkhand-lynching/62105

TNN (2017a, November 20). How a WhatsApp message can get you arrested. Times Now. Retrieved from https://timesofindia.indiatimes.com/india/how-a-whatsapp-message-can-get-you-arrested/articleshow/61718967.cms

Trends Desk. (2020, June 30). Memes flood social media as govt bans TikTok, 58 other Chinese apps. *The Indian Express.* Retrieved from https://indianexpress.com/article/trending/trending-in-india/govt-bans-59-chinese-apps-including-tiktok-memes-6482956/

Trepte, Sabine. (2020). The Social Media Privacy Model. *Communication Theory*, qtz035, https://doi.org/10.1093/ct/qtz035

United Nations. (2021). India: General Information. UNData App. Retrieved from http://data.un.org/en/iso/in.html

Unnithan, G. P. S. (2020, October 6). Kerala: 41, including IT professionals, arrested for creating, sharing child porn over WhatsApp, Telegram. *India Today*. Retrieved from https://www.indiatoday.in/crime/story/kerala-police-arrest-41-people-sharing-child-porn-whatsapp-instagram-telegram-1728978-2020-10-06

Veerappan, D. (2021, February 8). Tamil Nadu man arrested for watching child pornography. *The Times of India*. Retrieved from https://timesofindia.indiatimes.com/city/madurai/tamil-nadu-man-arrested-for-watching-child-pornography/articleshow/80746319.cms

Venkat, A., Pichandy, C., Barclay, F. P. & Jayaseelan, R. (2014). Facebook privacy management: An empirical study of awareness, perception and fears. *Global Media Journal-Indian Edition*, 5(1), Article 5: 1–20.

VID Community. (2020, May 8). How social media companies misuse your data. VID Community. Retrieved from https://vidcamera-community.medium.com/how-social-media-companies-misuse-your-data-9a53e459f02c

Wu, P. (2015). Impossible to regulate: Social media, terrorists, and the role for the UN. *Chicago Journal of International Law*, 16(1), 281–311. https://chicagounbound.uchicago.edu/cjil/vol16/iss1/11.

About the Editors and the Contributors

EDITORS

Francis P. Barclay is Assistant Professor in the Department of Media and Communication, School of Communication, Central University of Tamil Nadu, India. Dr Barclay has been a journalist, news artist and political cartoonist and is also a media researcher, psephologist and writer. He is the founder-editor of *Journal of Media and Communication*. He has published and contributed chapters to several books, apart from research articles in reputed journals. His research areas are media, politics and regulation, gender studies, contemporary journalism, new and social media, media usage and effects, media psychology, research methodology and immersive technologies. He has served several English newspapers in India. Some of his works are available at www.francisbarclay.com. (Orcid ID: 0000-0002-7361-9651)

Boobalakrishnan N. is Assistant Professor in the Department of Media and Communication, School of Communication, Central University of Tamil Nadu, India. He has published research articles on parental mediation, media and children, information and communication technologies and education. His current research addresses media, culture and communication; new media: usage and effects; social media; information and communication technologies. He has taught visual communication and electronic media courses and has technical proficiency in multimedia tools used for audio and non-linear video editing.

CONTRIBUTORS

I. Arul Aram is Professor and Head of the Department of Media Sciences, Anna University, Chennai. He was formerly Chief Sub-Editor with *The Hindu*, in Chennai and New Delhi. He was a postdoctoral fellow at the London School of Economics. He was Director of

UGC's Educational Multimedia Research Centre (EMMRC) during 2010–2011. He has published several research papers in national and international publications and has many book chapters and book publications to his credit. His areas of specialization and research interests include environmental communication, peace journalism, science communication and climate change communication.

Nikhil Kumar Gouda is Assistant Professor in the Department of Media and Communication, Central University of Tamil Nadu, India, and has a subject specialisation in Health Communication, with more than 15 years of experience in teaching, research and administration in communication.

Parama Gupta is UGC Junior Research Fellow in the Department of Media Sciences, Anna University, Chennai, India. She was formerly Assistant Professor in the Department of Communication, Women's Christian College, Chennai. Her areas of interest in research include ecological discourses, film studies and new media.

Anushiya K. is Research Assistant under an ICSSR-IMPRESS project in the Department of Media and Communication, Central University of Tamil Nadu, India.

V. Palaniappan is Research Scholar (part-time) in the Department of Communication, PSG College of Arts and Science (affiliated to the Bharathiar University, Coimbatore, Tamil Nadu, India). He is pursuing research in Media and Cultural Dynamics. He started his career as a journalist and served various regional and national newspapers as a reporter and photojournalist. Currently, he is in charge of public relations and corporate communications of a multinational company in Coimbatore, India.

Binish Parveen is Doctoral Scholar in the Department of Media and Communication, Central University of Tamil Nadu, India.

C. Pichandy specialized in Mass Communication from the University of Madras. His career spans over 40 years as an academic, researcher, administrator, teacher, leader and social worker, reflecting his commitment to higher education and society in general. He has made significant contributions to the field of mass communication and journalism and higher education in particular. He is the Founder-Head of the Department of Journalism and Mass Communication at PSG College of Arts and Science (affiliated to Bharathiar University, Coimbatore, Tamil Nadu, India) and made it into a centre for higher learning.

S. Ramamurthy is a critical theoretician and Former Head of the Department of Tamil Literature, TBML College, Porayar, Tamil Nadu, India.

C. J. Ravikrishnan is Assistant Professor in the Department of Visual Communication, PSG College of Arts and Science, Coimbatore, Tamil Nadu, India. His research areas are peace and conflict, an adaptation of artificial intelligence, machine learning and deep learning techniques for communication research and social media data mining. He has worked with editorial teams of leading vernacular and English newspapers at various levels.

Akhila S. is Doctoral Scholar in the Department of Media and Communication, Central University of Tamil Nadu, India. Her areas of interest are media and gender studies, communication methods and film studies.

Balashanmugam S. K. is Assistant Professor of Law at the Department of Law, School of Legal Studies, Central University of Tamil Nadu, India. His broad area of research includes corporate laws, banking laws and financial institutions, international trade laws, environmental law, biotechnology law, food laws and biodiversity laws. He was awarded a PhD from the prestigious Rajiv Gandhi School of Intellectual Property Law, Indian Institute of Technology Kharagpur, West Bengal, India. He has published his works in various international journals. He has participated in various international and national conferences focusing on international trade laws, international environmental law, biotechnology and law and public laws.

Malini Srinivasan is Research Scholar in the Department of Media and Communication, Central University of Tamil Nadu, India.

Index